FRANZ KAFKA

Roads grow
out of
travelling them!

MANFRED KRÖPLIN

Without attitude,
it's just shuffling
things around

STEVE MALKMUS

No more
absolutes,
no more
absolutes

TITLE

I used
to be
a design
student

AUTHORS AND EDITORS

Frank Philippin and
Billy Kiosoglou
Brighten the Corners
London / Darmstadt
United Kingdom / Germany

PUBLISHER

Laurence
King
Publishing

PUBLISHER LOGO

I used
to be
a design
student

Then   **Now**

CONTENTS PAGE

See back cover

IMPRINT INFORMATION

Published in 2013 by
Laurence King Publishing Ltd
361–373 City Road
London EC1V 1LR
United Kingdom
email: enquiries@laurenceking.com
www.laurenceking.com

ISBN
978 1 85669 898 6

AUTHORS & EDITORS
Frank Philippin &
Billy Kiosoglou

BOOK DESIGN
Brighten the Corners
www.brightenthecorners.com

PAPER
Yulong Pure & Thai Woodfree

TYPEFACE
Akzidenz Grotesk Medium

Printed in China

ACKNOWLEDGEMENTS

First of all, we'd like to thank the
Hochschule Darmstadt (Germany),
where Frank is a professor, for granting
the sabbatical during which the
research for this project took place.
Without this great academic tradition,
it would have been impossible to give
this book the kick-start, time and
attention it needed.

Thank you also to the tutors and
designers who were influential during
our studies. At Camberwell College of
Arts, London: primarily Andy Long but
also Alex Lumley, Jim Fielding and
Lawrence Zeegen; at the Royal College
of Art: Margaret Calvert, David Cross,
Dan Fern, Ian Gabb and Alan Kitching;
and, of course, all the other people in
both places who had an impact on us in
one way or another during our studies.

For later years, when we were trying
to find our way in the 'real world', we
have the following people to thank:
Jeremy Myerson at the Helen Hamlyn
Research Centre, Nina Lemmens at the
DAAD (German Academic Exchange
Service) and all our other clients who
have enabled us to run a successful
design studio for the last 13 years.

Regarding teaching, I (Frank) must
greatly thank (or perhaps blame)
Adrian Spaak, for without him I would
have never committed to it in the
way that I have done.

Our thanks also go to everyone at
Laurence King Publishing, especially
Jo Lightfoot who supported the project
from the start and Susie May for her
help in the editorial process.

Last, and definitely not least, a big
thank you goes to all the designers
who took part in this project. Finding
the time to patiently answer our
numerous questions and to track down
old student works while running an
established design practice isn't easy,
so we greatly appreciate their support
and contribution!

We would also like to thank all the
designers who contributed to our
research but whom we were not able
to feature in the final book.

Thank you all!

PHOTO CREDITS

Portrait photos on inside flaps,
comparative spread pages 22–23 and
on designer project spreads of António
S. Gomes (then/now) by José
Albergaria/Pedro Ca, Bernd Hilpert
(then/now) by Eibe Sönnecken,
Danijela Djokic (now) by Tom Ziora,
Emmi Salonen (now) by Jere Salonen,
Fons Hickmann (now) by Johannes
Bock, Kirsty Carter (now) by Martin
Hartley, Lars Harmsen (now) by Halim
Dogan, Laurent Lacour (then) by Meike
Lacour, Liza Enebeis by Dennis Koot,
Margaret Calvert (now) by Steven
Speller, Oliver Klimpel (now) by
Anna Gille and Sebastian Kissel,
Sascha Lobe (now) by Michael
Schnabel, Sven Voelker (then/now)
by Marcus Meyer/Frederik Busch.

Work photos on designer project
spreads of Emmi Salonen (now) by
Jere Salonen, Kristine Matthews (now)
by Doug Manelski (top and bottom two)
and Cassie Klingler (central two).

Portrait photos of the authors (page
256) by Tagore Leet (then) and
Kai von Rabenau (now).

The idea for this project came when we were invited to give a talk at our old college, Camberwell College of Arts (London, UK), 12 years after our graduation. For the talk, we presented old student projects alongside work we had done in the 'professional world' and looked for connections between them.

Initially, we weren't sure how fruitful this comparison would be, but we quickly realized that the connections were there once we started looking. These were sometimes conceptual, other times visual, but there was also a certain attitude that permeated the work. So, without necessarily being able to say exactly why, the work always felt that it belonged to the same people.

The students responded very well to the talk because they could relate to the college work and see how it fed into future projects. We also felt that it helped bridge the student and professional worlds a little, demistifying the transition from one to the other, reassuring students that they needn't tremble with awe at the professional world, but instead remember that most practising designers used to be design students too.

And it was also strangely reassuring for us to revisit old projects and see that no matter how much our lives and work may have changed and developed, there was something there that was still fundamentally the same.

Realizing that other people's work would also offer such insights, we invited graphic designers to share both a student project and a professional project with us. These two works could be similar conceptually or visually, or share a certain attitude or approach. They didn't have to be the designers' favourite projects but, rather, memorable projects of which they were fond, or which they considered to be defining in their development as a professional.

Our selection of contributors was pretty personal: some we had met during our studies (fellow students or tutors), others during our teaching (fellow tutors or students) and others are practising designers whose work we have always liked. Between them, the designers featured in this book have a total of 832 years of working experience and have spent 309½ years studying (see pages 20–21).

The aim of this publication is to trace the links between past and present work, and look at each designer's particular methodology and attitude. We see this book as a resource students can use and will hopefully learn from, as well as something teachers can use in their practice.

For professionals, the book provides a great opportunity to have a peek at colleagues' student work. And for the participating designers, it's an opportunity to get all those unseen student projects (brilliant or slightly confused) out of the black leather portfolio, and give them a much-deserved public platform.

Being a designer is often a vocation, so it's difficult to split the person from the work. We therefore asked contributors to give us feedback not only on their practice and influences, but on such incidental things as their weight, favourite food or their most valued possession, to help get a sense of what the person behind the work might be like. We decided to look at all these personal details alongside each other, comparing responses of different people to the same questions, for an overall 'portrait' of the design community (see pages 8–23 and 234–253).

TEACHING DESIGN
Teaching for the past 15 years has made me very interested in the different means by which good design finds its expression. What I often see is that attitude (towards design, and also towards life in general) plays a major role in the kind of solutions one finds, and consequently in the kind of designer one becomes. A better description for this is the German 'Haltung', which describes attitude and mindset, as well as one's posture – a person's stance, notional and physical. It is the 'Haltung' of each contributor that we are looking for in this project. What kind of 'Haltung' do different graphic designers have? How important is it in creating a piece of design? What role does it play in how one's work is received by others? Is it subject to change? Is 'Haltung' individual or can we adopt that of another? And most of all: does 'Haltung' visibly manifest itself in moments when things fall into place, when we realize and understand, when the penny drops?
– FRANK PHILIPPIN

A certain way of doing things

Preface

Wake-up time
Mode of transport
Favourite food
Weight
Exercise
Most valued possession
Student years
Portrait

Then

Wake-up time
Mode of transport
Favourite food
Weight
Exercise
Most valued possession
Professional years
Portrait

Now

ANDREAS GNASS	**ANDREW STEVENS**	**ANNELYS DE VET**	**ANTÓNIO S. GOMES**	**BEN BRANAGAN**	**BERND HILPERT**
08:00	08:30–09:00	09:00	10:00	Earlier than I wanted to	09:00
BRIAN WEBB	**CHRISTIAN HEUSSER**	**DANIEL EATOCK**	**DANIJELA DJOKIC**	**EMMI SALONEN**	**ÉRIC & MARIE GASPAR**
08:00	07:30	07:00–10:00	08:30–12:30	Around 08:00	08:00
FONS HICKMANN	**HANS DIETER REICHERT**	**HOLGER JACOBS**	**HOON KIM**	**HYOUN YOUL JOE**	**ISABELLE SWIDERSKI**
12:00	07:00	09:00	10:00	It depended on my daily condition and classes	07:00–07:30
JAMES GOGGIN	**JAN WILKER**	**JULIE GAYARD**	**KAI VON RABENAU**	**KEN GARLAND**	**KIRSTY CARTER**
09:00 or 10:00	10:00–11:00	09:00	09:00	Late	07:30
KRISTINE MATTHEWS	**LARS HARMSEN**	**LAURENT LACOUR**	**LIZA ENEBEIS**	**LUCINDA NOBLE**	**MAKI SUZUKI**
08:30ish	06:30	07:00	08:00	08:30	08:00
MARC VAN DER HEIJDE	**MARGARET CALVERT**	**MARION FINK**	**MARTIN LORENZ**	**MATTHIAS GÖRLICH**	**MICHAEL GEORGIOU**
08:00	It varied	09:00–09:30	09:00	Mostly around 08:00	10:00
NIKKI GONNISSEN	**OLIVER KLIMPEL**	**PAUL BARNES**	**PREM KRISHNAMURTHY**	**RENATA GRAW**	**RICHARD WALKER**
Around 08:00	07:00	07:00	09:00–11:00	07:00	10:00
SANDRA HOFFMANN	**SASCHA LOBE**	**STEFAN SAGMEISTER**	**SVEN VOELKER**	**TIM BALAAM**	**URS LEHNI**
Early	09:00	06:00	09:00	07:00–08:00	Around 08:00
YASMIN KHAN	**YVES FIDALGO**	**AVERAGE / EARLIEST / LATEST**			
Stayed up from night before	07:30 (train to catch)	A 08:46 E 06:00 L 12:30			

What time did you get up each morning?

▬▬▬

Then

ANDREAS GNASS	**ANDREW STEVENS**	**ANNELYS DE VET**	**ANTÓNIO S. GOMES**	**BEN BRANAGAN**	**BERND HILPERT**
07:00	09:30	07:00	06:00– 08:00	Later than I need to	07:00
BRIAN WEBB	**CHRISTIAN HEUSSER**	**DANIEL EATOCK**	**DANIJELA DJOKIC**	**EMMI SALONEN**	**ÉRIC & MARIE GASPAR**
07:45	08:15	07:00– 10:00	07:45	Around 08:00	07:00
FONS HICKMANN	**HANS DIETER REICHERT**	**HOLGER JACOBS**	**HOON KIM**	**HYOUN YOUL JOE**	**ISABELLE SWIDERSKI**
10:00	07:30	09:00	08:00	It depends on projects – usually at 08:30	05:30
JAMES GOGGIN	**JAN WILKER**	**JULIE GAYARD**	**KAI VON RABENAU**	**KEN GARLAND**	**KIRSTY CARTER**
07:00	07:00– 08:30	09:00	09:00	Not so late	07:30
KRISTINE MATTHEWS	**LARS HARMSEN**	**LAURENT LACOUR**	**LIZA ENEBEIS**	**LUCINDA NEWTON-DUNN**	**MAKI SUZUKI**
06:30ish	06:30	07:00	07:30	06:15	09:00
MARC VAN DER HEIJDE	**MARGARET CALVERT**	**MARION FINK**	**MARTIN LORENZ**	**MATTHIAS GÖRLICH**	**MICHAEL GEORGIOU**
07:30	It varies	07:30	07:00	08:00 at the latest	07:00
NIKKI GONNISSEN	**OLIVER KLIMPEL**	**PAUL BARNES**	**PREM KRISHNAMURTHY**	**RENATA GRAW**	**RICHARD WALKER**
Around 08:00	08:00	05:00– 07:00	07:00– 09:00	I don't use an alarm clock, but generally I wake up around 07:30	06:30
S. HOFFMANN ROBBIANI	**SASCHA LOBE**	**STEFAN SAGMEISTER**	**SVEN VOELKER**	**TIM BALAAM**	**URS LEHNI**
Very early	06:00	06:00	07:30	07:00	Around 08:00
YASMIN KHAN	**YVES FIDALGO**	**AVERAGE/EARLIEST/LATEST**			
05:30	No rule, I go to work by bike	A 07:22 E 05:00 L 10:00			

What time do you get up each morning?

Now

ANDREAS GNASS	ANDREW STEVENS	ANNELYS DE VET	ANTÓNIO S. GOMES	BEN BRANAGAN	BERND HILPERT
Muscle-driven transport	Bus	Train	The tram	Driving	Car

BRIAN WEBB	CHRISTIAN HEUSSER	DANIEL EATOCK	DANIJELA DJOKIC	EMMI SALONEN	ÉRIC & MARIE GASPAR
Train	Mountain bike	Walking	Train	Walking	The tube

FONS HICKMANN	HANS DIETER REICHERT	HOLGER JACOBS	HOON KIM	HYOUN YOUL JOE	ISABELLE SWIDERSKI
By foot	Car (VW Beetle, 1200cc), bus, train, tram	Bicycle (second-hand)	Bicycle	-	Walking

JAMES GOGGIN	JAN WILKER	JULIE GAYARD	KAI VON RABENAU	KEN GARLAND	KIRSTY CARTER
Bicycle or rail	Public transportation	Bus	Underground	-	In Brighton, I lived a stone's throw away from the university and walked every morning along the seafront… (Full answer, p. 228)

KRISTINE MATTHEWS	LARS HARMSEN	LAURENT LACOUR	LIZA ENEBEIS	LUCINDA NOBLE	MAKI SUZUKI
Bus (in British style)	1: Bicycle 2: Car	-	Walking	Public transport	Bicycle

MARC VAN DER HEIJDE	MARGARET CALVERT	MARION FINK	MARTIN LORENZ	MATTHIAS GÖRLICH	MICHAEL GEORGIOU
Bicycle (of course – being Dutch and poor)	Train	Bicycle	Car or bike	Walking	Car

NIKKI GONNISSEN	OLIVER KLIMPEL	PAUL BARNES	PREM KRISHNAMURTHY	RENATA GRAW	RICHARD WALKER
Bicycle	Bicycle	Walking, running and train	Walking	Walking, biking	Walking

SANDRA HOFFMANN	SASCHA LOBE	STEFAN SAGMEISTER	SVEN VOELKER	TIM BALAAM	URS LEHNI
Bicycle	Flying	Train	Bicycle	Foot	Bicycle

YASMIN KHAN	YVES FIDALGO	RANKING LIST
Car	My red Peugeot 205 GTI	1 CYCLE 2 WALK 3 TRAIN, CAR

What was your favoured mode of transport?

—

Then

ANDREAS GNASS Transport with no system-forced stop-overs	**ANDREW STEVENS** Bus	**ANNELYS DE VET** Train	**ANTÓNIO S. GOMES** Imperial Speeder Bike or any other form of individual transportation	**BEN BRANAGAN** Walking	**BERND HILPERT** Car
BRIAN WEBB Train	**CHRISTIAN HEUSSER** Race bike	**DANIEL EATOCK** Walking	**DANIJELA DJOKIC** Car and train	**EMMI SALONEN** Cycling	**ÉRIC & MARIE GASPAR** Le métro
FONS HICKMANN By foot	**HANS DIETER REICHERT** Car (Volvo V50), bus, train, tube, plane	**HOLGER JACOBS** There are several bicycles to choose from (mostly new)	**HOON KIM** Car	**HYOUN YOUL JOE** -	**ISABELLE SWIDERSKI** Walking
JAMES GOGGIN Bicycle or high-speed rail	**JAN WILKER** Public transport	**JULIE GAYARD** Bicycle	**KAI VON RABENAU** Bicycle	**KEN GARLAND** -	**KIRSTY CARTER** I walk to work every day – I live really close to our East London studio, it's a ten-minute walk
KRISTINE MATTHEWS Car (in American style)	**LARS HARMSEN** 1: Bicycle 2: Walking 3: Train 4: Aeroplane Cars don't mean much to me. Walking is about having time	**LAURENT LACOUR** -	**LIZA ENEBEIS** Walking	**LUCINDA NEWTON-DUNN** By foot (but currently have to drive everywhere)	**MAKI SUZUKI** Four bicycles
MARC VAN DER HEIJDE Car; I don't drive much but really enjoy it when I do. I have a 1976 gold metallic Mercedes-Benz 280 SE (it's a classic)	**MARGARET CALVERT** Train	**MARION FINK** Bicycle	**MARTIN LORENZ** Walking	**MATTHIAS GÖRLICH** Taking the train and walking	**MICHAEL GEORGIOU** Bicycle
NIKKI GONNISSEN Bicycle	**OLIVER KLIMPEL** Walking	**PAUL BARNES** Walking, running, cycling and train	**PREM KRISHNAMURTHY** Walking	**RENATA GRAW** Walking, biking, flying across oceans	**RICHARD WALKER** Taxi
S. HOFFMANN ROBBIANI Bicycle and train	**SASCHA LOBE** Flying	**STEFAN SAGMEISTER** Train	**SVEN VOELKER** Porsche	**TIM BALAAM** Car	**URS LEHNI** Bicycle
YASMIN KHAN Car	**YVES FIDALGO** My Cannondale	**RANKING LIST** 1 CYCLE 2 WALK 3 TRAIN			

What is your favoured mode of transport?

—

Now

ANDREAS GNASS	ANDREW STEVENS	ANNELYS DE VET	ANTONIO S. GOMES	BEN BRANAGAN	BERND HILPERT
I didn't have a favourite food	Rigatoni Siciliana	-	Pasta fredda	Bacon sandwich	Kellogg's Smacks

BRIAN WEBB	CHRISTIAN HEUSSER	DANIEL EATOCK	DANIJELA DJOKIC	EMMI SALONEN	ÉRIC & MARIE GASPAR
Chinese	Pasta pesto	Fruit	Fast food	Vegetarian	Cadbury's

FONS HICKMANN	HANS DIETER REICHERT	HOLGER JACOBS	HOON KIM	HYOUN YOUL JOE	ISABELLE SWIDERSKI
Cake	German (Currywurst mit Fritten)	German potato pancakes	Korean BBQ	Korean	Good home-made food

JAMES GOGGIN	JAN WILKER	JULIE GAYARD	KAI VON RABENAU	KEN GARLAND	KIRSTY CARTER
Japanese	Anything from the students' cafeteria	-	Pasta with tuna	Tomato Soup	I've always kept a very balanced diet. It makes me happy to eat well. When I had little money, food was… (Cont. opposite – now)

KRISTINE MATTHEWS	LARS HARMSEN	LAURENT LACOUR	LIZA ENEBEIS	LUCINDA NOBLE	MAKI SUZUKI
Pasta	Pasta	Tafelspitz	Marmite	Probably pasta	Being French and being a vegetarian was a national joke… (Full answer, p. 229)

MARC VAN DER HEIJDE	MARGARET CALVERT	MARION FINK	MARTIN LORENZ	MATTHIAS GÖRLICH	MICHAEL GEORGIOU
Pasta	Pasta	Hummus, and the soups and spicy sauces of my Korean flatmate	All kinds	Whatever was available within a limited budget	Spaghetti bolognese

NIKKI GONNISSEN	OLIVER KLIMPEL	PAUL BARNES	PREM KRISHNAMURTHY	RENATA GRAW	RICHARD WALKER
Indonesian (my mother comes from Indonesia)	Cheap	Pasta	Taco Bell bean burritos	I love all things food, but I am addicted to just one: coffee	Indian food

SANDRA HOFFMANN	SASCHA LOBE	STEFAN SAGMEISTER	SVEN VOELKER	TIM BALAAM	URS LEHNI
Canadian	Italian cuisine	Zürich veal with cream sauce and mushrooms	Käsespätzle (Thimble dumplings made with cheese)	Bread	-

YASMIN KHAN	YVES FIDALGO	RANKING LIST
Anything that wasn't dehydrated	Pasta	1 PASTA 2 CHEAP, CHOCOLATE, KOREAN, VEGETARIAN 3 ALL OTHER FOOD

What was your favourite food?

ANDREAS GNASS	ANDREW STEVENS	ANNELYS DE VET	ANTÓNIO S. GOMES	BEN BRANAGAN	BERND HILPERT
Still don't have a favourite food. I do like fish, different kinds of pasta and good entrecôte and lamb though	Home-cooked peasant food (pasta, rice)	-	Spaghetti alle vongole	Rendang	Good restaurant food (typical local kitchen – all over the world)

BRIAN WEBB	CHRISTIAN HEUSSER	DANIEL EATOCK	DANIJELA DJOKIC	EMMI SALONEN	ÉRIC & MARIE GASPAR
Japanese	Anything that has been prepared in the oven	Fruit	Slow food	Vegetarian	Le pot-au-feu

FONS HICKMANN	HANS DIETER REICHERT	HOLGER JACOBS	HOON KIM	HYOUN YOUL JOE	ISABELLE SWIDERSKI
Cake	Italian (pasta, antipasti and salad)	Anything Japanese, except for the crab brain that my wife's relatives invited me to taste once	Korean BBQ	Seafood, Korean and Japanese	Good home-made food

JAMES GOGGIN	JAN WILKER	JULIE GAYARD	KAI VON RABENAU	KEN GARLAND	KIRSTY CARTER
Probably still Japanese – or Korean	Anything but from the students' cafeteria	-	Schnitzel	Gambas al aquillo (giant prawns in garlic)	…never cut, it was always my top priority. I perhaps eat out a little more now. In terms of favourites, it has always been chocolate

KRISTINE MATTHEWS	LARS HARMSEN	LAURENT LACOUR	LIZA ENEBEIS	LUCINDA NEWTON-DUNN	MAKI SUZUKI
Pasta	Home-cooking and good restaurants. There is a great Lebanese restaurant here in Karlsruhe I love to go to	Tafelspitz	Marmite	Japanese food of various kinds	Fish, still

MARC VAN DER HEIJDE	MARGARET CALVERT	MARION FINK	MARTIN LORENZ	MATTHIAS GÖRLICH	MICHAEL GEORGIOU
Thai food	Pasta	Pasta and good wine	All kinds	Whatever is available	Spaghetti bolognese

NIKKI GONNISSEN	OLIVER KLIMPEL	PAUL BARNES	PREM KRISHNAMURTHY	RENATA GRAW	RICHARD WALKER
Indonesian, Japanese, French	Japanese	Sushi and home-made bread	Chicken shawarma	I love all things food, but I am addicted to just one: coffee	Cheese

S. HOFFMANN ROBBIANI	SASCHA LOBE	STEFAN SAGMEISTER	SVEN VOELKER	TIM BALAAM	URS LEHNI
Italian, Ticinese	Japanese cuisine	Tiny bow Shanghainese soup dumplings	Käsespätzle (thimble dumplings made with cheese)	Bread	-

YASMIN KHAN	YVES FIDALGO	RANKING LIST
Peaches in pie, in cobbler, in anything or just by themselves	Pasta	1 JAPANESE 2 PASTA 3 KOREAN

What is your favourite food?

Now

ANDREAS GNASS	ANDREW STEVENS	ANNELYS DE VET	ANTÓNIO S. GOMES	BEN BRANAGAN	BERND HILPERT
75kg	67kg	Same (as now)	68kg	Lighter (than now)	Approx. 70kg

BRIAN WEBB	CHRISTIAN HEUSSER	DANIEL EATOCK	DANIJELA DJOKIC	EMMI SALONEN	ÉRIC & MARIE GASPAR
60kg	70kg	54kg	10kg less	-	64kg/50kg

FONS HICKMANN	HANS DIETER REICHERT	HOLGER JACOBS	HOON KIM	HYOUN YOUL JOE	ISABELLE SWIDERSKI
70kg	66kg	75kg	65kg	Approx. 61kg	50kg

JAMES GOGGIN	JAN WILKER	JULIE GAYARD	KAI VON RABENAU	KEN GARLAND	KIRSTY CARTER
70kg	72kg	52kg	75kg	57kg	53kg

KRISTINE MATTHEWS	LARS HARMSEN	LAURENT LACOUR	LIZA ENEBEIS	LUCINDA NOBLE	MAKI SUZUKI
58kg	Not enough	71kg	A bit less (than now)	51kg	65kg

MARC VAN DER HEIJDE	MARGARET CALVERT	MARION FINK	MARTIN LORENZ	MATTHIAS GÖRLICH	MICHAEL GEORGIOU
75kg	-	-	72kg	Too much	70kg

NIKKI GONNISSEN	OLIVER KLIMPEL	PAUL BARNES	PREM KRISHNAMURTHY	RENATA GRAW	RICHARD WALKER
71kg	60kg	65kg	63kg	I was 4kg lighter than now	80kg

SANDRA HOFFMANN	SASCHA LOBE	STEFAN SAGMEISTER	SVEN VOELKER	TIM BALAAM	URS LEHNI
62kg (of which 10kg was 'Schoggi' after moving to Switzerland…)	Not enough…	82kg	74kg	60kg	67kg

YASMIN KHAN	YVES FIDALGO	AVERAGE/HEAVIEST/LIGHTEST
48kg	Can't remember really	A 65KG H 82KG L 48KG

How much did you weigh?

Then

ANDREAS GNASS	ANDREW STEVENS	ANNELYS DE VET	ANTÓNIO S. GOMES	BEN BRANAGAN	BERND HILPERT
75 kg	73 kg	Same (as then)	78 kg	Heavier (than then)	Approx. 75 kg

BRIAN WEBB	CHRISTIAN HEUSSER	DANIEL EATOCK	DANIJELA DJOKIC	EMMI SALONEN	ÉRIC & MARIE GASPAR
73 kg	75 kg	54 kg	10 kg more	-	64 kg / 50 kg

FONS HICKMANN	HANS DIETER REICHERT	HOLGER JACOBS	HOON KIM	HYOUN YOUL JOE	ISABELLE SWIDERSKI
80 kg	77 kg	80 kg	65 kg	66 kg	59 kg (all muscle of course)

JAMES GOGGIN	JAN WILKER	JULIE GAYARD	KAI VON RABENAU	KEN GARLAND	KIRSTY CARTER
80 kg	75 kg	56 kg	80 kg	64 kg	53 kg

KRISTINE MATTHEWS	LARS HARMSEN	LAURENT LACOUR	LIZA ENEBEIS	LUCINDA NEWTON-DUNN	MAKI SUZUKI
61 kg	A little more, but still not enough	75 kg	A bit more (than then)	54 kg	73 kg

MARC VAN DER HEIJDE	MARGARET CALVERT	MARION FINK	MARTIN LORENZ	MATTHIAS GÖRLICH	MICHAEL GEORGIOU
80 kg	-	-	75 kg	Far too much	85 kg

NIKKI GONNISSEN	OLIVER KLIMPEL	PAUL BARNES	PREM KRISHNAMURTHY	RENATA GRAW	RICHARD WALKER
67 kg	65 kg	75 kg	86 kg	I am 4 kg heavier than then	80 kg

S. HOFFMANN ROBBIANI	SASCHA LOBE	STEFAN SAGMEISTER	SVEN VOELKER	TIM BALAAM	URS LEHNI
52 kg	Too much…	89 kg	77 kg	70 kg	71 kg

YASMIN KHAN	YVES FIDALGO	AVERAGE / HEAVIEST / LIGHTEST
50 kg	I don't weigh myself, really. Don't have scales at home…	A 70 KG H 89 KG L 50 KG

How much do you weigh?

Now

ANDREAS GNASS	ANDREW STEVENS	ANNELYS DE VET	ANTONIO S. GOMES	BEN BRANAGAN	BERND HILPERT
Skiing, skateboarding	Football	Trampolining	None	Dancing	Freeclimbing

BRIAN WEBB	CHRISTIAN HEUSSER	DANIEL EATOCK	DANIJELA DJOKIC	EMMI SALONEN	ÉRIC & MARIE GASPAR
Walking	Nothing	Cycling, walking	Roller-skating, biking, swimming, jogging	Yoga, swimming and running	None/None

FONS HICKMANN	HANS DIETER REICHERT	HOLGER JACOBS	HOON KIM	HYOUN YOUL JOE	ISABELLE SWIDERSKI
None	Running, Taekwondo	Occasionally yoga for stress relief	Push-ups in dorm	-	Football, strength training

JAMES GOGGIN	JAN WILKER	JULIE GAYARD	KAI VON RABENAU	KEN GARLAND	KIRSTY CARTER
Walking and cycling as a mode of transport	Very little daily exercise, smoking over a pack a day	-	None	Table tennis	Tennis

KRISTINE MATTHEWS	LARS HARMSEN	LAURENT LACOUR	LIZA ENEBEIS	LUCINDA NOBLE	MAKI SUZUKI
Not much	Cycling, mountain-biking, swimming, surfing, skiing, cross-country, sailing… (Cont. opposite – now)	Windsurfing, mountain-biking, funsports	-	Walking quickly everywhere	Cycling

MARC VAN DER HEIJDE	MARGARET CALVERT	MARION FINK	MARTIN LORENZ	MATTHIAS GÖRLICH	MICHAEL GEORGIOU
I played some squash; the only sport I enjoy	Walking	None (apart from cycling to college)	Taekwondo	None	None

NIKKI GONNISSEN	OLIVER KLIMPEL	PAUL BARNES	PREM KRISHNAMURTHY	RENATA GRAW	RICHARD WALKER
Basketball	Football (very rarely) and a lot of walking	Running	None	Capoeira	Cycling, walking

SANDRA HOFFMANN	SASCHA LOBE	STEFAN SAGMEISTER	SVEN VOELKER	TIM BALAAM	URS LEHNI
Cycling, hiking, swimming, wandering, water-skiing	Skiing, tennis	None	None	Running and swimming	Skateboarding

YASMIN KHAN	YVES FIDALGO	RANKING LIST			
Cigarette breaks	Not sure	1 NONE 2 CYCLE 3 WALK			

What type of exercise did you do?

Then

ANDREAS GNASS

Badminton, snowboarding

ANDREW STEVENS

Football

ANNELYS DE VET

Bicycling my son to school every day

ANTÓNIO S. GOMES

Aikido (but haven't done any sports since my daughter's birth)

BEN BRANAGAN

Running

BERND HILPERT

-

BRIAN WEBB

Walking

CHRISTIAN HEUSSER

Cycling

DANIEL EATOCK

Cycling, walking, running

DANIJELA DJOKIC

Roller-skating, biking, swimming, jogging

EMMI SALONEN

Yoga and climbing

ÉRIC & MARIE GASPAR

None/ Aikido

FONS HICKMANN

None

HANS DIETER REICHERT

Running, swimming

HOLGER JACOBS

Cycling, jogging

HOON KIM

Overall exercise at a gym three times a week

HYOUN YOUL JOE

-

ISABELLE SWIDERSKI

Track, conditioning, strength training

JAMES GOGGIN

Walking and cycling as a mode of transport

JAN WILKER

Tennis in the early mornings during summer season, no more smoking

JULIE GAYARD

Kalaripayattu

KAI VON RABENAU

Cycling, swimming, Feldenkrais

KEN GARLAND

Walking

KIRSTY CARTER

Tennis

KRISTINE MATTHEWS

Not much

LARS HARMSEN

…I just love sport, but I would never go to a gym

LAURENT LACOUR

Jogging, snoring every night

LIZA ENEBEIS

-

LUCINDA NEWTON-DUNN

Yoga occasionally

MAKI SUZUKI

Cycling

MARC VAN DER HEIJDE

I have stopped going to the gym, as it gives me no pleasure – so currently I am a lazy bastard

MARGARET CALVERT

Walking

MARION FINK

Running, cycling

MARTIN LORENZ

Gym

MATTHIAS GÖRLICH

Still nothing

MICHAEL GEORGIOU

Cycling

NIKKI GONNISSEN

Basketball, rowing, the gym

OLIVER KLIMPEL

Swimming (if at all) and a lot of walking

PAUL BARNES

Running, swimming, gym and cycling

PREM KRISHNAMURTHY

None

RENATA GRAW

Sometimes I catch a yoga class, but mostly I just move the mouse around

RICHARD WALKER

Cycling, walking

S. HOFFMANN ROBBIANI

Bird-watching, cross-country skiing, cycling, gliding, hiking, ice skating, kayaking, snowshoeing, strolling, swimming, wandering, yoga

SASCHA LOBE

Tennis, skiing

STEFAN SAGMEISTER

Running

SVEN VOELKER

None

TIM BALAAM

Not enough running and swimming

URS LEHNI

Running

YASMIN KHAN

Yoga

YVES FIDALGO

Cycling

RANKING LIST

1 CYCLE
2 NONE, RUN
3 WALK

What type of exercise do you do?

Now

ANDREAS GNASS
Bike

ANDREW STEVENS
Sony Walkman

ANNELYS DE VET
-

ANTÓNIO S. GOMES
At the time I didn't care much about stuff

BEN BRANAGAN
No one thing really comes to mind

BERND HILPERT
My professional equipment

BRIAN WEBB
Books

CHRISTIAN HEUSSER
My Mac G4

DANIEL EATOCK
None

DANIJELA DJOKIC
My bike, my pictures and one piece of art

EMMI SALONEN
iMac G3

ÉRIC & MARIE GASPAR
Camera

FONS HICKMANN
-

HANS DIETER REICHERT
VW Beetle 1200cc

HOLGER JACOBS
My sketchbooks – I was pretty poor and can't remember owning anything else of real value

HOON KIM
Family and one external hard drive that had all the data in my life

HYOUN YOUL JOE
Books

ISABELLE SWIDERSKI
Walkman

JAMES GOGGIN
My Ricoh GR 35mm camera

JAN WILKER
My computer

JULIE GAYARD
-

KAI VON RABENAU
My Nikon camera

KEN GARLAND
My portable radio

KIRSTY CARTER
All my Apple products and I am not ashamed to admit it. I love my iPad, iPhone, MacBook Pro. I have had a Mac since I was 13 years old

KRISTINE MATTHEWS
My latest design project

LARS HARMSEN
My camera and my first computer

LAURENT LACOUR
-

LIZA ENEBEIS
My books

LUCINDA NOBLE
My family, my photos, my Mac (sad but true), my ability to see things in a certain way

MAKI SUZUKI
Comic books collection

MARC VAN DER HEIJDE
A German Perzina piano from the 1920s

MARGARET CALVERT
My work

MARION FINK
Computer + Sony camera

MARTIN LORENZ
Comic collection

MATTHIAS GÖRLICH
-

MICHAEL GEORGIOU
A watch

NIKKI GONNISSEN
If family is a possession, my family

OLIVER KLIMPEL
-

PAUL BARNES
-

PREM KRISHNAMURTHY
My 4×5 camera

RENATA GRAW
My camera

RICHARD WALKER
I had an original copy of How to Have a Number One the Easy Way by the KLF

SANDRA HOFFMANN
A toolbox with instruments (Swann-Morton scalpel, marble, roller, Caran… (Full answer, p. 231)

SASCHA LOBE
Books

STEFAN SAGMEISTER
Silkscreen equipment

SVEN VOELKER
My most expensive asset at the time was a Paul Smith suit – actually, it was the first G3 PowerBook for approx. £4,000

TIM BALAAM
Sepak takraw ball

URS LEHNI
Self-restored Vespa Tourist 150 (1960)

YASMIN KHAN
Not sure

YVES FIDALGO
My comics collection

RANKING LIST
1 COMPUTER
2 CAMERA
3 BOOKS

What was your most valued possession?

▬▬▬▬

Then

ANDREAS GNASS	ANDREW STEVENS	ANNELYS DE VET	ANTÓNIO S. GOMES	BEN BRANAGAN	BERND HILPERT
Family	Camper van	-	My young daughter	No one thing really comes to mind	The studio in which I am a partner

BRIAN WEBB	CHRISTIAN HEUSSER	DANIEL EATOCK	DANIJELA DJOKIC	EMMI SALONEN	ÉRIC & MARIE GASPAR
Books	My vinyl collection	None	My watch, my bike, my pictures and one piece of art	MacBook Pro	Computer

FONS HICKMANN	HANS DIETER REICHERT	HOLGER JACOBS	HOON KIM	HYOUN YOUL JOE	ISABELLE SWIDERSKI
-	House, office	Hand-built Italian racing bicycle	Family and four external hard drives that sync twice a day automatically and still contain all the data in my life	Books and my works	MacBook Pro (sad, I know)

JAMES GOGGIN	JAN WILKER	JULIE GAYARD	KAI VON RABENAU	KEN GARLAND	KIRSTY CARTER
My Ricoh GR Digital II camera	My health	-	My Leica camera	My cheap digital camera	Documenta 5 poster by Ed Ruscha in 1972 – it's my favourite piece of graphic design. I love that he made type up out of little ants

KRISTINE MATTHEWS	LARS HARMSEN	LAURENT LACOUR	LIZA ENEBEIS	LUCINDA NEWTON-DUNN	MAKI SUZUKI
My children Finn and Nell	It's not a 'valued possession', but my family is something very important to me now, more than anything else	My kids (but – oh – I don't possess them)	My books	Same as then	A copy of Steal This Book by Abbie Hoffman

MARC VAN DER HEIJDE	MARGARET CALVERT	MARION FINK	MARTIN LORENZ	MATTHIAS GÖRLICH	MICHAEL GEORGIOU
A Japanese Yamaha grand piano from the 1990s	My work	My flat	Book collection	-	My art collection

NIKKI GONNISSEN	OLIVER KLIMPEL	PAUL BARNES	PREM KRISHNAMURTHY	RENATA GRAW	RICHARD WALKER
Family, books, shields, ceremonial outfits, bis poles from the Asmat	Currently my new sofa, otherwise a painting by Peter McDonald and a few books	-	My notebooks from the past years	My hands	I have an original May '68 poster. It's the one with the riot policeman holding a baton… (Full answer, p. 230)

S. HOFFMANN ROBBIANI	SASCHA LOBE	STEFAN SAGMEISTER	SVEN VOELKER	TIM BALAAM	URS LEHNI
The diamond necklace from my husband	Books	My dad's watch	My most beautiful material thing is a 40-year-old Porsche	Sepak takraw ball	Wedding ring

YASMIN KHAN	YVES FIDALGO	RANKING LIST
Not sure	My bike	1 BOOKS, FAMILY/CHILDREN 2 COMPUTER 3 CAMERA

What is your most valued possession?

Now

ANDREAS GNASS	ANDREW STEVENS	ANNELYS DE VET	ANTÓNIO S. GOMES	BEN BRANAGAN	BERND HILPERT
4	7	8	5	6	5

BRIAN WEBB	CHRISTIAN HEUSSER	DANIEL EATOCK	DANIJELA DJOKIC	EMMI SALONEN	ÉRIC & MARIE GASPAR
6	8	5	8	3	8 (×2)

FONS HICKMANN	HANS DIETER REICHERT	HOLGER JACOBS	HOON KIM	HYOUN YOUL JOE	ISABELLE SWIDERSKI
6	7	8	7	6	7

JAMES GOGGIN	JAN WILKER	JULIE GAYARD	KAI VON RABENAU	KEN GARLAND	KIRSTY CARTER
6	6	5	6	6	6

KRISTINE MATTHEWS	LARS HARMSEN	LAURENT LACOUR	LIZA ENEBEIS	LUCINDA NOBLE	MAKI SUZUKI
6	6½	6	6	6	7

MARC VAN DER HEIJDE	MARGARET CALVERT	MARION FINK	MARTIN LORENZ	MATTHIAS GÖRLICH	MICHAEL GEORGIOU
6	4	7	10	7	5

NIKKI GONNISSEN	OLIVER KLIMPEL	PAUL BARNES	PREM KRISHNAMURTHY	RENATA GRAW	RICHARD WALKER
6	7	4	5½	6	4

SANDRA HOFFMANN	SASCHA LOBE	STEFAN SAGMEISTER	SVEN VOELKER	TIM BALAAM	URS LEHNI
10½	5	7	6	7	6

YASMIN KHAN	YVES FIDALGO	AVERAGE / LONGEST / SHORTEST
6	4	A 6¼ L 10½ S 3

How many years did you study?

────────

Then

ANDREAS GNASS	ANDREW STEVENS	ANNELYS DE VET	ANTÓNIO S. GOMES	BEN BRANAGAN	BERND HILPERT
13	22	12	15	8	15

BRIAN WEBB	CHRISTIAN HEUSSER	DANIEL EATOCK	DANIJELA DJOKIC	EMMI SALONEN	ÉRIC & MARIE GASPAR
44	10	13	17	10	10 (×2)

FONS HICKMANN	HANS DIETER REICHERT	HOLGER JACOBS	HOON KIM	HYOUN YOUL JOE	ISABELLE SWIDERSKI
21	25	15	9	7	16

JAMES GOGGIN	JAN WILKER	JULIE GAYARD	KAI VON RABENAU	KEN GARLAND	KIRSTY CARTER
13	10	13	11	58	9

KRISTINE MATTHEWS	LARS HARMSEN	LAURENT LACOUR	LIZA ENEBEIS	LUCINDA NEWTON-DUNN	MAKI SUZUKI
22	19	16	16	12	11

MARC VAN DER HEIJDE	MARGARET CALVERT	MARION FINK	MARTIN LORENZ	MATTHIAS GÖRLICH	MICHAEL GEORGIOU
16	53	13	13	12	19

NIKKI GONNISSEN	OLIVER KLIMPEL	PAUL BARNES	PREM KRISHNAMURTHY	RENATA GRAW	RICHARD WALKER
19	12	19	12	12	15

S. HOFFMANN ROBBIANI	SASCHA LOBE	STEFAN SAGMEISTER	SVEN VOELKER	TIM BALAAM	URS LEHNI
26	20	23	11	11	13

YASMIN KHAN	YVES FIDALGO	AVERAGE/LONGEST/SHORTEST
12	9	A 16¾ L 58 S 7

How many years have you been working?
—

Now

ANDREAS GNASS ('98) ANDREW STEVENS ('94) ANNELYS DE VET ('95) ANTÓNIO S. GOMES ('95) BEN BRANAGAN ('97) BERND HILPERT ('96)

BRIAN WEBB ('68) CHRISTIAN HEUSSER ('99) DANIEL EATOCK ('98) DANIJELA DJOKIC ('98) EMMI SALONEN ('00) ÉRIC & MARIE GASPAR ('99)

FONS HICKMANN ('93) HANS D. REICHERT ('82) HOLGER JACOBS ('97) HOON KIM ('07) HYOUN YOUL JOE ('03) ISABELLE SWIDERSKI ('96)

JAMES GOGGIN ('97) JAN WILKER ('98) JULIE GAYARD ('95) KAI VON RABENAU ('98) KEN GARLAND ('53) KIRSTY CARTER ('93)

KRISTINE MATTHEWS ('96) LARS HARMSEN ('94) LAURENT LACOUR ('00) LIZA ENEBEIS ('96) LUCINDA NOBLE ('99) MAKI SUZUKI ('98)

MARC V. D. HEIJDE ('93) MARGARET CALVERT ('62) MARION FINK ('99) MARTIN LORENZ ('97) MATTHIAS GÖRLICH ('00) MICHAEL GEORGIOU ('84)

NIKKI GONNISSEN ('93) OLIVER KLIMPEL ('96) PAUL BARNES ('92) P. KRISHNAMURTHY ('98) RENATA GRAW ('08) RICHARD WALKER ('96)

SANDRA HOFFMANN ('90) SASCHA LOBE ('90) STEFAN SAGMEISTER ('84) SVEN VOELKER ('99) TIM BALAAM ('98) URS LEHNI ('99)

YASMIN KHAN ('04) YVES FIDALGO ('00)

Portrait

Then

ANDREAS GNASS ('09) · ANDREW STEVENS ('10) · ANNELYS DE VET ('10) · ANTÓNIO S. GOMES ('10) · BEN BRANAGAN ('10) · BERND HILPERT ('10)

BRIAN WEBB ('09) · CHRISTIAN HEUSSER ('10) · DANIEL EATOCK ('10) · DANIJELA DJOKIC ('10) · EMMI SALONEN ('10) · ÉRIC & MARIE GASPAR ('10)

FONS HICKMANN ('10) · HANS D. REICHERT ('10) · HOLGER JACOBS ('10) · HOON KIM ('11) · HYOUN YOUL JOE ('10) · ISABELLE SWIDERSKI ('10)

JAMES GOGGIN ('10) · JAN WILKER ('10) · JULIE GAYARD ('10) · KAI VON RABENAU ('10) · KEN GARLAND ('11) · KIRSTY CARTER ('11)

KRISTINE MATTHEWS ('10) · LARS HARMSEN ('11) · LAURENT LACOUR ('10) · LIZA ENEBEIS ('11) · L. NEWTON-DUNN ('10) · MAKI SUZUKI ('10)

MARC V. D. HEIJDE ('10) · MARGARET CALVERT ('04) · MARION FINK ('10) · MARTIN LORENZ ('10) · MATTHIAS GÖRLICH ('11) · MICHAEL GEORGIOU ('10)

NIKKI GONNISSEN ('10) · OLIVER KLIMPEL ('11) · PAUL BARNES ('11) · P. KRISHNAMURTHY ('10) · RENATA GRAW ('11) · RICHARD WALKER ('10)

S. HOFFMANN ROBBIANI ('10) · SASCHA LOBE ('11) · STEFAN SAGMEISTER ('10) · SVEN VOELKER ('09) · TIM BALAAM ('10) · URS LEHNI ('10)

YASMIN KHAN ('10) · YVES FIDALGO ('10)

Portrait

Now

Student work of 50 graphic designers

Projects Then

Professional work of 50 graphic designers

Projects Now

Andreas Gnass

Shout out loud when your idea is good, shut up if not + Don't take yourself too seriously

YEAR OF PROJECT
1999

STUDENT PROJECT BRIEF
Self-initiated diploma project to design a fashion publication that had nothing to do with fashion

COLLEGE
Hochschule Darmstadt (Germany)

TUTOR(S)
Prof. Sandra Hoffmann Robbiani (see also pp. 194–197)

COLLABORATOR(S)
Brita Wiesbach (design), Marijan Kojic (text)

TECHNOLOGY
Brain

TIME SPENT
200 hours

TYPEFACE
Monospace 821, animated Helvetica

WHY DO YOU LIKE THIS PROJECT?
Because it was a jump in at the deep end – I had no contacts and no ideas about business. I like the self-made aspects and that the project is taken beyond the pure design aspects. The project was also the starting point of the collaboration with Brita Wiesbach, which is still ongoing.

WHAT DO YOU DISLIKE ABOUT IT?
To have worked on the project after our diploma. We only managed a short comeback as a T-shirt warehouse called 'sheeg.com'.

OUTCOMES
Brief yourself!

FEEDBACK
It worked – we got the industry contacts and realized a nearly 'real' photoshoot and a printed supplement.

PROJECT SIMILARITIES THEN AND NOW
Our goal was to make a real-life project as a diploma project, not a fantasy project. A fashion magazine in Darmstadt was a really absurd idea in the Darmstadt of 1999. The aesthetics grew around the plan of connecting with fashion people but with nearly no budget to spend. So at the end there was no style/look that we liked because of its beauty or coolness – it had one story, a basis and was still fragile and searching – not like a dogma. The sum of elements and media made the message.

The Hafen 2 project developed in a similar way. In the beginning, the client had different ideas on how to establish a new urban place with music/café/art in Offenbach am Main (Germany). But there was no clear idea of where exactly the journey would lead. Like our diploma project, the Hafen 2 was considered as temporary – based in a harbour wasteland, the buildings should have been demolished within a few years. While searching and specifying its way of being the design grew and changed. It was distorted and rebuilt. For me it's great to see design as a vivid aspect, not as the end of a road.

FAVOURITE FOOD THEN
I didn't have a favourite food

YOUR MOST VALUED POSSESSION THEN
Bike

Project Then

Andreas Gnass (U9 visuelle Allianz)

A VALUABLE QUALITY FOR A DESIGN STUDENT + A DESIGN PROFESSIONAL

Curiosity and a little bit of modesty + Staying relaxed

YEAR OF PROJECT
2004–ongoing

PROFESSIONAL PROJECT BRIEF
Corporate identity for Hafen 2, a non-profit association 'suesswasser e.V. – Art and Culture in Offenbach's harbour' plus a network of many associated creative minds

CLIENT
Hafen 2, Offenbach am Main (Germany)

COLLABORATOR(S)
Brita Wiesbach Gnass, Sabrina Hahn, Valerie Rapp

TECHNOLOGY
Brain

TIME SPENT
100 hours

TYPEFACE
OSK, Akzidenz Grotesk

WHY DO YOU LIKE THIS PROJECT?
We support this cultural project with special pricing, but have a lead position according to every question of visual communication. I also like the fact that it is playful.

OUTCOMES
Expand the briefing!

FEEDBACK
The brand is well known and highly recognizable while being in constant flow.

DO YOU TEACH?
Typography – one year in Darmstadt, three years at the Free University of Bolzano. I stopped in 2010 because I was a little bit bored of not having enough time for designing, and it was a very long way to travel between Bolzano (Italy) and Offenbach (Germany).

IS IT POSSIBLE TO TEACH DESIGN?
The main aspect in teaching design is to sensitize the students to ask the important questions. The second point is to give answers to some basic questions. That's all.

FAVOURITE FOOD NOW
I still don't have a favourite food. I do like fish, different kinds of pasta and good entrecôte and lamb, though

YOUR MOST VALUED POSSESSION NOW
Family

Project Now

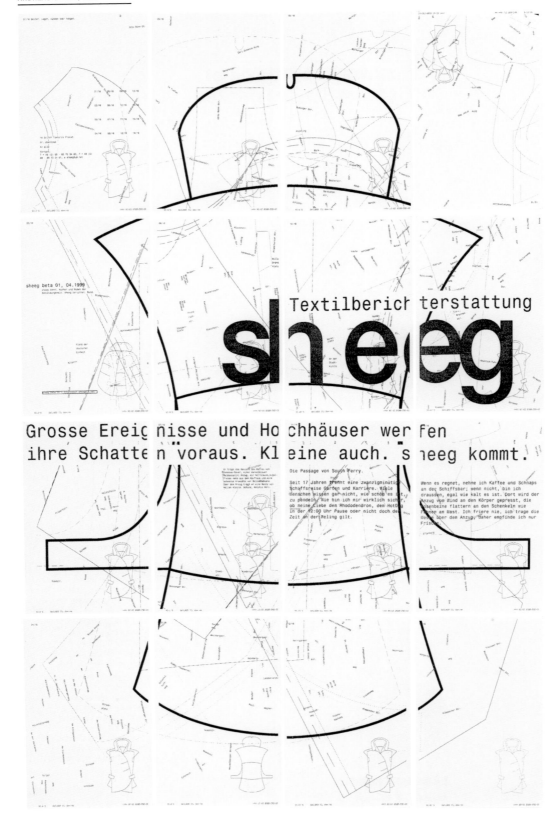

Textilbericht terstattung

sheeg

Grosse Ereignisse und Hochhäuser werfen
ihre Schatten voraus. Kleine auch. sheeg kommt.

sheeg beta 01, 04.1999

Die Passage von South Ferry.

Seit 17 Jahren trennt eine zwanzigminütige
Schiffsreise Garten und Karriere. Viele
Menschen wissen gar nicht, wie schön es ist,
zu pendeln. Nie bin ich mir wirklich sicher,
ob meine Liebe dem Rhododendron, dem HotDog
in der 12:00 Uhr Pause oder nicht doch der
Zeit an der Reling gilt.

Wenn es regnet, nehme ich Kaffee und Schnaps
an der Schiffsbar, wenn nicht, bin ich
draussen, egal wie kalt es ist. Dort wird der
Anzug vom Wind an den Körper gepresst, die
Hosenbeine flattern an den Schenkeln wie
Fahnen am Mast. Ich friere nie, ich trage die
Wärme über dem Anzug, daher empfinde ich nur
Frische.

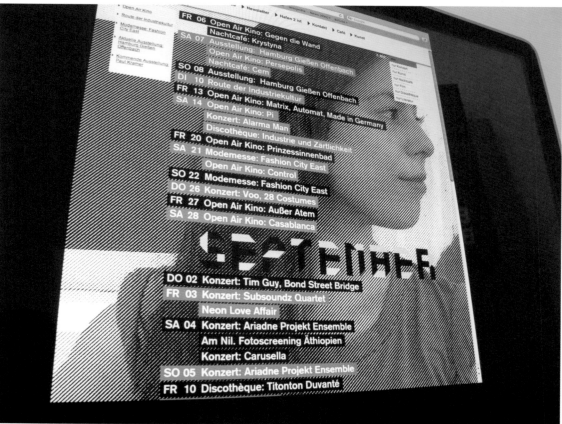

Andrew Stevens

Learn the basics of good type, layout and colour – it won't make you a mundane designer. It will give you a foundation and a better chance to get a job + Don't forget there are students in other departments – you may find yourself working with them after college

YEAR OF PROJECT
1990

STUDENT PROJECT BRIEF
Invite a speaker to college and design a poster for it. I chose the photographer Paul Reas

COLLEGE
Royal College of Art, London (United Kingdom)

TUTOR(S)
Margaret Calvert was head of course then, Derek Birdsall was head the previous year, but mostly I spoke with peers on this project

TECHNOLOGY
Litho and silkscreen

TIME SPENT
2–3 months

TYPEFACE
Snell Roundhand (an unrefined vision of refinement)

WHY DO YOU LIKE THIS PROJECT?
I grew up when photographers like Paul Reas, Paul Graham and Martin Parr were working, photographing the dusty corners of places, rather than the Henri Cartier-Bresson traditional black-and-white approach to the world, and in that work I could see a Britain that I recognized. This is something I also try to do with my work, and that is very much present in this project: observation, reference to the vernacular. I also like the use of the typeface Snell Roundhand – a very unrefined vision of refinement.

WHAT DO YOU DISLIKE ABOUT IT?
The overprinted typography should dominate more; it should have been stronger. Also, I kept the box white so that the images would read better but that wasn't necessary, and in retrospect I see it was a compromise. I should have left it brown, and just printed onto it as it was.

FEEDBACK
Some posters fell down during the degree-show exhibition and the cleaners binned them, so I guess that's a negative feedback. My peers liked it, although I don't think it has much commercial appeal.

FAVOURITE FOOD THEN
Rigatoni Siciliana

YOUR MOST VALUED POSSESSION THEN
Sony Walkman

Project Then

PROJECT SIMILARITIES THEN AND NOW
Physicality, reference to the vernacular, mixing rawness with graphic things.

Andrew Stevens (Graphic Thought Facility)

A VALUABLE QUALITY FOR A DESIGN STUDENT + A DESIGN PROFESSIONAL

Energy + Clarity

YEAR OF PROJECT
1999

PROFESSIONAL PROJECT BRIEF
Design the prospectus for the Royal College of Art, working within an existing budget and with the different college departments

CLIENT
Royal College of Art, London (United Kingdom)

COLLABORATOR(S)
GTF members + illustrator Kam Tang

TECHNOLOGY
Offset

TIME SPENT
At least 6 months

TYPEFACE
Futura Bold and a monospace font (I think Souvenir)

FAVOURITE FOOD NOW
Home-cooked peasant food (pasta, rice)

YOUR MOST VALUED POSSESSION NOW
Camper van

WHY DO YOU LIKE THIS PROJECT?
It was the first time we were given the whole budget for design and production, and could really consider a project in its entirety. We were able to change the usual full-colour, coated-paper approach and instead print the job in a single colour, but use the money saved to print on good paper. Then, full colour came in at the start of the prospectus, for the illustrations of Kam Tang, a visual journey of the MA course. I especially like the treatment of the imagery for each department, as this can be very tricky when dealing with different departments from within the college with different ideas about the type of images required. Instead, we proposed to scan the college's press clippings (of which the RCA has a rich archive). This was more relevant as it showed the scope of the work, but crucially tied the whole prospectus together graphically, as every department was described through photocopied press clippings. I especially like the presence of a News of the World clipping for the Vehicle Design spread (not sophisticated, but important) and the map of the RCA building, essentially a scan of the previous year's prospectus.

WHAT DO YOU DISLIKE ABOUT IT?
Nothing really.

OUTCOMES
We were asked to do the prospectus for the following year.

FEEDBACK
Good, as we were also asked to do it for the following year. I don't know if it increased or decreased application numbers, though.

DO YOU TEACH?
I have been external examiner at Chelsea College of Art and Design, London (UK). More recently at the National College of Art and Design (NCAD) in Dublin (Ireland).

IS IT POSSIBLE TO TEACH DESIGN?
It's not possible to teach a sensibility, but by encompassing creativity, resource-fulness and originality you can create the framework for someone to develop.

Project Now

Paul Reas

• Photographer • Graphic Design Paul Reas, Paul Reas •

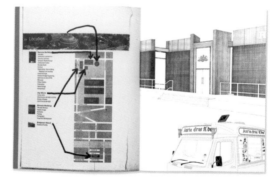

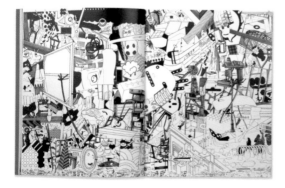

Annelys de Vet

Use your own vision and mentality in order to form design decisions + Don't believe your professor

YEAR OF PROJECT
1995

STUDENT PROJECT BRIEF
Make different sequences within the theme of 'climax'. I chose to focus on the concept of 'orgasm'.

COLLEGE
Hogeschool voor de Kunsten (HKU), Utrecht (The Netherlands)

TUTOR(S)
Paul Gofferjé

TIME SPENT
3 months

WHY DO YOU LIKE THIS PROJECT?
The image is about pop culture and the representation of sex. It's a still of Madonna's 'Like a Virgin' video clip that has been repeated only by zooming in. Nothing changes, but the repetition makes the story. The other image is a remake with a remake. A sex doll is photographed from the same perspective as Madonna in her clip, and that image is screenprinted on tiles, referring to traditional 'Delftsblauwe' tiles. Again, the repetition changes the representation and makes the vulgar images safe and normal.

FEEDBACK
Invitation to exhibit it at two external places.

FAVOURITE FOOD THEN
-

YOUR MOST VALUED POSSESSION THEN
-

Project Then

PROJECT SIMILARITIES THEN AND NOW
The quality of repetition, the strength of patterns.

Annelys de Vet

Same for both: Use your own vision and mentality in order to form design decisions

YEAR OF PROJECT
2011

PROFESSIONAL PROJECT BRIEF
Develop a calendar for a new area in the Dutch village Puttershoek. I designed 12 tea towels, one for each month, with regional lists of words that express the cultural or botanical characteristics of the village. The tea towels were produced by the Textile Museum in Tilburg.

CLIENT
Binnenmaas (village) & SKOR

TIME SPENT
3 years

TYPEFACE
Ceacilia by Matthias Noordzij

WHY DO YOU LIKE THIS PROJECT?
This is a set of 12 tea towels that together create a calendar of the Dutch village Puttershoek. Each towel represents a local theme or story that is specific for the month. So in September it shows the types of apples and potatoes that are being picked in that month; in October it shows the process of making sugar in approximately 30 words because the village is famous for its sugar factory. The calendar as a whole puts the normal at the centre and shows how special and characteristic that is. The graphic design is based on old Dutch tea towels.

FEEDBACK
The local people appreciate the project a lot; much more than they realized before it was finished – they never could imagine what the full project actually meant. There is also a website, big monthly banners in the quarter, a publication for all new citizens and a website, www.kalenderputtershoek.nl. The locals were proud and excited that 'their' story was woven in the towels. At the same time, people who are not connected to the village appreciate the set of towels for the design and the particular stories. I've sold more towels to outsiders than to insiders. The project was shortlisted for the Dutch Design Awards.

FAVOURITE FOOD NOW
-

YOUR MOST VALUED POSSESSION NOW
-

Project Now

DO YOU TEACH?
Previously: Design Academy Eindhoven (The Netherlands), Communication Department
Currently: Head of Design Department, Sandberg Instituut Amsterdam (The Netherlands).

IS IT POSSIBLE TO TEACH DESIGN?
Yes.

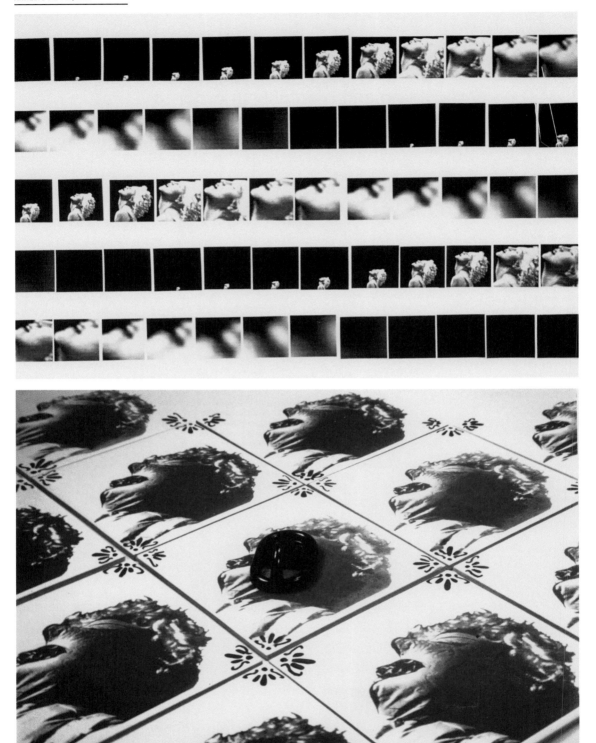

António Silveira Gomes

Design affects the way we perceive information. Students must understand the consequences of their work before placing a new artefact into the world + I would like to quote Cedric Price: 'Technology is the answer, but what was the question?'

YEAR OF PROJECT
1995

STUDENT PROJECT BRIEF
To make a short documentary film to be presented in a class critique simulating a festival ambience, for which we also had to design a poster and a booklet

COLLEGE
Faculdade de Belas Artes da Universidade de Lisboa, Lisbon (Portugal)

TUTOR(S)
Aurelindo Ceia

COLLABORATOR(S)
José Albergaria (co-author) Pedro Correia (voice dubbing and translations)

TITLE OF PROJECT
b.b.w: The Life and Times of Bill Burst Williams

TECHNOLOGY
Hi8 amateur camcorder, Polaroid Sx70 film, Letraset, photocopied images, Rotring artpen, Indian ink, Tipp-Ex, sticky tape, watercolours, paintbrushes, a PC and an overused Epson jet printer, scenery paper and glue.

FAVOURITE FOOD THEN
Pasta fredda

YOUR MOST VALUED POSSESSION THEN
At the time I didn't care much about stuff

TIME SPENT
1 month

TYPEFACE
Letraset, hand-lettering (mostly scrawl), system font (probably Arial)

WHY DO YOU LIKE THIS PROJECT?
Our response to the brief was inadvertently closer to the mockumentary form, which made the whole experience more interesting as a learning device – playing with narrative to reach a critical understanding of an artist's work, in this case, that of the artist Bob Flanagan.

WHAT DO YOU DISLIKE ABOUT IT?
Nothing.

OUTCOMES
The storyline for the film was a fake (five-minute) biopic constructed around the artist and poet Bob Flanagan in an attempt to understand the relationship between his art and the excruciating pain he felt during his performances. We first traced his identity (under a fictitious name) and then cross-examined his work through the eyes of four stereotypical art-scene characters. Due to technical restrictions, the film was shot in one take. We designed a huge map/collage to be the main scenery and making

the film involved walking over it, shooting one continuous take, and dubbing live music from tapes and doing sound effects like a bad Kung Fu movie. We had to shoot the film more than once to get it right, so in a way it was like choreography. It was a physically tiring project and we felt a certain satisfaction when we managed to get it right. Making the scenery – a 4×2-metre illustrated chart – and then walking all over it as we filmed also put us in a destructive relationship with our own work, echoing Flanagan's sadomasochism. We never had any particular fondness for Flanagan's performance work, yet as we delved deeper into his writings we encountered an incredible consistency in his thought.

FEEDBACK
There were some negative responses, given the brutality of Flanagan's work. Still, the film was later chosen for an experimental video festival and it now belongs to the Lisbon Municipal Videotheque archives. We never got to send the film to Bob Flanagan because he passed away soon after, in 1996.

PROJECT SIMILARITIES THEN AND NOW
The contexts were very different, but there were nonetheless natural similarities between the projects. The student project is about a body of work that spreads over 20 years of suffering; the professional one is a moment in time where two communities mingle and celebrate over a thousand years of difference. Both challenge us as designers to represent problems of identity: an artist with a chronic disease and the identity he constructs through his work; the autonomy of a Gypsy community that bought land in a European country and began to settle. Each problem is addressed in both projects through a mapping device: a family tree, a street map or an imaginary cartography functions as scenery. And both projects were made with minimal costs in resources such as fonts and paper output. In the case of the Baralha project, we worked not-for-profit.

Project Then

António Silveira Gomes
(barbara says… Projecto Próprio)

A VALUABLE QUALITY FOR A DESIGN STUDENT + A DESIGN PROFESSIONAL

To approach any exercise with a serious attitude even in the simulated scenarios that are common in design schools + To be able to listen even if you feel you know what a client is about to say

YEAR OF PROJECT
2010

PROFESSIONAL PROJECT BRIEF
To design a book, map, website and signage for a street performance festival that took place within a Gypsy family commune

CLIENT
Marco Martins (film director and scenographer)

COLLABORATOR(S)
Claudia Castelo (art direction and production) Alexandre Castro (web and graphic design), Patrícia Maya (graphic design), Maiadouro (printing)

TITLE OF PROJECT
Baralha

TECHNOLOGY
2 iMacs, laser printer, desktop publishing software: CS3, Fontographer, Google Earth

TIME SPENT
3 months

TYPEFACE
Gentium + 2 custom fonts (Cristiana, Deus Viveaqi), hand-lettering sampled from the walls of the Gypsy dwellings

FAVOURITE FOOD NOW
Spaghetti alle vongole

YOUR MOST VALUED POSSESSION NOW
My young daughter

WHY DO YOU LIKE THIS PROJECT?
The fact that the book embodied a powerful visual statement for the identity of this particular Gypsy family: their need for territorial autonomy as a sedentary group, going against their natural nomadic heritage. We as Europeans become more nomadic as the Gypsy community becomes sedentary. We designed a tree showing the 70 family members and shaped it to resemble the official flag of this ethnic Gypsy group.

WHAT DO YOU DISLIKE ABOUT IT?
A few insignificant technical details in the binding and layout.

OUTCOMES
The performance comprised a series of documentary videos and live shows with actors, musicians and choreographers. These were made within the gypsy dwellings and in the surrounding woods. Some were the result of workshops with the community and others were interviews. I visited the camp before our work on the book started and quickly realized that the context wasn't about performance but about understanding and interacting with an incredibly autonomous culture. The project opened my mind towards the complex issues regarding Gypsy integration in Portugal, to their semantic and cultural codes (the Portuguese word for 'gypsy' is quite demeaning) and their social organization as a tribe.

FEEDBACK
Most responses were positive.

DO YOU TEACH?
Currently guest lecturer at the Universidade de Coimbra – Faculty of Computer Sciences (Portugal). Lecturing Design III (studio practice).

IS IT POSSIBLE TO TEACH DESIGN?
Yes. I am a teacher. As a design student, I learned how to appreciate design thinking as an autonomous discipline, to defend my work reasonably and respectfully, accepting an honest critique from my tutors, distinguishing between good and bad ideas, working on developing an idea through creative speculation, working and sharing ideas collaboratively. I also mastered drawing (even though I don't practise it much). Apart from this, a copious amount of theory solidified my understanding of philosophy and history. Nevertheless, I still feel I should have learned more practical skills in school.

Project Now

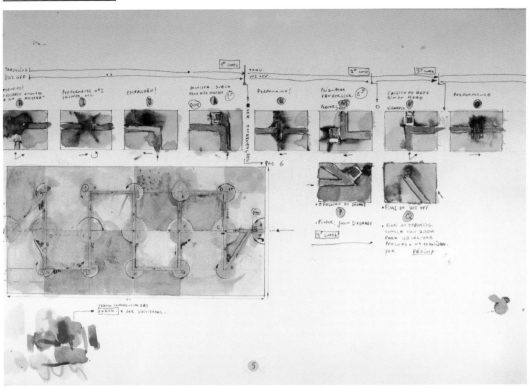

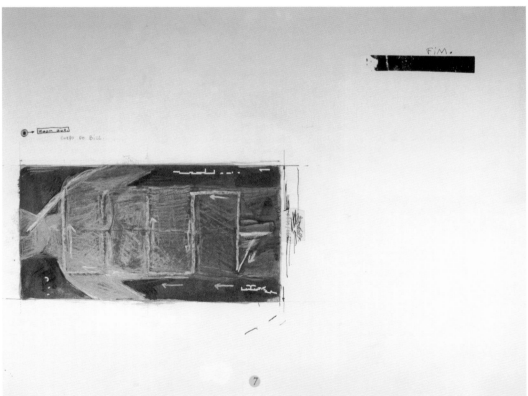

Ben Branagan

A PIECE OF SOUND ADVICE + A SINGLE WARNING TO A DESIGN STUDENT

Enjoy yourself + Don't do what you think your tutor wants to see

YEAR OF PROJECT
1997

STUDENT PROJECT BRIEF
Produce a typographic poster using one of a selection of poems

COLLEGE
Kingston University, London (United Kingdom)

TUTOR(S)
Chris Draper

TECHNOLOGY
Letterpress proofing printer, photocopier, Mac

TIME SPENT
1 day

TYPEFACE
Impact

WHY DO YOU LIKE THIS PROJECT?
This is one of the first pieces of graphic design I made as a student – I was doing my foundation at the time. It has a loose and casual feel, largely inspired by not knowing what I was doing, which I like a lot. I had a lot of fun in the print workshop making the backgrounds – I still like experimenting with different materials and processes in both my professional and personal work today.

WHAT DO YOU DISLIKE ABOUT IT?
The way the typography reads across the page needs a lot of work, and I am not keen on Impact as a font.

PROJECT SIMILARITIES THEN AND NOW
There are lots of similarities between the two – a limited colour palette, use of overprinting and processes – these are things that crop up quite a lot in my work. Despite this visual overlap they are, for me, emblematic of two different areas of my practice as a designer. The one from my student days is more indicative of personal motivations and interests in my work that extend beyond a professional context; an outlook on design and communication that really began during my time at art school. The later one is typical of lots of the work I have done while running a small, one-man studio; it's not one of the big or more involving projects that I would naturally refer back to when thinking about my work. It's a smaller, more everyday project that, while much more practical than the first, shares a common outlook.

FAVOURITE FOOD THEN
Bacon sandwich

YOUR MOST VALUED POSSESSION THEN
No one thing really comes to mind

Project Then

LONDON, UNITED KINGDOM

Ben Branagan

A VALUABLE QUALITY FOR A DESIGN STUDENT + A DESIGN PROFESSIONAL

Openness + Resilience

YEAR OF PROJECT
2010

PROFESSIONAL PROJECT BRIEF
Design of template and initial poster for a series of talks organized by the Graphic Design Department at Epsom University

CLIENT
UCA Epsom Graphic Design Department

TECHNOLOGY
Mac, offset litho

TIME SPENT
2 days

TYPEFACE
Franklin Gothic

WHY DO YOU LIKE THIS PROJECT?
This was a small project I undertook alongside some teaching I was doing on the design communication course at Epsom. I originally suggested a different solution for the posters, which at the time I felt was far more interesting and exciting graphically. However, for one reason or another that one didn't make it and this solution emerged in a kind of ad-hoc manner after further discussions with staff at the college. I like solutions that emerge in this organic way. Looking back at it now, I think it works a lot better than the original proposal I submitted. As a simple typographic piece, it's something I am very pleased with.

WHAT DO YOU DISLIKE ABOUT IT?
The intention for the project was to produce a template or system that would allow posters to be produced at short notice for upcoming talks. Exploiting the positioning and the colour of the overprinted section would give each poster an individual quality while creating a set of posters that worked as a family. Due to complications, the subsequent series never happened, so I was left with a single poster rather than the multiple configurations and versions I had in mind when designing it.

DO YOU TEACH?
Design Communication, Bachelor & Master of Arts, Chelsea College of Art & Design (UK); Graphic Design Bachelor of Arts, UCA Epsom (UK).

IS IT POSSIBLE TO TEACH DESIGN?
You can teach design, certainly the technical aspects; the creative side of it is harder. I learned a lot at college, but I have also learned a lot since – I don't see them as two really distinct periods but part of the same development. The most important thing to take from college is an understanding of your own practice, understanding the type of work you want to be involved in and how you will approach it.

FAVOURITE FOOD NOW
Rendang

YOUR MOST VALUED POSSESSION NOW
No one thing really comes to mind

Project Now

and I've
done nearly

nothing
all day,

nearly
nothing all day.

If get my way.

When it's six o'clock

Yes six p.m.
done

I'll do half as much tomorrow

JONATHAN BARNBROOK U.C.A. EPSOM 15.10.08

The first of this years EPSOM lecture series.

Jonathan Barnbrook has emerged in the past two decades as one of the UK's most consistently innovative graphic designers. Pioneering graphic design with a social conscience, Barnbrook makes powerful statements about corporate culture, consumerism, war and international politics. Through his work in both commercial and non-commercial spheres he combines wit, political savvy and bitter irony in equal measures.

Signed copies of 'Barnbrook Bible' will be available.

Tickets & information:

Contact: Maxine Alexander
malexander1@ucreative.ac.uk

University for the Creative Arts, Epsom
www.ucreative.ac.uk/epsom

Venue: Epsom Playhouse
Ashley Avenue, Epsom KT18 5AL
14:30 | 15.10.08

university for the creative arts

Bernd Hilpert

Be sure that your work is relevant + Never think you are the benchmark of the things you do

YEAR OF PROJECT
1996

STUDENT PROJECT BRIEF
We often had very open briefs that dealt with essential questions of our daily life – tools or spaces. The brief for this project was 'thinking about the future way of housing and living'.

COLLEGE
ENSCI Les Ateliers, Paris (France)

TUTOR(S)
Prof. Marc Bertier

COLLABORATOR(S)
The student team and my professor (see above)

TECHNOLOGY
The most important tool was my fineliner (today the Penxacta). Besides that, it was the Mac with its software (Mac LC III)

TIME SPENT
6 months, as one of two projects (and without really finishing it)

WHY DO YOU LIKE THIS PROJECT?
The most important part of the project was to look into a subject: to reflect the background, to discuss the statement, to answer the question. During my student time, we were pushed to open our minds and to look for solutions that were not obvious. Today this is still the basis of my work.

WHAT DO YOU DISLIKE ABOUT IT?
Nothing. But the result depends on the time of its origin. It reflects your personal background and experience, but is also influenced by trends and the general spirit of the time.

OUTCOMES
A new level of experience. Each project is a step forwards regardless of whether you think that the result is OK.

FEEDBACK
The students' work was shown on several occasions, but only in the context of the college.

FAVOURITE FOOD THEN
Kellogg's Smacks

YOUR MOST VALUED POSSESSION THEN
My professional equipment

Project Then

PROJECT SIMILARITIES THEN AND NOW
Apart from an approach that was similar, both projects deal with space, perception and context.

Bernd Hilpert (unit-design)

A VALUABLE QUALITY FOR A DESIGN STUDENT + A DESIGN PROFESSIONAL

To have your own idea +
To have your own idea and
to be able to realize it

YEAR OF PROJECT
2009

PROFESSIONAL PROJECT BRIEF
Design of a visitor
information system for a
Nazi concentration camp.

CLIENT
Mahn- und Gedenkstätte
Ravensbrück (The
Ravensbrück National
Memorial)

COLLABORATOR(S)
The team in the studio
and the project partners,
the client and the architect
(Wolfgang Lorch + Niko
Hirsch), other specialized
designers and – not to
forget – the people who
did the production.
The idea of co-operation
is essential to my work
as a designer.

TECHNOLOGY
The most important tool is my
Penxacta. Besides that, it is
the Mac with its software
(Powerbook G4). Interestingly,
I still use software I learned
to use during my time as a
student – with the old serial
version.

TIME SPENT
6 months; as one of
15 projects

TYPEFACE
FF Unit

WHY DO YOU LIKE THIS PROJECT?
For this project, the main
question was to find a design
expression that suits the
sensitive and serious context
of the site. To bring together all
dimensions of design to a well-
balanced and appropriate
setting; the product and its
making, the positioning, colour,
surface, type and the graphic
layout.

WHAT DO YOU DISLIKE ABOUT IT?
See answer opposite (then).

OUTCOMES
See answer opposite (then).

FEEDBACK
Besides the feedback within
the team, from colleagues or
in the specialized press,
I know that each day there is
somebody using or reflecting
the design products I realized
(without getting the reaction
of the recipients in most
cases…).

FAVOURITE FOOD NOW
Good restaurant food
(typical local kitchen –
all over the world)

YOUR MOST VALUED
POSSESSION NOW
The studio in which
I am a partner

DO YOU TEACH?
No.

IS IT POSSIBLE TO
TEACH DESIGN?
Yes, it's possible and
necessary. The designer
has to be formed on
different levels:
personally, technically
and culturally.

Project Now

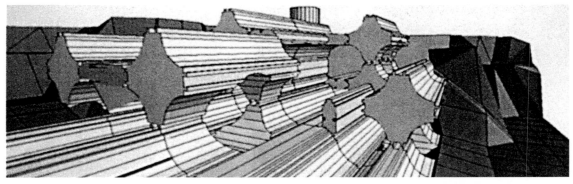

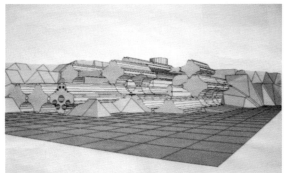 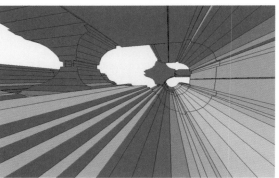

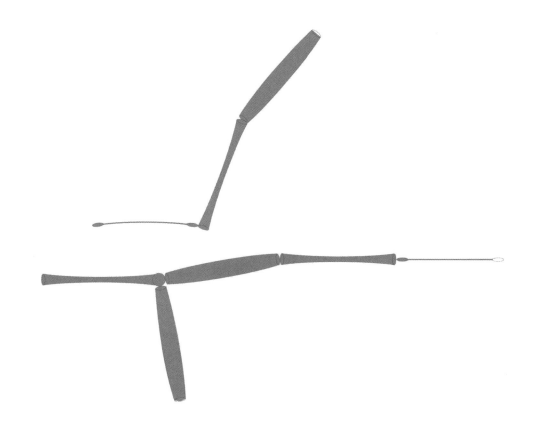

31

»Erschießungsgang« | 1959

Der als »Erschießungsgang« ausgewiesene Gang
zwischen der Rückseite des Garagentraktes und
der Lagermauer entstand im Zuge einer baulichen
Umplanung. Seine Nutzung als Erschießungsort
ist allerdings durch Quellen historisch nicht
nachweisbar. Er war zeitweise zugemauert. Da
ehemalige Häftlinge berichteten, Schüsse im
Krematoriumsbereich gehört zu haben, wurde
in dieser baulichen Lücke ein »Todes« oder
»Erschießungsgang« vermutet und deshalb 1959
hier der Gedenkstein aufgestellt.

Commemorative Stone Marking the
"Execution Passage" | 1959

The passage between the garage complex's rear
wall and the camp wall was created by structural
alterations and became known as the "execution
passage". There is, however, no historical
evidence to prove that it was actually used for
executions. The passage was temporarily bricked
up. It was assumed that this gap between the
two structures formed a "death" or "execution
passage" because survivors had remembered
hearing shots in the area near the crematorium,
and therefore the commemorative stone was
set up here in 1959.

29

Gaskammer
Gas Chamber |
1944–45

das Haftling
stattfindenden entv
der Häftlinge erhiel
vieler überlebende
Mauerreste, der Bo

Brian Webb

A PIECE OF SOUND ADVICE + A SINGLE WARNING TO A DESIGN STUDENT

Don't ever apologize for a job + If you're not enjoying it, don't do it

YEAR OF PROJECT
1966

STUDENT PROJECT BRIEF
Design a poster for a lecture

COLLEGE
Canterbury College of Art (United Kingdom)

TUTOR(S)
Stanley Hickson, Head of College

TECHNOLOGY
5×4 negative and photographic print, Letraset type

TIME SPENT
2 weeks thinking, 2 days doing

TYPEFACE
Cooper Black Italic

WHY DO YOU LIKE THIS PROJECT?
My student piece isn't one of the best things I did at college, but it is memorable for several reasons. It was designed in 1966. It's a poster for a lecture by Arnold Schwartzman, who had been at college a few years before me. He was working at ATV television at the time and went on to win an Oscar for his Los Angeles Olympics film. The reason it's memorable for me is that it was about that time I discovered ideas rather than decorating the surface. The lecture was going to be on TV graphics. I thought if I photographed a TV screen (ideally with an image of Schwartzman on it), enlarged it to poster size and called it Between the Lines, that it would make an interesting poster. First problem: I didn't own a TV set. The photographing of TV screens was hit and miss with a 5×4 plate camera and I only had a couple of sheets of film.

A friend at college had an old portable TV. There was a lunchtime news programme; I wanted a face and Harold Wilson (the prime minister at the time) appeared on the screen and I took two quick shots. The negatives were very thin when I processed them, but enough to get an image – now I could do it easily on a computer. As I looked at it, I thought the prime minister should be announcing the lecture in a TV-screen-shaped speech bubble. In close up the image was pretty crude. I had thought of putting the type between the lines. As a large poster you could read the face; close up you could read the type, and the image at 425 lines per inch became a pattern. I began to like design with several layers of meaning.

OUTCOMES
Design is more than surface decoration.

FEEDBACK
Arnold liked it.

ANYTHING ELSE
Most of the projects I did at college were typeset and printed letterpress.

FAVOURITE FOOD THEN
Chinese

YOUR MOST VALUED POSSESSION THEN
Books

Project Then

PROJECT SIMILARITIES
THEN AND NOW
An idea doesn't have to be instant; it can sneak up and tap you on the shoulder.

Brian Webb (Webb & Webb Design)

A VALUABLE QUALITY FOR A DESIGN STUDENT + A DESIGN PROFESSIONAL

Insatiable curiosity +
See above plus a bit of
diplomacy

YEAR OF PROJECT
2009

PROFESSIONAL PROJECT BRIEF
**Design a piece to
illustrate a lost or
forgotten word**

CLIENT
**The Art of Lost Words
(The National Literacy
Trust)**

TECHNOLOGY
Letterpress/inkjet

TIME SPENT
**2 weeks thinking,
2 days doing**

TYPEFACE
**Wood Letter Grotesque,
Gill Sans Bold**

WHY DO YOU LIKE THIS PROJECT?
**As then (see answer opposite)
– using type elements to add
a layer of meaning.**

OUTCOMES
**Using letterpress to solve
a plegnic (adjective: acting
by a blow, striking like a
hammer) process.**

FEEDBACK
**A couple of magazines
reproduced it.**

ANYTHING ELSE
**After 30 years of using
computer type, I now use
letterpress and computers.**

DO YOU TEACH?
**Visiting Professor at
University of the Arts
London (UK), Honorary
Fellow at University
College of the Creative
Arts London (UK) and
lectures, assessing, etc.**

IS IT POSSIBLE TO
TEACH DESIGN?
**Yes, if you're lucky. It
took me five years to
meet a tutor (Edward
Hughes) who talked
about ideas and
problem analysis.**

FAVOURITE FOOD NOW
Japanese

YOUR MOST VALUED
POSSESSION NOW
Books

Project Now

Between the lines
*Arnold Schwartzman
on TV graphics*
**School of Graphic Design
2.15pm October 11**

PLEGNIC

HER PLEGNIC POUNDING OF THE PIANO KEYS CONTRASTED SHARPLY WITH HER TINY FRAME

Christian Heusser

Try as many disciplines as the school offers, especially those that do not seem to fit your tastes at first glance, and be bold + The first idea isn't always the best one

YEAR OF PROJECT
1999

STUDENT PROJECT BRIEF
To translate an object of choice only in black and white. After that, design an F4 poster for the chosen object on a freely chosen topic.

COLLEGE
Hochschule für Gestaltung und Kunst Basel (Switzerland)

TUTOR(S)
Michael Renner

TECHNOLOGY
At first drawing by hand, then using Illustrator

TIME SPENT
2 days a week over one semester

TYPEFACE
Frutiger

WHY DO YOU LIKE THIS PROJECT?
It was my first poster. I like the size of it.

WHAT DO YOU DISLIKE ABOUT IT?
The influence of the school is too visible. Nowadays I would certainly design it differently.

OUTCOMES
The most important thing was to learn that the sketches had to match the end result in size in order to get a feeling for the proportions.

FEEDBACK
At the time, a fellow student asked me if I had won a contest with that poster. I had to admit that I hadn't sent it in.

FAVOURITE FOOD THEN
Pasta pesto

YOUR MOST VALUED POSSESSION THEN
My Mac G4

PROJECT SIMILARITIES THEN AND NOW
Both posters deal with contemporary expressions of art, music and dance. The way the type has been used is similar. The main message is big and not set horizontally.

Project Then

Christian Heusser (Equipo)

The drive to explore and solve problems – to want to discover something new + The ability to throw a good idea overboard and start afresh, even when pressed for time

YEAR OF PROJECT
2010

PROFESSIONAL PROJECT BRIEF
Design the visual concept for the Contemporary Dance Festival in Neuchâtel. Elaborate a low-cost concept, adaptable to several formats, in this case F4.

CLIENT
ADN Neuchâtel

COLLABORATOR(S)
I discussed the sketches with my partners at Equipo (Roman Schnyder and Dirk Koy). Photography: Anja Fonseka.

TECHNOLOGY
Photography, Photoshop, Illustrator, InDesign

TIME SPENT
3 days

TYPEFACE
DIN

WHY DO YOU LIKE THIS PROJECT?
The colours, the silence and the space.

WHAT DO YOU DISLIKE ABOUT IT?
Unfortunately, the picture does not capture the essence of the movement of the dancers.

OUTCOMES
Working with a client you get along with – amusing, entertaining – is sometimes worth more than making lots of money.

FEEDBACK
The client still likes it.

DO YOU TEACH?
Hochschule für Gestaltung und Kunst Basel, Hochschule für Technik Rapperswil, Universität Basel (both Switzerland): a seminar in visual communication in the degree programme of Human Computer Interaction Design.

IS IT POSSIBLE TO TEACH DESIGN?
I believe it is possible to sensitize students to topics such as type, form, space, images, etc. Then they'll need some time to 'exercise' designing.

FAVOURITE FOOD NOW
Anything that has been prepared in the oven

YOUR MOST VALUED POSSESSION NOW
My vinyl collection

Project Now

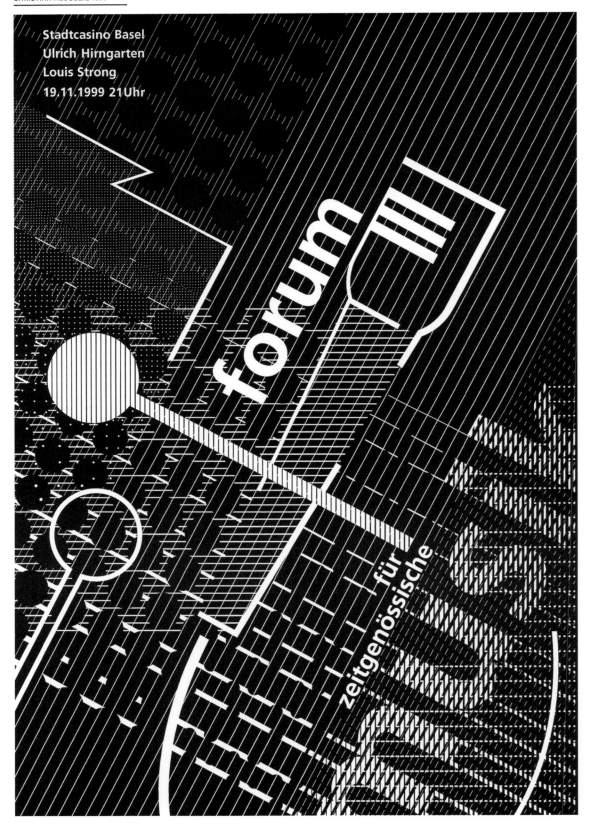

Stadtcasino Basel
Ulrich Hirngarten
Louis Strong
19.11.1999 21Uhr

forum III

für
zeitgenössische

Daniel Eatock

A PIECE OF SOUND ADVICE + A SINGLE WARNING TO A DESIGN STUDENT

Explore, invent +
Scalpels are very sharp

YEAR OF PROJECT
1998

STUDENT PROJECT BRIEF
Self-initiated

COLLEGE
**Royal College of Art,
London (United Kingdom)**

TUTOR(S)
No tutor

TECHNOLOGY
Brain & hands

TIME SPENT
5 minutes

WHY DO YOU LIKE THIS PROJECT?
Sculpture as a punchline.

OUTCOMES
Life affirmation.

FEEDBACK
Smile.

FAVOURITE FOOD THEN
Fruit

YOUR MOST VALUED
POSSESSION NOW
None

Project Then

PROJECT SIMILARITIES
THEN AND NOW
**Both responses
to givens.**

Daniel Eatock

For both: curiosity

YEAR OF PROJECT
2010

PROFESSIONAL PROJECT BRIEF
Self-initiated

CLIENT
**Made for Book Show at
Eastside Projects**

TECHNOLOGY
Brain & hands

TIME SPENT
5 hours

WHY DO YOU LIKE THIS PROJECT
Sculpture as a punchline.

OUTCOMES
Life affirmation.

FEEDBACK
Smile.

FAVOURITE FOOD NOW
Fruit

YOUR MOST VALUED
POSSESSION NOW
None

Project Now

DO YOU TEACH?
Yes, at many places.

IS IT POSSIBLE TO
TEACH DESIGN?
50% possible.

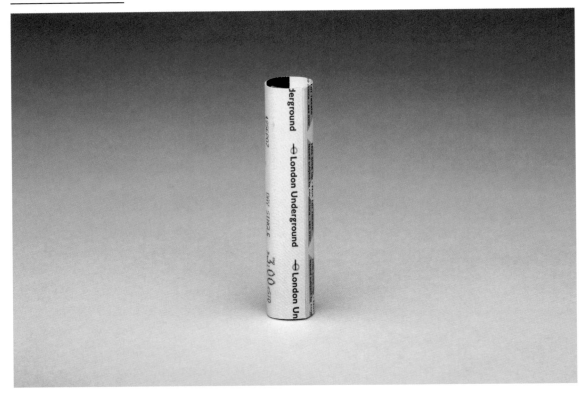

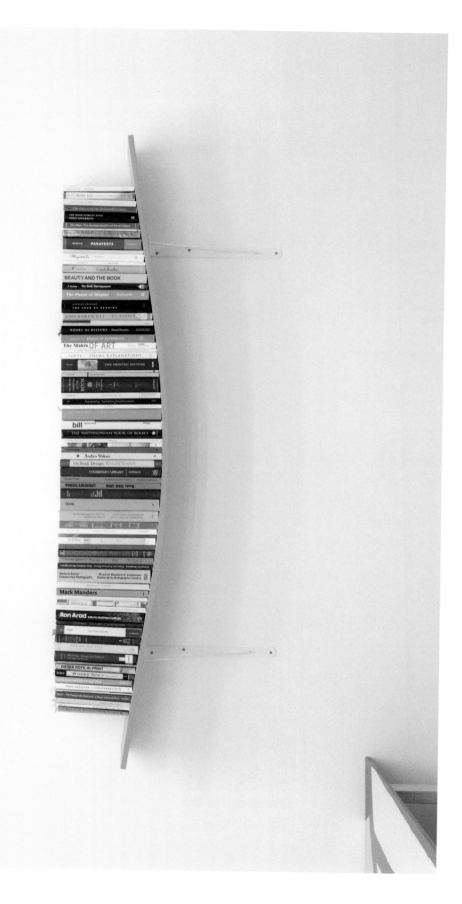

ORIGINALLY YUGOSLAVIAN, GERMAN FOR 11 YEARS

Danijela Djokic

A PIECE OF SOUND ADVICE + A SINGLE WARNING TO A DESIGN STUDENT

Do everything with passion +
Don't be lazy

YEAR OF PROJECT
1998

STUDENT PROJECT BRIEF
**Design a new information
system**

COLLEGE
**Hochschule für
Gestaltung Schwäbisch
Gmünd (Germany)**

TUTOR(S)
Prof. Frank Zebner

TECHNOLOGY
Director

TIME SPENT
4 months

TYPEFACE
Arial

WHY DO YOU LIKE THIS PROJECT?
**The simplexity: the simplicity
of the visualization and the
complexity of the information;
the design, that I made it alone,
that there are no unexplained
questions.**

WHAT DO YOU DISLIKE ABOUT IT?
Nothing.

OUTCOMES
I discovered my profession.

FEEDBACK
Diploma grade 1,0.

FAVOURITE FOOD THEN
Fast food

YOUR MOST VALUED
POSSESSION THEN
**My bike, my pictures and
one piece of art**

Project Then

PROJECT SIMILARITIES
THEN AND NOW
**The challenge to present
highly complex themes
simply, in terms of
visualization and
content; to maintain a
subtly playful approach;
to make the information
architecture clear.
The enthusiasm the
applications evoke
in the user.**

Danijela Djokic (Projekttriangle)

A VALUABLE QUALITY FOR A DESIGN STUDENT + A DESIGN PROFESSIONAL

Ambition and passion +
See above and business sense

YEAR OF PROJECT
2010

PROFESSIONAL PROJECT BRIEF
**Design a multi-touch table
with 5 applications**

CLIENT
**Milla & Partner GmbH and
E.ON Kraftwerke GmbH**

COLLABORATOR(S)
**Freelancer: Florian
Streckenbach**

TECHNOLOGY
Flash

TIME SPENT
4 months

TYPEFACE
Polo

WHY DO YOU LIKE THIS PROJECT?
**The fun in using it, the easy
way of explaining complex
data, the collaboration between
designer, programmer, sound
designer, conceptual designer,
client, etc.**

WHAT DO YOU DISLIKE ABOUT IT
**The colour, but it is the
brand colour…**

OUTCOMES
I learned new skills.

FEEDBACK
**Red Dot Award 'Best of the
Best' 2010, iF Award 2011,
Designpreis Deutschland
2012 nomination.**

DO YOU TEACH?
**Yes, at Fachhochschule
Potsdam (Germany),
Interface Design,
Information Architecture
and Visualization.**

IS IT POSSIBLE TO
TEACH DESIGN?
**The basis of all is to
learn the basics. This is
what you can teach.
To get another point of
view is what students
can learn. But creativity
and an aesthetic feeling
is something you
can't learn.**

FAVOURITE FOOD NOW
Slow food

YOUR MOST VALUED
POSSESSION NOW
**My watch, my bike,
my pictures and
one piece of art**

Project Now

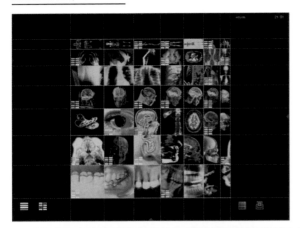

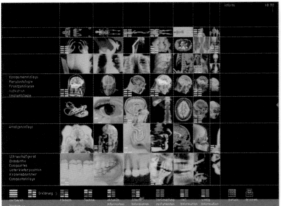

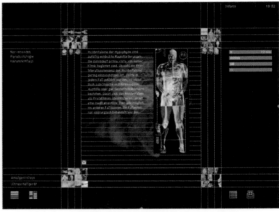

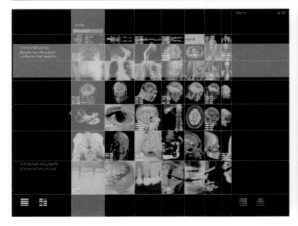

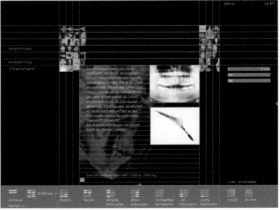

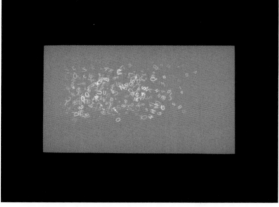

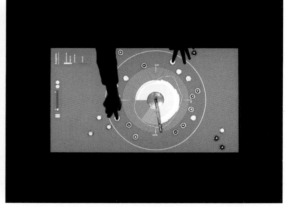

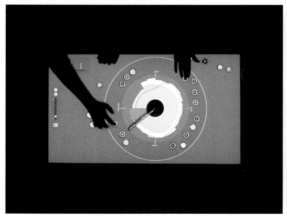

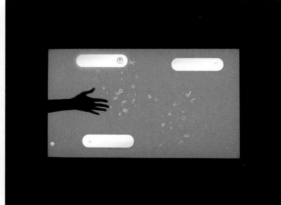

FINNISH

Emmi Salonen

A PIECE OF SOUND ADVICE + A SINGLE WARNING TO A DESIGN STUDENT

Avoid automatically applying your 'style' to a project – let each assignment influence you, your approach and the way you work + Be nice to people, be respectful

YEAR OF PROJECT
2000

STUDENT PROJECT BRIEF
Editorial design: design a front cover for Baseline magazine, for a feature on a chosen subject. Mine was excessive packaging.

COLLEGE
University of Brighton (United Kingdom)

TUTOR(S)
Lawrence Zeegen

TECHNOLOGY
QuarkXPress

WHY DO YOU LIKE THIS PROJECT?
I like the simplicity of the outcome. It also talks about the same issue that is at the core of my practice over a decade later: environment and sustainability.

WHAT DO YOU DISLIKE ABOUT IT?
I don't like the lack of attention to detail on the student work. But I suppose I didn't know what to look for. Now I would remake the label and shoot the image, not scan it and do the work in Photoshop.

OUTCOMES
I learned something.

FEEDBACK
I can't remember.

FAVOURITE FOOD THEN
Vegetarian

YOUR MOST VALUED POSSESSION THEN
iMac G3

PROJECT SIMILARITIES THEN AND NOW
I like that both of the designs have an idea behind them, a reasoning. Both editorial design briefs, that required a captive cover design. Neither has decorative trims added to the final layout, playing with core elements and simplicity. Both deal with environmental and sustainability issues.

Project Then

Emmi Salonen (Studio Emmi)

For both: listening and a willingness to learn

YEAR OF PROJECT
2008

PROFESSIONAL PROJECT BRIEF
Year Book conveying information about the past and future of the Finnish Institute in London (United Kingdom)

CLIENT
The Finnish Institute in London (United Kingdom)

TECHNOLOGY
InDesign

WHY DO YOU LIKE THIS PROJECT?
Because it is an example of current work that I like style-wise, and it's designed with the environment in mind; printed with vegetable-based inks on recycled stock, with minimum print. In fact, there is no print at all on the cover.

OUTCOMES
I learned something and got paid.

FEEDBACK
People seem to like the simplicity of the solution.

DO YOU TEACH?
Yes. I lecture in graphic design at various universities, including Nottingham Trent, Ravensbourne and Brighton (all UK).

IS IT POSSIBLE TO TEACH DESIGN?
Of course you can teach design. It helps if one wants to learn it. There is no real right or wrong way of designing, but you can help with pointing out what to look for as a tutor, in order to make things look good or look a certain way.

FAVOURITE FOOD NOW
Vegetarian

YOUR MOST VALUED POSSESSION NOW
MacBook Pro

Project Now

baseline

international typographics magazine   no31 2000

WASTE   98%

0755966413264000 2491
SECONDARY PACKAGING
326400   B Q0 250
664132CD   3

Éric & Marie Gaspar

Try all the techniques you can while you are at college; try not to be afraid of design solutions that look bizarre and weird and don't match the surrounding visual landscape + Don't forget humour and fantasy in your work

YEAR OF PROJECT
1999

STUDENT PROJECT BRIEF
To design the degree show catalogue of the graphic design department

COLLEGE
Central Saint Martins College of Art & Design, London (United Kingdom)

TUTOR(S)
Geoff Fowle

COLLABORATOR(S)
Holly Mackenzie and Tomako Takasu for the photographs

TECHNOLOGY
Offset printing and die-cutting

TIME SPENT
5 months

TYPEFACE
Officina

WHY DO YOU LIKE THIS PROJECT?
We like the way the objects, printed scale 1, are very simply displayed on the page. Objects are juxtaposed without any commentary. The viewer is engaged to think his own narration.

WHAT DO YOU DISLIKE ABOUT IT?
The cover of the inside brochure is weak.

OUTCOMES
It was basically our first printed project, so we learned a lot while conceiving it. It eventually figured in the D&AD annual the year after.

FEEDBACK
'We don't see the work of the students so this catalogue is useless.'

FAVOURITE FOOD THEN
Cadbury's

YOUR MOST VALUED POSSESSION THEN
Camera

PROJECT SIMILARITIES THEN AND NOW
On both projects, objects are displayed on the pages in a very simple way. Texts concerning those pictures are placed at the end of the publications to allow pictures a wider life. The chronology of the work of the Bouroullecs is erased, the property of the students' objects also.

Project Then

Éric & Marie Gaspar (ÉricandMarie)

Openness – students shouldn't wear the graphic designer jacket + Punctuality, reliability

YEAR OF PROJECT
2008

PROFESSIONAL PROJECT BRIEF
To design a catalogue for an exhibition about two designers

CLIENT
Ronan & Erwan Bouroullec

COLLABORATOR(S)
Ronan & Erwan Bouroullec

TECHNOLOGY
Offset printing

TIME SPENT
3 months

TYPEFACE
Century Schoolbook, Monotype Grotesk

WHY DO YOU LIKE THIS PROJECT?
Similarly (see answer opposite – then), we like the dialogue we built between drawings and photographs.

WHAT DO YOU DISLIKE ABOUT IT?
The photoengraving is not optimal.

OUTCOMES
We got a better comprehension of the two designers.

FEEDBACK
'What have you done for this project, really?'

FAVOURITE FOOD NOW
Le pot-au-feu

YOUR MOST VALUED POSSESSION NOW
Computer

DO YOU TEACH?
No.

IS IT POSSIBLE TO TEACH DESIGN?
The best tutors we had in the two colleges we attended were not practitioners. What they taught was about ideas and concepts. They told us how to re-question a brief and how to structure an idea. If we had to teach, we would follow this. How a project finally looks is the student's concern, not really the tutor's.

Project Now

Ronan & Erwan Bouroullec   *Objets Dessins Maquettes*

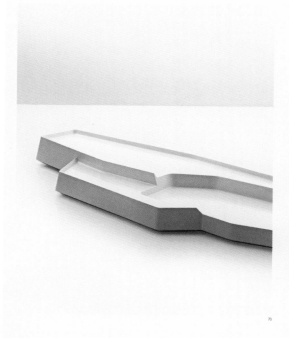

Fons Hickmann

Be curious + Be afraid but go for it nonetheless

YEAR OF PROJECT
1993

STUDENT PROJECT BRIEF
Create a poster on the theme of 'ideology and planning concepts before and after 1945'

COLLEGE
Fachhochschule Düsseldorf (Germany)

TUTOR(S)
Can't remember

COLLABORATOR(S)
Oliver Iserloh, Stefan Nowak

TECHNOLOGY
Screenprinting

TIME SPENT
4 weeks

TYPEFACE
Typewriter

WHY DO YOU LIKE THIS PROJECT?
Because of its complexity.

WHAT DO YOU DISLIKE ABOUT IT?
The bad printing. We didn't have enough money and had to squeegee it ourselves.

OUTCOMES
A poster.

FEEDBACK
Uwe Loesch said, 'Ah, you did that!'

ANYTHING ELSE
I am using the question to say that nuclear energy isn't a good idea.

FAVOURITE FOOD THEN
Cake

YOUR MOST VALUED
POSSESSION THEN
-

Project Then

PROJECT SIMILARITIES
THEN AND NOW
Birds

Fons Hickmann (Fons Hickmann m23)

A VALUABLE QUALITY FOR A DESIGN STUDENT + A DESIGN PROFESSIONAL

Curiosity + Curiosity

YEAR OF PROJECT
2010

PROFESSIONAL PROJECT BRIEF
Create a poster on the theme of 'search for freedom and hunt it down!'

CLIENT
Labor für Soziale und Ästhetische Entwicklung (Laboratory for Social and Aesthetic Development)

TECHNOLOGY
Screenprinting

TIME SPENT
1 day

TYPEFACE
Helvetica

WHY DO YOU LIKE THIS PROJECT?
Because of its simplicity.

WHAT DO YOU DISLIKE ABOUT IT?
The uncertainty whether it is brilliant or banal.

OUTCOMES
A poster.

FEEDBACK
Thorsten Nolting said 'Thanks', Lena said 'Burner!' and Uma said 'Oha'.

ANYTHING ELSE
See answer opposite.

FAVOURITE FOOD NOW
Cake

YOUR MOST VALUED POSSESSION NOW
-

DO YOU TEACH?
Professor at the University for Applied Arts Vienna (Austria) until 2007. Since 2007, Professor at Universität der Künste Berlin (Germany) in Graphic Design.

IS IT POSSIBLE TO TEACH DESIGN?
It's not possible to teach someone how to be talented, but one can encourage students to explore new paths and show them where the entrances to those paths might be.

Project Now

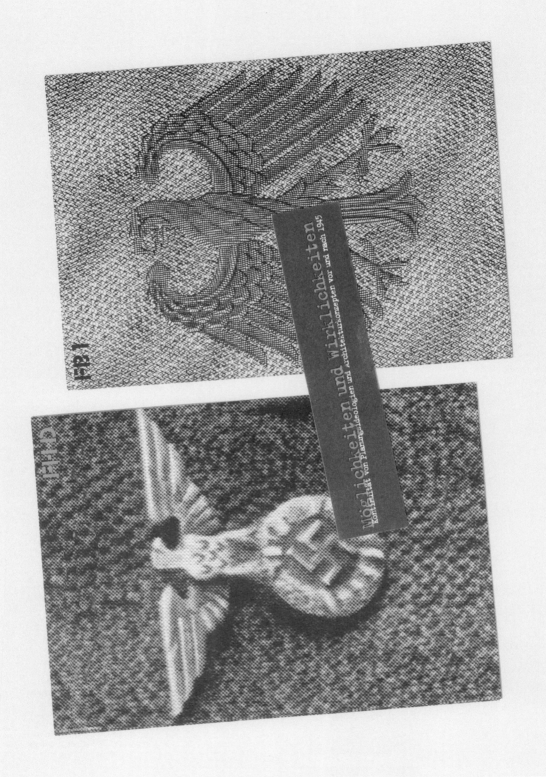

Suche Frieden und jage ihm nach!
Eine konspirative Kochübung in friedlicher Absicht
von, mit und ohne Thorsten Nolting und Team
7. Dezember 2010 um 12 Uhr und 18 Uhr

Labor
für soziale und ästhetische Entwicklung
vor der Bergerkirche Düsseldorf

Hans Dieter Reichert

Sometimes it's hard, but hang in there; be true to yourself; earn less money but do better work; think about your responsibility within society + 'Anyone who has never made a mistake has never tried anything new' and 'Only a life lived for others is a life worthwhile' (Albert Einstein)

YEAR OF PROJECT
1983

STUDENT PROJECT BRIEF
Type studies

COLLEGE
Universität-
Gesamthochschule
Essen (Germany)

TUTOR(S)
Hans Nienheysen,
Lazló Lakner,
Willy Fleckhaus

TECHNOLOGY
Paste-up, photocopy,
PMT darkroom, Letraset,
photo composition

TIME SPENT
Forgot

TYPEFACE
Hand-rendered

FAVOURITE FOOD THEN
German (Currywurst
mit Fritten)

YOUR MOST VALUED
POSSESSION THEN
VW Beetle 1200cc

WHY DO YOU LIKE THIS PROJECT?
Designing, experimenting,
thinking, creating.

OUTCOMES
Learning a skill, self-esteem.

FEEDBACK
Encouraging remarks and
constructive critique,
good mark.

PROJECT SIMILARITIES
THEN AND NOW
In my view, there are
similarities or traces
in my approach between
1983 and 2011: then,
I drew my freehand
constructed letterforms
in an analytical style.
I tried to understand,
tried to make the infor-
mation transparent and
tried to communicate
my thoughts. I still work
this way today. There
are also similarities or
traces in my attitude
towards design. In the
abstraction exercise
'Life, death, eternity',
it is the aim of designing
something that has
moral undertones,
even philosophical
tendencies, and to be
honest and straight.
In terms of style, there
are similarities between
then and now too – the
use of a crafted (striving
for perfection) linear,
straight, reductionist,
clean design – 'almost
Calvinistic'. I do like
engineered, electronic
and hand-produced

products. The reason
I publish Baseline
magazine and related
items in printed and
in electronic form is
that I believe in
communicating and
sharing views, thoughts,
experiences and, if you
like, philosophies.
Although that deeper
thought, the moral
purpose of publishing,
was not apparent to me
when I was studying, it
just led towards it later
on in my professional
life. It is a bit like
'one follows one's
inner voice'. Also life
'suggests' the way one
takes! It seems to me
that I approach graphic
design from a point of
view that relates more
to 'thinking/calculating,
analyzing, reducing,
simplifying, structuring,
planning', rather than
emotional graphic
design. Its roots might
be in my cultural
upbringing – but in the
field of graphic design
I have a tendency to
approach graphic
solution mostly with
typography/photography
rather than illustration
and painting.

Project Then

Hans Dieter Reichert
(HDR Visual Communication)

A VALUABLE QUALITY FOR A DESIGN STUDENT + A DESIGN PROFESSIONAL

Idealism, motivation, perseverance, talent, honesty, curiosity + Communication skills, open-mindedness, willingness to learn, ability to see one's place and responsibility within society and to provide a good service as well as explaining it

YEAR OF PROJECT
2011

PROFESSIONAL PROJECT BRIEF
Design of a magazine
(Baseline)

CLIENT
Bradbourne Publishing Ltd.

COLLABORATOR(S)
Clients, office staff,
authors, printers,
programmers. (Designer:
Johnathon Hunt; design
assistants: Peter Barnes,
Luke Borgust, Chloe
Wooldridge; contributing
editor: Arnold
Schwartzman)

TECHNOLOGY
Apple Mac, programming

TIME SPENT
Several days/weeks
per issue

TYPEFACE
Various – mainly
Akkurat (sans serif) and
Kingfisher (serif)

WHY DO YOU LIKE THIS PROJECT?
Interaction between author,
designer, printer and
distributor. Learning about the
various subjects. Baseline
discussions (subject: editorial
contents and its visual
interpretation/design among
members of staff). Educational
purpose. Knowledge transfer
and how to communicate in
a visually effective and
purposeful way.

OUTCOMES
Pleasure, intellectual
exchange.

FEEDBACK
Compliments, increased sales
and invitations to guest
lectures, professional
recognition in the academic
and professional world.

DO YOU TEACH?
I taught Visual
Communication at:
Bath Spa University
(UK), 1989–99; Reading
University (UK), 1999–
2005; assessor at
Northampton University
(UK), 2000–05; guest
lectures in the UK,
USA, Switzerland and
Gerrmany.

IS IT POSSIBLE TO
TEACH DESIGN?
Yes, you can teach
various elements of
design: discipline,
how to see things
differently, how to
develop responsibility
in communication,
how to develop
personality. I teach
students to become
self-motivated and see
design as a valuable
profession/service
to society. I teach
them to see design
as holistic, and
encourage them to
be curious about
everything.

FAVOURITE FOOD NOW
Italian (pasta, antipasti
and salad)

YOUR MOST VALUED
POSSESSION NOW
House, office

Project Now

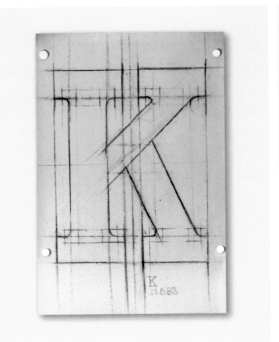

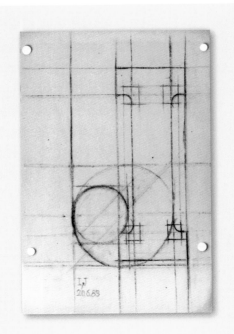

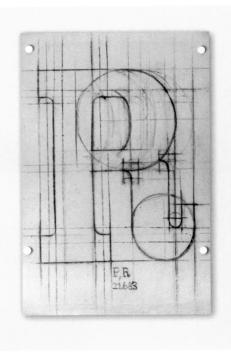

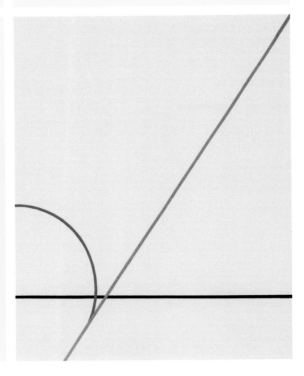

Holger Jacobs

Learn the basics of typography, punctuation and printing. Experiment and don't rush into producing 'professional'-looking work. If you are committed, hard-working and love what you do, things will happen + Never follow a particular style just because it seems popular

YEAR OF PROJECT
1997

STUDENT PROJECT BRIEF
Self-initiated

COLLEGE
**Royal College of Art,
London (United Kingdom)**

TUTOR(S)
Russell Warren-Fisher

COLLABORATOR(S)
**Matthew Rudd was my
first-year 'assistant' at the
college and he helped
me a great deal**

TECHNOLOGY
**Laser-cut vinyl letters on
painted wooden blocks**

TIME SPENT
Just a few days

TYPEFACE
Helvetica

WHY DO YOU LIKE THIS PROJECT?
**It was a simple project (but
had a complex meaning).**

OUTCOMES
**It was the last project I did in
college and somehow marks
the end of a journey exploring
the relationship between
content and form.**

FEEDBACK
**The fashion chain Whistles
showed my work in their shop
windows.**

FAVOURITE FOOD THEN
German potato pancakes

YOUR MOST VALUED
POSSESSION THEN
**My sketchbooks – I was
pretty poor and can't
remember owning
anything else of real value**

PROJECT SIMILARITIES
THEN AND NOW
**Both projects deal with
materiality. In Splitwords
I was curious to explore
the 'physical' aspect
of words and how their
meaning can change.
For the Paramount
signage, we printed
patterns on the front of
thick blocks of clear
acrylic while the actual
information went on
the back. Depending
on the angle of view,
this information is more
or less obstructed.**

Project Then

Holger Jacobs (Mind Design)

Never, ever think it's 'cool' being a designer + Willingness to take risks

YEAR OF PROJECT
2008

PROFESSIONAL PROJECT BRIEF
Identity and signage for a club and restaurant occupying the top three floors of a London skyscraper

CLIENT
Paramount

COLLABORATOR(S)
My colleague Craig Sinnamon

TECHNOLOGY
Screenprinting on acrylic

TIME SPENT
About 3 months

TYPEFACE
Futura

FAVOURITE FOOD NOW
Anything Japanese, except for the crab brain that my wife's relatives once invited me to taste

YOUR MOST VALUED POSSESSION NOW
Hand-built Italian racing bicycle

WHY DO YOU LIKE THIS PROJECT?
It was a complex project (but had a simple meaning).

OUTCOMES
The design for Paramount was our first attempt to develop a visual identity that was not based on a singular logo. Instead we developed a flexible system of abstract patterns that express the height of the building.

FEEDBACK
The project was published in several books and magazines.

ANYTHING ELSE
As in college, I am still suspicious of the idea of a fixed 'meaning'. Working mostly on identity projects, I often reject concepts that aim to be a visual translation of 'brand values' and look for a certain honesty and directness in form.
The Paramount identity is a good example, as it relates to architecture and certain features of the building. It was difficult to explain this to the client, who originally wanted to put more emphasis on 'exclusivity' and communicate a certain 'up-market feel'.

DO YOU TEACH?
Currently Visiting Professor for Typography at Fachhochschule Düsseldorf (Germany).

IS IT POSSIBLE TO TEACH DESIGN?
My college education was not very systematic. In Germany I started studying illustration because graphic design seemed very technical and boring to me at the time. It was only when I came to England that I became interested in typography, because it was taught in a more experimental way as a form of self-expression. Actually, it was not taught at all; our tutors just encouraged us to mess around with type on the photocopier. During my MA, I focused more on ideas than on style and used the time to teach myself the typographic basics I rejected so much in Germany. Looking back at my education, I think it is very important to teach the basics of typography and go through simple exercises of 'form finding'. This might be boring and hard work, but many ideas develop through experimentation with form, not just through concept development and research.

Project Now

HOLGER JACOBS, 1997

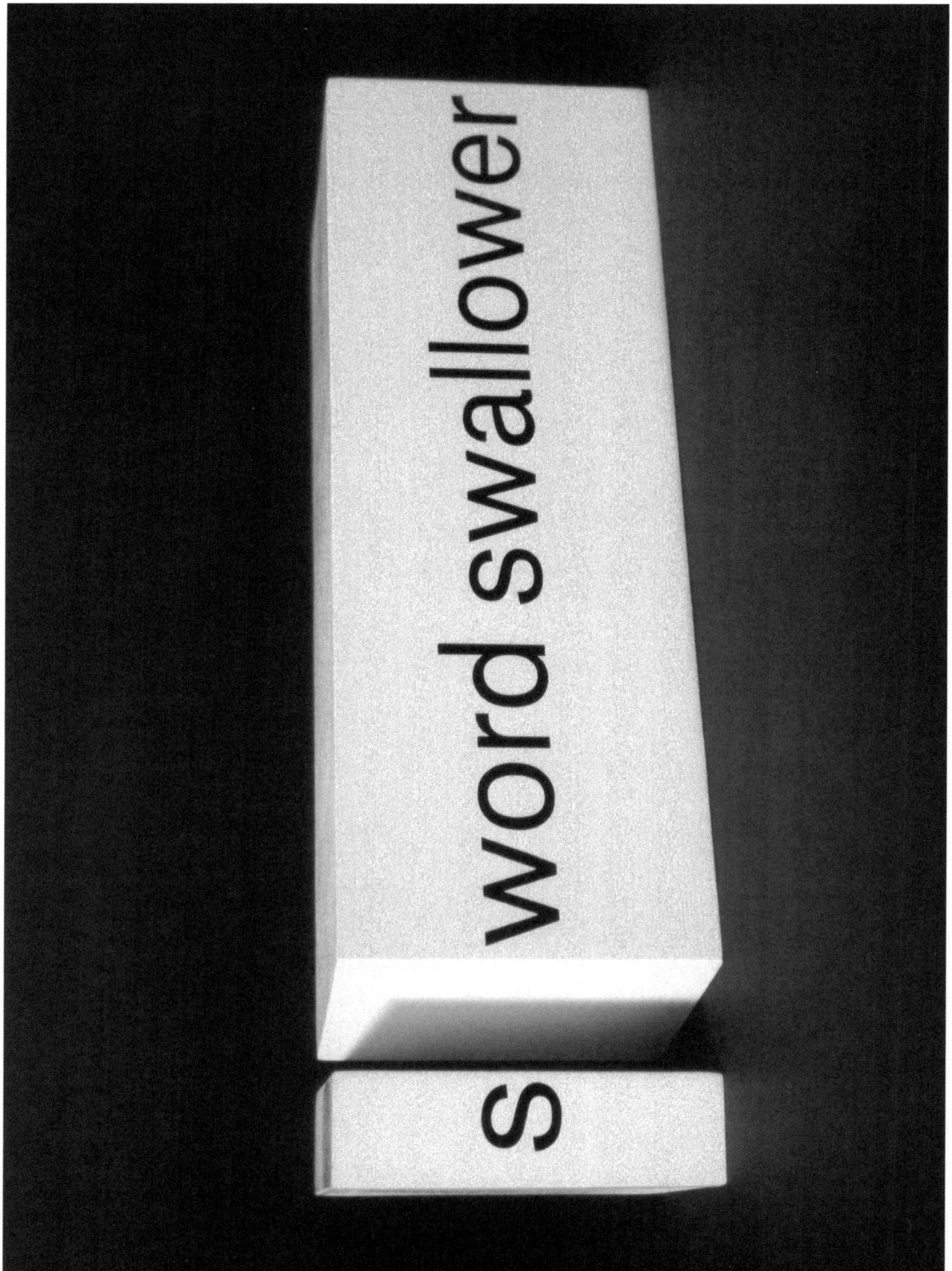

Hoon Kim

Build up broad possibilities for your future, but those possibilities and goals should be specific + Everyone changes every single second – your thoughts may change as you grow

YEAR OF PROJECT
2006

STUDENT PROJECT BRIEF
'I am the place where I am' – a map of Providence onto which are transposed the symbols of aural memories of places. This project explores the possibilities of bridging the gap between public space and personal space. This map provides subjective representations of personal memories of places, inviting users to visit them, to revisit the artist's memories, and experience their own auditory sense of the area.

COLLEGE
Rhode Island School of Design, Providence (USA)

TUTOR(S)
David Reinfurt

TECHNOLOGY
Digital print, hand binding, etc.

TIME SPENT
4 months

TYPEFACE
Univers Mono and Courier – Univers Mono is a customized typeface for Wire, a British magazine I worked on as a designer. James Goggin (see also pages 98–101) was an art director for the magazine and my boss at his studio (Practise).

WHY DO YOU LIKE THIS PROJECT?
School projects always encourage an experimental approach, which enables the designer to think and act more deeply and more broadly with enough time.

WHAT DO YOU DISLIKE ABOUT IT?
If I had had a bigger fund, I would have spread the map books out throughout public places for free to encourage citizens to linger and engage in public spaces.

OUTCOMES
I learned how spaces, people and sounds are related and interact with each other. Also, how to represent the topic in print media with paper quality – size, weight, thickness, texture and sound.

PROJECT SIMILARITIES THEN AND NOW
Both projects are firmly related to the relationships between real spaces and spaces of graphic media. I believe designing graphic media is comparable to constructing and composing architectonic elements. A piece of paper, an interactive and scrollable browser, or a transforming print format is a space given to designers. To get the essence of an idea, the designer must guide the audience to explore and experience the surrounding spaces.

FAVOURITE FOOD THEN
Korean BBQ

YOUR MOST VALUED POSSESSION THEN
Family and one external hard drive that had all the data in my life

Project Then

Hoon Kim (Why Not Smile)

Curiosity + Punctuality

YEAR OF PROJECT
2011

PROFESSIONAL PROJECT BRIEF
A Sustainable Future for the Exumas – Environmental Management, Design, and Planning is an international conference addressing both current strategies and future possibilities for the Exumas. The event was held by the Ministry of the Environment of the Commonwealth of the Bahamas in conjunction with the Bahamas National Trust and the Harvard University Graduate School of Design.

CLIENT
Harvard University Graduate School of Design, Cambridge (USA)

COLLABORATOR(S)
Two senior designers, one developer and one intern

FAVOURITE FOOD NOW
Korean BBQ

YOUR MOST VALUED POSSESSION NOW
Family and four external hard drives that sync twice a day automatically and still contain all the data in my life

TECHNOLOGY
Offset print, etc.

TIME SPENT
3 months

TYPEFACE
Pin – a typeface that Why Not Smile has been working on for many months; 15 weights in its family will be published soon. It is inspired by Pinball, a classic typeface found in an old Letraset catalogue.

WHY DO YOU LIKE THIS PROJECT?
Projects with real clients require a logical approach through specific processes and methodology, which leads to the best result within a given timeline.

WHAT DO YOU DISLIKE ABOUT IT?
We preferred a specific print skill for gradation colours, but couldn't find any printer to do it in the States. Consequently, the print quality was not that good. Now for the book, which is the last part of the project, we are trying to find better ways to represent gradations by mixing PMS and CMYK.

OUTCOMES
How to visualize space within various media is still something I am learning. I have thought a lot about how features can illustrate the real space: a minimal identity, print media with multiple pages that reflect the dimension of time, a website requiring various interaction and kinetic hierarchy, etc.

DO YOU TEACH?
Pratt Institute, New York (USA), Graduate Visual Communication Design Department, Graduate Thesis, and Harvard University, Cambridge (USA), Graduate School of Design, Portfolio and Graphic Design.

IS IT POSSIBLE TO TEACH DESIGN?
I always encourage students to be critical thinkers, focusing on design philosophy and methodology, as well as design authorship, as I learned at school. Graphic design is not only about visual substances. It meets a wide variety of studies and fields such as technology, new media, public environments, language, literature, philosophy, psychology and architecture. Hence, in courses, students need an organized curriculum focusing on how to analyze and establish correlations judiciously as an author and director.

Project Now

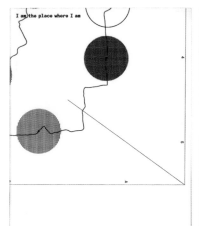

I am the place where I am

my short-winded breathing
the blinking traffic signals
the trail of footprints having
various tempos
humid air and stillness

A1

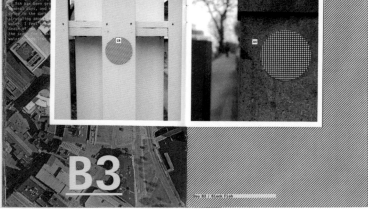

B3

B3

A SUSTAINABLE FUTURE
FOR THE EXUMAS
Environmental Management,
Design, and Planning
Conference

8 July, 2011
sustainableexumas.org

ABSTRACTS

Visible and Invisible Aspects of
Architecture and Urbanism
Mohsen Mostafavi

Architecture and urbanism are both
visual practices. They involve the
construction of artefacts—buildings,
infrastructure, etc.—that visibly
transform the environment. The beauty
of architecture affects our apprehension
of the built environment and improves
our quality of life. But architecture and
urbanism possess a nonvisual or invisible
dimension as well. The aim of this talk is
to explore the relationship between
these two aspects of architecture and
urbanism. How do buildings as physical
objects contribute to constructing our
lives? How can designers, planners, and
government agencies create the
appropriate frameworks for the most
productive articulation of the relationship
between visible and invisible dimensions
of our environments?

A SUSTAINABLE FUTURE
FOR THE EXUMAS
Environmental Management,
Design, and Planning
Conference

8 July, 2011
sustainableexumas.org

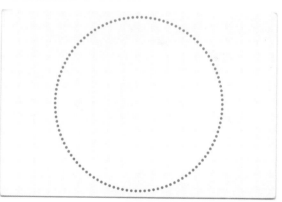

Hyoun Youl Joe

A PIECE OF SOUND ADVICE + A SINGLE WARNING TO A DESIGN STUDENT

Be generous in experimentation and have confidence + Be honest about your work

YEAR OF PROJECT
2003

STUDENT PROJECT BRIEF
A research project about Hanguel's each-phoneme system. For the project, I designed a new font based on the typeface that Kim-Do-Bong designed as a proposal for the each-phoneme writing system.

COLLEGE
Dankook University, Seoul (South Korea)

TUTOR(S)
Professors at the college and classmates of mine

COLLABORATOR(S)
Mostly classmates

TECHNOLOGY
Offset print for the poster and book

TIME SPENT
Approx. 3 months as a research project

TYPEFACE
Kim-Do-Bong Bold. I designed the font and, based on that, have since proposed a new Korean typeface system.

WHY DO YOU LIKE THIS PROJECT?
I was totally into the Korean typography system at that time. I wrote a B.F.A. thesis entitled The Possibility of Each-Phoneme System of Hanguel. I also designed a Korean typeface – Kim-Do-Bong, which has a different typographic system. I spent a lot of time writing the research paper and designing the font.

WHAT DO YOU DISLIKE ABOUT IT?
This was very time-consuming and I feel that it needs even more research to support the point I was trying to make.

OUTCOMES
Understanding Korean typography – its character, structure, system and history.

FEEDBACK
Positive: modernity, simplicity, dryness. Negative: simplicity, dryness, lack of function.

FAVOURITE FOOD THEN
Korean

YOUR MOST VALUED POSSESSION THEN
Books

Project Then

PROJECT SIMILARITIES THEN AND NOW
Formal approach of dealing with typography.

Hyoun Youl Joe (Hey Joe)

A VALUABLE QUALITY FOR A DESIGN STUDENT + A DESIGN PROFESSIONAL

Confidence and experimentation + Understanding co-workers' needs and thoughts (clients, editors, curators, artists, etc. ...)

YEAR OF PROJECT
2010

PROFESSIONAL PROJECT BRIEF
To design a poster, a postcard and the exhibition graphics for the exhibition The Letter from Huynh Mai. This exhibition was created to remember the Vietnamese woman Huynh Mai, who was killed by her Korean husband.

CLIENT
The independent curator Jihye Kim

COLLABORATOR(S)
Curator: Jihye Kim; co-ordinators: Yoonyoung Kim, Hayoung Lee; photo and documentation: Jihye Ahn; artists: Kyungmi Kim, Sunmi Kim, Soorin Kim, Jisu Kim, Jin Kim, Junghyun Park, Hyewon Park, Jangmi Beak, Yurim Song, Hyejung Shim, Hyesook Yong, Jinsuk Kim, Gahyun Yoon, Woonyung Ja, Jangeun Cho, Nguyen Thi Chau Giang, Inkyung Huh

TECHNOLOGY
Offset printing for the book and poster, copperplate stamp for the postcard, rubber stamp for the exhibition design

TIME SPENT
Approx. 1 month

TYPEFACE
SM Gung Seo Regular, Courier Regular

WHY DO YOU LIKE THIS PROJECT?
I could somewhat understand how hard Vietnamese people's life is in Korea as foreigners, because I studied in the USA. The exhibition The Letter from Huynh Mai communicates not only a Korean bias towards strangers, but also the political-social tension between Korea and Vietnam.

WHAT DO YOU DISLIKE ABOUT IT?
After completing this project, I visited Vietnam for another related project. The work was done without having visited/experienced Vietnam before. Now that I have been there, I would totally redesign it all.

OUTCOMES
An understanding of how to work/collaborate with others (curators, artists, photographers, clients).

FEEDBACK
Simplicity, symbolic meaning.

FAVOURITE FOOD NOW
Seafood, Korean and Japanese

YOUR MOST VALUED POSSESSION NOW
Books and my works

DO YOU TEACH?
Graphic Design and Editorial Design at Dankook University and Kookmin University, Seoul (South Korea).

IS IT POSSIBLE TO TEACH DESIGN?
Most Korean students studying graphic design have great difficulty in solving problems by themselves, since their attitude to learning is a passive one. I quite often see beautifully executed results, but the causal relationship between process and outcome is unclear and insufficient. As a tutor at college, I try to create an active environment through diverse discussions.

Project Now

CANADIAN/FRENCH

Isabelle Swiderski

A PIECE OF SOUND ADVICE + A SINGLE WARNING TO A DESIGN STUDENT

Sketch, sketch, sketch +
Don't fall in love with your ideas

YEAR OF PROJECT
1996

STUDENT PROJECT BRIEF
As part of a year-long graduation project, we were meant to identify a need or issue and propose a solution. The brief I set for myself was to shed some light on the reasons behind the impending collapse of wild salmon stocks on the western coast of Canada. Title of work: Spirit in the Water.

COLLEGE
Emily Carr Institute of Art & Design, Vancouver (Canada)

TUTOR(S)
Deborah Shackleton

TECHNOLOGY
Pen and paper, Macromedia Director

TIME SPENT
No idea

TYPEFACE
Officina

WHY DO YOU LIKE THIS PROJECT?
I still think the concept is strong.

WHAT DO YOU DISLIKE ABOUT IT?
I would design it differently.

OUTCOMES
It is one of the most memorable 'aha!' moments of my student life. I would say I learned the meaning of concept while working on that project. What you might call the 'penny dropping'.

FEEDBACK
Mostly positive due to the use of technology and the ties between native folklore and scientific reality.

FAVOURITE FOOD THEN
Good home-made food

YOUR MOST VALUED POSSESSION THEN
Walkman

PROJECT SIMILARITIES THEN AND NOW
Both display a desire to balance concept/idea and craft/materials. I still believe that strong ideas can be rendered beautifully and that this combination is the most desirable. This is not an original thought, but nevertheless it's one that fuels my approach to design. When I further develop my processes and technical abilities, the work steadily improves and remains fulfilling.

Project Then

Isabelle Swiderski (Seven25)

A VALUABLE QUALITY FOR A DESIGN STUDENT + A DESIGN PROFESSIONAL

Curiosity + Tact

YEAR OF PROJECT
2010

PROFESSIONAL PROJECT BRIEF
**To design a functional
programme for the CPA's
biennial conference**

CLIENT
**Canadian Payments
Association**

TECHNOLOGY
Pen and paper, CS4

TIME SPENT
About 45 hours

TYPEFACE
Akkurat

WHY DO YOU LIKE THIS PROJECT?
**The cover works nicely
by subtly underlining the
theme of the conference.**

WHAT DO YOU DISLIKE ABOUT IT?
**There are always details I wish
to tweak after the fact.**

OUTCOMES
**That having clients who trust
you and value your work leads
to more enjoyable and better
work.**

FEEDBACK
**Positive feedback for use of
materials and usability.**

DO YOU TEACH?
**Varied course at Emily
Carr University of Art &
Design (Canada).
Currently 4th year of
BA, Advanced Print
Publications.**

IS IT POSSIBLE TO
TEACH DESIGN?
**It is possible to teach
the principles of design
as well as its history and
evolution in context.
A student only becomes
a designer when they
internalize the principles
and connect them to
their own life experience
and approach to develop
their own voice. But
that's only my opinion.
I happen to teach design
and try to balance
technical apprenticeship
with idea development
methodologies. I've
observed that there
seems to be no time
for formal client-
management tips.
Perhaps that's for
the best?**

FAVOURITE FOOD NOW
Good home-made food

YOUR MOST VALUED
POSSESSION NOW
**MacBook Pro
(sad, I know)**

Project Now

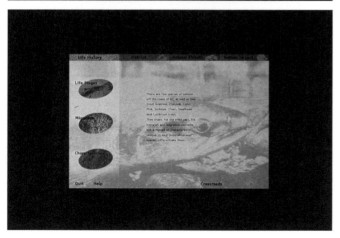

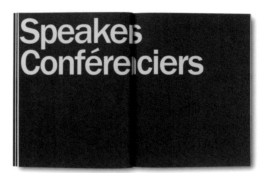

BRITISH (BORN AUSTRALIAN)

James Goggin

A PIECE OF SOUND ADVICE + A SINGLE WARNING TO A DESIGN STUDENT

Keep studying + Beware of graphic design

YEAR OF PROJECT
1998

STUDENT PROJECT BRIEF
Open brief, edition of 5×50 postcards printed during letterpress classes at RCA with Alan Kitching. My idea was to take the grid of a revolving postcard rack (5 columns by 10 rows = 50 cards) and place it over a map of the world. From each grid square, a major city or body of water was chosen. Each name was typeset letter-press – cities printed with red, waters with blue. Five sets of 50 postcards were produced, and then set out geographically onto the rack, top to bottom (north to south) and around the five columns, east to west. A 51st card was also printed, titled In Transit. This was the name of the project, but also documented the unseen transit of a postcard navigating its way from the sender to the recipient.

FAVOURITE FOOD THEN
Japanese

YOUR MOST VALUED POSSESSION THEN
My Ricoh GR 35mm camera

COLLEGE
Royal College of Art, London (United Kingdom)

TUTOR(S)
Alan Kitching

TECHNOLOGY
Letterpress

TIME SPENT
2 weeks (approx.)

TYPEFACE
Helvetica

WHY DO YOU LIKE THIS PROJECT?
This is a project I could still imagine doing today; there is nothing I would change. A lot of my work relies on serendipity and chance. Here it involved coming across an old postcard rack in the Holborn area of London, outside a pharmacy that had closed down. I eventually pulled it in to my studio at the RCA, and it sat there for many months before I came up with a project to make use of it. The postcard project involved many themes that recur in my work: the postcard as a valid medium, alternative carto-graphic representations of the world, attempts at making graphic manifestations of a sense of place, and at making the intangible visible (the transitional state of a postcard between dispatch and delivery).

Project Then

OUTCOMES
An appreciation for letterpress, and the basic act of actually printing the work you've typeset as a designer. The project was one of several I made at the RCA that connected printed matter to a conceptually logical spatial situation: here, a revolving postcard rack, suggesting a spinning globe.

FEEDBACK
No negative feedback.

PROJECT SIMILARITIES THEN AND NOW
There is a certain consistent logic in typeface choice, which you can find in a lot of my projects. For In Transit, I wanted the postcards to feel generic, the idea of the postcard as a touristic proof of location ('I was really here') distilled to its logical graphic conclusion: just a place name printed on a blank card, no picture necessary. Helvetica Bold worked for this, and, if I recall correctly, the main reason could well have been the fact that the set of Helvetica lead type contained enough characters for me to set up all 50 postcards without having to take the settings apart for different place names. The two colours of red for cities and blue for seas were borrowed from general map and atlas colour palettes. For Interstate, the road signage of the USA and The Netherlands dictated type choice without having to really think about it. The colours were an admittedly obvious combination of stars and stripes, Dutch flag and a slight De Stijl reference with the yellow. Again, these self-determined parameters set up a rational system that allowed me to avoid worrying about such design distractions as typeface and colour choice.

James Goggin (Museum of Contemporary Art Chicago)

For both: Studiousness

YEAR OF PROJECT
2010

PROFESSIONAL PROJECT BRIEF
Self-published postcard, announcing my studio and family move from Arnhem to Chicago, printed on a Ricoh colour stencil duplicator at Knust in Nijmegen, The Netherlands, on my very last day before leaving for the USA.

CLIENT
Myself

TECHNOLOGY
Ricoh Priport JP8500 Digital Duplicator

TIME SPENT
1 day (approx.)

TYPEFACE
Interstate

WHY DO YOU LIKE THIS PROJECT?
I'll take any chance I can get to make more postcards, and it is of course a logical format for a moving card. Since high school, the typefaces I have most appreciated have been vernacular, engineered (rather than necessarily 'designed') specimens. Having moved around a lot growing up, the subtle differences in commonplace typographies like road signage and car licence plates drew my attention as the first indicators of cultural difference when arriving in a new country.

FAVOURITE FOOD NOW
Probably still Japanese – or Korean

YOUR MOST VALUED POSSESSION NOW
My Ricoh GR Digital II camera

The typeface (actually the FHWA Series fonts, aka 'Highway Gothic' developed by the United States Federal Highway Administration in the 1940s) is one that I grew up with when visiting the USA, and from my early years in Australia and New Zealand, where the font is also used for road signage. In its contemporary Hoefler & Frere-Jones redrawn format, the font was overused (UK supermarket chain Sainsbury has plastered its branches with it for years) and is therefore not one I would ever really use myself. But given that the font is also used on Dutch road signage, it seemed appropriate to acknowledge this little-known Dutch–American design connection. Hence the postcard's title: Arnhem–Chicago Interstate.

WHAT DO YOU DISLIKE ABOUT IT?
The Ricoh's yellow ink is slightly too bright, making 'Chicago' a bit difficult to read.

OUTCOMES
I was finally able to spend some time at Knust, the stencil-printing part of Extrapool, an experimental art/sound/print arts and residency centre in Nijmegen. It was a place I'd admired from afar, and then visited a few times with Werkplaats students. But it

Project Now

was only in my last days of living in The Netherlands that I was finally able to print a project with them. I asked Joyce, the resident printing expert, a lot of questions about stencil printers, inks and comparisons between Ricoh and Riso models (the two main Japanese companies that manufacture stencil printers). As a result, I hired a new Riso MZ 1090U – one of my first acts as Director of Design, Publishing and New Media upon arriving at the Museum of Contemporary Art Chicago.

FEEDBACK
No negative feedback.

DO YOU TEACH?
Intermittent and itinerant visiting critic and lecturing. Most recently: CalArts (California Institute of the Arts), Valencia (USA); Elam School of Fine Arts, Auckland (NZ); Konstfack, Stockholm (SE); ISIA (Istituto Superiore Industrie Artistiche), Urbino (Italy); Werkplaats Typografie, Arnhem (NL); ArTEZ Institute of the Arts, Arnhem (NL); ECAL (Ecole cantonale d'art de Lausanne), Lausanne (CH). Lecturing about typography, graphic design, contemporary art, design history and theory, and architecture.

IS IT POSSIBLE TO TEACH DESIGN?
I think there has to be something to start with, a certain instinct, motivation and interest. A lot of what I consider to be good design involves a capacity for reading, critical thought, writing and research. And a wide-ranging knowledge of design and art history, history in general, politics, philosophy, critical theory, cultural studies, literature, film, etc. I'm still trying to catch up in this regard, and think that a much more rounded liberal arts programme should be taught as a fundamental part of any graphic design programme. It is possible to teach typography, however, and I'm amazed how many contemporary graphic design courses seem to leave this part out. In the same way that I think graphic design study should involve all of the aforementioned fields, I also think typography should be taught across all other fields: in art, architecture, English literature, law, science, etc. It's the foundation of written language, crucial for everyone to have a good understanding of.

In transit

Barents Sea

Los Angeles

James Goggin
~~Course Director~~
~~Werkplaats Typografie~~
~~Agnietenplaats 2~~
~~6822 JD Arnhem~~
~~The Netherlands~~
~~james@~~
~~werkplaatstypografie.org~~

James Goggin
Shan Connell
Beatrix & Audrey

Design Director
Museum of
Contemporary Art
220 East Chicago Avenue
Chicago IL 60611
United States of America
jgoggin@mcachicago.org

5320 Thayer Street
Evanston IL 60210
United States of America
studio@practise.co.uk

www.practise.co.uk

Jan Wilker

A PIECE OF SOUND ADVICE + A SINGLE WARNING TO A DESIGN STUDENT

You suck – use this status wisely, then it's only temporary + It's a long-distance run, not a sprint

YEAR OF PROJECT
1998

STUDENT PROJECT BRIEF
Create a magazine, with cover and interior spreads

COLLEGE
Staatliche Akademie der Bildenen Künste Stuttgart (Germany)

TUTOR(S)
Prof. Pospischil

TECHNOLOGY
Freehand/Photoshop

TIME SPENT
1 week

TYPEFACE
Handwriting in Freehand with Wacom tablet

WHY DO YOU LIKE THIS PROJECT?
Other than a faint romantic feeling for my first cover design assignment in school, nothing.

OUTCOMES
I remember that specific little rush one gets when creating.

FEEDBACK
Nothing in particular.

FAVOURITE FOOD THEN
Anything from the students' cafeteria

YOUR MOST VALUED POSSESSION THEN
My computer

Project Then

PROJECT SIMILARITIES THEN AND NOW
Obviously the reduced colour palette, with mainly black type on white, as well as a generally very playful approach. I am still not good with colours, it seems.

A VALUABLE QUALITY FOR A DESIGN STUDENT + A DESIGN PROFESSIONAL

Curiosity and openness +
Staying open and curious

YEAR OF PROJECT
2006

PROFESSIONAL PROJECT BRIEF
**Catalogue design for the
Guggenheim's biannual
Hugo Boss Art Prize**

CLIENT
**The Guggenheim
Foundation**

TECHNOLOGY
Illustrator/InDesign

TIME SPENT
3 months, on and off

TYPEFACE
Akzidenz Grotesk

WHY DO YOU LIKE THIS PROJECT?
**This is still one of my favourite
projects, due to the complete
lack of intellectual construct
in its creation.**

OUTCOMES
**See opposite page (then),
only stronger.**

FEEDBACK
Positive throughout.

FAVOURITE FOOD NOW
**Anything but from the
students' cafeteria**

YOUR MOST VALUED
POSSESSION NOW
My health

DO YOU TEACH?
**I teach at Parsons
School of Design in
New York (USA),
a class about 'process',
and I frequently hold
workshops, also on
'process'.**

IS IT POSSIBLE TO
TEACH DESIGN?
**Yes, but I can't offer
any proof yet.**

Project Now

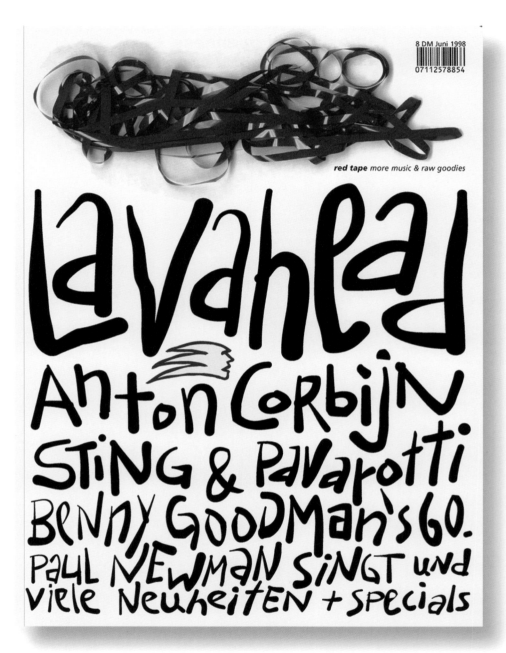

Alora &
Calzadilla
Bock
Dean
THE HUGO BOSS PRIZE 2006
Ortega
Ruilova
Sehgal

GERMAN-FRENCH

Julie Gayard

A PIECE OF SOUND ADVICE + A SINGLE WARNING TO A DESIGN STUDENT

Have fun with the projects and your fellow students + Take the fun seriously

YEAR OF PROJECT
1994

STUDENT PROJECT BRIEF
**Describe your journey
to college through
typography**

COLLEGE
**Camberwell College
of Arts, London (United
Kingdom)**

TUTOR(S)
Darren Lago

TECHNOLOGY
Pen on paper, photocopier

TIME SPENT
2 weeks

TYPEFACE
**No particular fonts –
photocopied fonts, drawn
fonts, handwriting,
typewriter (no computer
yet)…**

WHY DO YOU LIKE THIS PROJECT?
**The directness of it. I took
the brief literally, with a twist:
I let the journey describe
itself through typography:
the movements of the tube
itself are drawing the lines of
the letters; my hand is just
holding the pen.**

WHAT DO YOU DISLIKE ABOUT IT?
**Why is it just a big page
full of sketches? Why didn't
I turn it into a font?**

OUTCOMES
**I remember enjoying the
looseness of the lines, and the
fact that I was not controlling
the pen but the shakings of
the tube was. It felt childish
but good. Maybe it felt
refreshing compared to other
projects that were usually
more idea-based.**

FEEDBACK
**My friend Ed Gill, also a
student at Camberwell and
a graffiti artist, really liked an
'F' of it. I enlarged it.**

ANYTHING ELSE
**Sometimes the pressures
of a deadline force you to be
intuitively effective with
minimum effort and time!**

FAVOURITE FOOD THEN
-

YOUR MOST VALUED
POSSESSION THEN
-

PROJECT SIMILARITIES
THEN AND NOW
**Obviously the hand-
drawn type, both small
doodles blown up
much bigger. But also:
the stripped-bare
looseness and lightness
of both of them,
the childish style.**

Project Then

Julie Gayard (Jutojo)

For both: Enthusiasm

YEAR OF PROJECT
2008

PROFESSIONAL PROJECT BRIEF
Design record sleeves for a series of 12-inches called Based On Misunderstandings – with a crafty feel and cheap production

CLIENT
Sonar Kollektiv Records

COLLABORATOR(S)
Jutojo Partners Toby Cornish and Johannes Braun

TECHNOLOGY
Pen on paper, scanner, Photoshop and InDesign, press plant for record sleeves

TIME SPENT
2 weeks

TYPEFACE
Avenir, Akzidenz Grotesk, Century Gothic…

WHY DO YOU LIKE THIS PROJECT?
The lightness of it. And the fact that I did it almost absent-mindedly, like a doodle, and they liked it instantly.

WHAT DO YOU DISLIKE ABOUT IT?
The fact that the three covers from the series are all slightly different on the back. I don't remember why; I think the artist wanted slight changes, or it was cheaper to not print the whole back solidly? I wonder…

OUTCOMES
Finding that I should draw more often and that it is refreshing to do something very intuitive and quick, effortless yet effective.

FEEDBACK
It's unreadable! But that's the point ('based on misunder-standings') – so it's OK.

ANYTHING ELSE
See answer opposite (then).

DO YOU TEACH?
No.

IS IT POSSIBLE TO TEACH DESIGN?
I think teaching design should be a mix of design theory, technical and craft skills, and learning how to develop ideas. At Camberwell College I learned to think of graphic design in a wider sense – that it is not just layout and typography, but also an idea, which can be communicated through a performance, a song, a photo, a film… which was mind-opening, but also confusing some-times. I think I got lost in all the possibilities sometimes and probably that's why my projects never came to an actual final stage!

FAVOURITE FOOD NOW
-

YOUR MOST VALUED POSSESSION NOW
-

Project Now

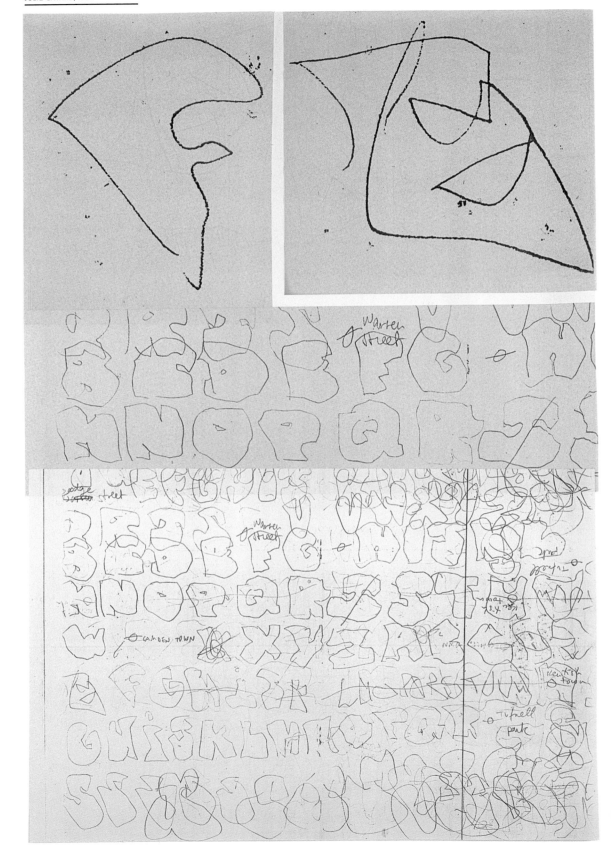

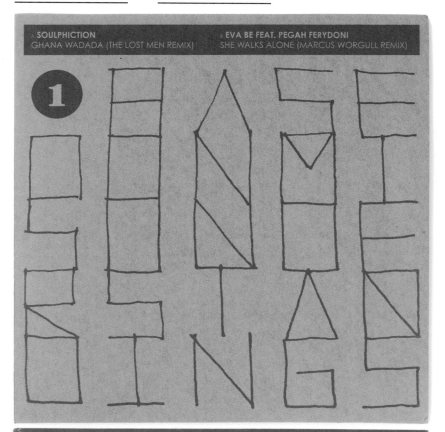

A SOULPHICTION
GHANA WADADA (THE LOST MEN REMIX)

B EVA BE FEAT. PEGAH FERYDONI
SHE WALKS ALONE (MARCUS WORGULL REMIX)

1

BASED ON MISUNDERSTANDINGS 1

SONAR KOLLEKTIV

BASED ON MISUNDERSTANDINGS 1

Kai von Rabenau

Follow your own path + Don't do it for the money or glamour – neither will come true

YEAR OF PROJECT
1998

STUDENT PROJECT BRIEF
The visualization of music, taking three different genres (pop, jazz, classical); this work represents the album Tabula Rasa by Arvo Pärt

COLLEGE
Central Saint Martins College of Art & Design, London (United Kingdom)

TUTOR(S)
Chris Corr

TECHNOLOGY
35mm black-and-white photography and screenprint

TIME SPENT
1 month

TYPEFACE
If only I could remember… maybe Times?

FAVOURITE FOOD THEN
Pasta with tuna

YOUR MOST VALUED POSSESSION THEN
My Nikon camera

WHY DO YOU LIKE THIS PROJECT?
I like the simplicity of it, which works well with the music it is meant to capture; the bowls were photographed in a staircase in Prague, where they were placed to catch raindrops leaking through the ceiling – in the last piece of Tabula Rasa is a passage that is very reminiscent of dripping water.

WHAT DO YOU DISLIKE ABOUT IT?
I would probably change the typography a little now, but on the whole, I still like it very much.

OUTCOMES
I learned that you can't control everything: I had gone through a long and tedious process of setting up an image that I had had in my mind to capture the mood of the music; it was a staged studio shot that finally felt lifeless and contrived and had very little in common with the recording I tried to visualize, which has a certain lightness and depth hard to put into two dimensions. At the end of the album, if you listen very carefully, you can hear the musicians leave the room one by one – it was that sort of 'reality' that was missing.

Desperate for some sort of solution, I went through my archives of photographs and came across this image, which I'd taken on a spur of the moment, and I realized that this photograph had everything that I'd wanted to recreate in the studio. In short, it was perfect, and I learned that sometimes you have to discard all your previous ideas and let life take over to find a solution to a project. I also believe that it was this image that got me accepted to the MA course at the RCA, since the head of the course back then was a huge fan of the album by Arvo Pärt and could obviously relate to my interpretation.

FEEDBACK
The image was part of the visual aspect of my BA thesis on the visualization of sound; it received very good feedback from my tutors, as far as I can remember.

PROJECT SIMILARITIES THEN AND NOW
Visually, they definitely share a certain aesthetic that is reduced and controlled, but also very graphic and composed. Even though I was a student in graphic design, I quickly discovered that I was more interested in the image-making side of design – namely photography – than in typography or layout. At college, I still wanted to learn as much as possible about everything, so I tried to combine photography with other areas, such as typography and screenprinting in this example. Later you learn that you need to focus to go further, deeper, so I eventually decided to concentrate on photography. But I think that my background in graphic design is still very visible in the work that I produce today, even though I do not consider myself to be a designer anymore.

Project Then

Kai von Rabenau (mono.graphie)

A VALUABLE QUALITY FOR A DESIGN STUDENT + A DESIGN PROFESSIONAL

Insistence and genuineness + Insistence and detachment

YEAR OF PROJECT
2010

PROFESSIONAL PROJECT BRIEF
One image from the self-initiated portraits series Typologies 03: The Nameless – Iran Orphans, which assembles portraits according to varying parameters

CLIENT
Self-initiated

TECHNOLOGY
Medium-format colour photography

TIME SPENT
3 weeks

WHY DO YOU LIKE THIS PROJECT?
I like the simplicity of it, where you rely simply and purely on your subject, without any additional effects or tricks; the distanced posture of the photographer versus the obvious humanity of the portrayed.

OUTCOMES
This image and this series made me change my mind about where I want to go with my photography; after working for ten years in mainly editorial photography, which is very close to graphic design in terms of working to a given brief, finding the best possible solution to a problem within a given set of circumstances, this series made me want to work in a different environment to have more freedom to produce images that will stand on their own.

FEEDBACK
The image hasn't really been exhibited yet, so there's been little feedback so far.

ANYTHING ELSE
Funnily enough, with mono.kultur, we just finished our latest issue on ECM records, who published the Tabula Rasa album. So another circle comes to an end.

DO YOU TEACH?
No – only individual workshops, mainly at Bezalel Academy in Jerusalem (Israel).

IS IT POSSIBLE TO TEACH DESIGN?
Yes, I do. I learned a lot at college, namely to sharpen a sense for aesthetics and composition, but also how to develop and edit ideas, to find my own personal approach. I think design teaching needs to maintain an individual approach, to let students build their own style and creative process. And to develop a sense for quality – what is good and what isn't.

FAVOURITE FOOD NOW
Schnitzel

YOUR MOST VALUED POSSESSION NOW
My Leica camera

Project Now

Ken Garland

A PIECE OF SOUND ADVICE + A SINGLE WARNING TO A DESIGN STUDENT

Acquire skills +
No warning

YEAR OF PROJECT
1953

STUDENT PROJECT BRIEF
**Experimental typography
project using found items
of letterpress**

COLLEGE
**Central School of Arts &
Crafts, London (United
Kingdom)**

TUTOR(S)
Edward Wright

TECHNOLOGY
Letterpress

TIME SPENT
3 hours

WHY DO YOU LIKE THIS PROJECT?
**Because I like making
creatures out of anything.**

WHAT DO YOU DISLIKE ABOUT IT?
Nothing, I love it.

FEEDBACK
**Edward Wright, who ran the
project, loved it.**

ANYTHING ELSE
**I have always seen monsters
(and I'm sure I'm not the only
one) in the most mundane of
materials. In 1953 it was spare
bits of type matter; in 2009
it was fire hydrants.**

FAVOURITE FOOD THEN
Tomato soup

YOUR MOST VALUED
POSSESSION THEN
My portable radio

Project Then

PROJECT SIMILARITIES
THEN AND NOW
Monsters.

LONDON, UNITED KINGDOM

Ken Garland

A VALUABLE QUALITY FOR A DESIGN STUDENT + A DESIGN PROFESSIONAL

For both: An open mind

YEAR OF PROJECT
2009

PROFESSIONAL PROJECT BRIEF
**I set my own brief.
Wherever I go in the
world, I look out for fire
hydrants that excite me**

CLIENT
Self-initiated

TECHNOLOGY
Photography

TIME SPENT
3 months

WHY DO YOU LIKE THIS PROJECT?
**The Jewish fire hydrant
excited me particularly,
as it had 'chutzpah'.**

FEEDBACK
**People email me about
the book to tell me they
love it.**

FAVOURITE FOOD NOW
**Gambas al aquillo
(giant prawns in garlic)**

YOUR MOST VALUED
POSSESSION NOW
My cheap digital camera

Project Now

DO YOU TEACH?
**Currently at University
of Brighton (UK),
Visiting Professor in
Graphic Design. Overall
53 years as a teacher.**

IS IT POSSIBLE TO
TEACH DESIGN?
**Skills and relations
between arts.**

Kirsty Carter

A PIECE OF SOUND ADVICE + A SINGLE WARNING TO A DESIGN STUDENT

None

YEAR OF PROJECT
2001

STUDENT PROJECT BRIEF
This project was set to choose an example of rationalist graphic communication and a contrasted example of its 'irrational' counterpart. I chose Tufte/Duchamp, Duchamp/Tufte, Esoteric/Exoteric. Edward Tufte (author of Visual Explanations) represents for me the extreme of the scientific analysis of visual problems. He intends a clarity of expression, an immediacy of communication. Marcel Duchamp intended his Large Glass to reveal its secrets through slow release with a deliberate obscurity of expression. His analysis of visual problems was highly personal, even eccentric.

STUDENT PROJECT BRIEF CONT.
What if Tufte chose to express a visual analysis using Duchamp and vice versa? My study of the two artists suggests that my previous perception of them as extremes was an over-simplification. They share similar methods of creativity.

COLLEGE
University of Brighton (United Kingdom)

TUTOR(S)
Daniel Eatock (see also pp. 58–61), Frank Philippin (see also p. 256), Lawrence Zeegen

TECHNOLOGY
Freehand, QuarkXpress

TYPEFACE
Helvetica Neue Bold, Helvetica Neue Medium

WHY DO YOU LIKE THIS PROJECT?
This was the beginning of many projects in my last year at Brighton University where I was exploring my interest in conceptual art, reading, gaining knowledge about contemporary art. This was a very positive time.

WHAT DO YOU DISLIKE ABOUT IT?
The visual language of this project is very pragmatic, dry and lacks real feeling; the visualization of the design was not my top priority. It was an exercise in research and dealing with information. Of course now, both the concept and visualization of my projects fit better together, I am more confident designing. My last year at Brighton was a lot about experiments and research and why I wanted to continue my education and go straight into postgraduate studies, as it was clear to me I was still developing, and my very particular way of being a designer, bringing together my interests.

PROJECT SIMILARITIES THEN AND NOW
The strongest similarity is of course the subject matter. I never wanted our studio or myself to develop a distinct visual style; the project is born from research and content that determines its form. For example, each of the projects are approached typograph-ically in very different ways, a justified sans-serif compared with a sans-serif left-aligned book and that is just the beginning. People work with us because of our approach, not because they want a particular visual style. Every project ends up looking so different because they are often very different projects. More importantly, the book feels more confident and uses colour!

FAVOURITE FOOD THEN
I've always kept a very balanced diet. It makes me happy to eat well. When I had little money, food was…
(Cont. opposite – now)

YOUR MOST VALUED POSSESSION THEN
All my Apple products and I am not ashamed to admit it. I love my iPad, iPhone, MacBook Pro. I have had a Mac since I was 13 years old

Project Then

Kirsty Carter (A Practice for Everyday Life)

To explore +
To keep exploring

YEAR OF PROJECT
2010/11

PROFESSIONAL PROJECT BRIEF
Exhibition Histories book series. To produce 15 books, each dedicated to a contemporary art exhibition since 1955, publishing 3 books per year and feeling like a book series with a target audience of academics, curators and students.

CLIENT
Lucy Steeds, Teresa Gleadsowe, Pablo Lafuente, Charles Esche (Afterall Books)

COLLABORATOR(S)
A Practice For Everyday Life (the whole studio was involved in some shape or form)

TECHNOLOGY
Adobe InDesign, Photoshop

TYPEFACE
Adobe Garamond Regular,
Adobe Garamond Italic,
Neuzeit Office Bold,
Neuzeit Office Italic,
Neuzeit Office Regular

WHY DO YOU LIKE THIS PROJECT?
This was one of my favourite projects we produced in 2010 – the series seems to sum up our passion, love and interest in contemporary art. The research/history and our growing knowledge of this subject is what perhaps makes our studio somewhat specialist in this field. This is one of the first publications we have designed that is now printing its 2nd edition; I am sure that is a sign of success!

FAVOURITE FOOD NOW
...never cut, it was always my top priority. I perhaps eat out a little more now. In terms of favourites, it has always been chocolate

YOUR MOST VALUED POSSESSION NOW
Documenta 5 poster by Ed Ruscha in 1972 – it's my favourite piece of graphic design. I love that he made type up out of little ants

DO YOU TEACH?
I have never had a regular teaching position at any college, but I have been a visiting lecturer and lectured at many. One or two years into A Practice for Everyday Life, we were regularly asked to teach, but we (Emma Thomas and I) both felt we weren't ready to teach then and how much knowledge we could really pass on at that point. Now it's perhaps a different story. We did and still do often teach in the capacity of lecturing and workshops. I have taught at many different institutions and different kinds of students all over the world. We love this way of teaching, where you can set workshops, give a huge amount of enthusiasum and input into a brief to get the students thinking; it makes us excited to see what they will produce. The only trouble is that we never build up a relationship with any of the students, which I am sure is where the real joy begins!

IS IT POSSIBLE TO TEACH DESIGN?
Of course! I think it is an incredible education, a design education. It was time to evolve, experiment, research, collect, investigate and learn. Some of my teaching was quite formal; we learned typography formally at Brighton in workshops about 'Typographic detailing' but also had time to just explore my concepts. At the Royal College I had access to an incredible library of books and periodicals and other designers' archives. I would have never had this without a design education. Throughout my education I had conversations, dialogues and critiques with some of the most inspiring design practitioners, which I learned a lot from, both what I wanted to be and want I didn't want to be. But most importantly, I was taught by the great people around me – the fellow design students I was at college with.

Project Now

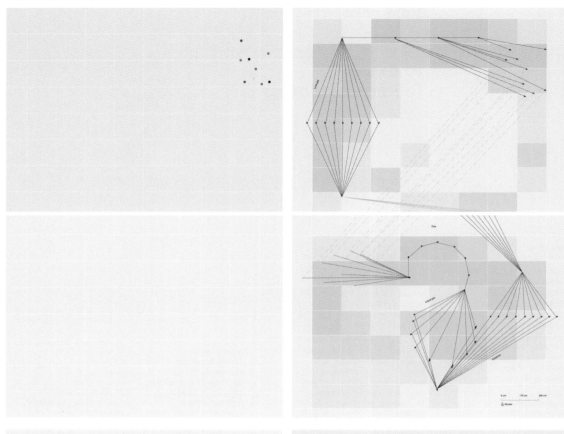

Kristine Matthews

a: To American students in particular: Travel the world. Live in another country b: Take risks. Now is the time to do it + Don't let your fears get in the way of admitting what you really want – then go after that thing

YEAR OF PROJECT
1996

STUDENT PROJECT BRIEF
A self-initiated project. A brief to myself. Coming out of a more commercial design background and entering grad school, I was interested in the idea of introducing chance/luck/randomness to my work. I wanted to create a project to let loose in the world and see what came back. (Also, other people have more interesting ideas than I do, so I thought I would ask lots of people to send me theirs.)

COLLEGE
Royal College of Art, London (United Kingdom)

TUTOR(S)
Siobhan Keaney, Margaret Calvert, Richard Bonner-Morgan, Russell Warren-Fisher (I can't remember if one in particular was offering significant critique on this project…; they each tutored me at various times at the Royal College)

COLLABORATOR(S)
My collaborators were the 100 people I sent cards to (especially the ones who responded…)

TECHNOLOGY
Postcards printed letterpress. Book cover printed letterpress, inside pages printed offset (printing donated by the White Dove Press)

TIME SPENT
Oh goodness, I can't remember. It lasted at least three or four months altogether, I think. (Long, pleasant hours in the letterpress studio making the cards and cover / Happy times at the postbox collecting replies as they trickled in / Forever trying to make the handwriting look good in the book before hitting on the idea of translating handwriting to its typeset equivalent.)

TYPEFACE
Helvetica Compressed (title), Bell Gothic (body)

WHY DO YOU LIKE THIS PROJECT?
I like that the book is now all around the world, tucked onto various people's bookshelves. Even for non-designers, people tend to remember it, as the content is so personal.

WHAT DO YOU DISLIKE ABOUT IT?
I'd probably change the title of Now Here This. Then again… maybe not.

OUTCOMES
Good fodder for some handwriting analysis.

FEEDBACK
Positive: I think people were pleasantly surprised to find that if they made the effort to fill in and send back the card, they eventually got a book in return. Negative: Some friends of my parents accused me of incorrect spelling (in the title). It's supposed to be word-play, referring to where you are (not what you hear). Makes me wonder how many other people silently pity my spelling faux pas.

ANYTHING ELSE
Looking at Now Here This and the subsequent global onslaught of email, social media, blah blah, I lament the rapid decline of the postal service and the personal letter. The variety of stamps that I received on the replies to Now Here This could have merited their own project. Some students of mine recently did a project on this subject, which I love: www.positivepost.org Long live the stamp!

PROJECT SIMILARITIES THEN AND NOW
Both feature content collected from the audience of the project itself. Maybe it's laziness, but I always find that if you ask the right question of your audience, you will get unexpected results that are much more interesting than what you would come up with yourself, even if you stared hard at a blank sheet of paper for days on end. Now Here This certainly proved that to me, and I have returned to the idea for various professional projects. There is nothing better than crafting the right question (and by that I mean, not too specific, but not too general), then waiting to see what people come up with. I never cease to be entertained and inspired.

FAVOURITE FOOD THEN
Pasta

YOUR MOST VALUED POSSESSION THEN
My latest design project

Project Then

Kristine Matthews (Studio Matthews)

A VALUABLE QUALITY FOR A DESIGN STUDENT + A DESIGN PROFESSIONAL

Willingness to work hard and at the same time take risks + Ability to read people well

YEAR OF PROJECT
2010

PROFESSIONAL PROJECT BRIEF
The SCIDpda (Seattle Chinatown International District Preservation & Development Authority) wanted to create a resource centre for the neighbourhood, which includes Chinese, Japanese and Korean communities. It would become the go-to spot for business owners and residents to find out about local programmes and resources. In line with SCIDpda's mission, it would work to improve the local neighbourhood and build cross-cultural communities.

CLIENT
SCIDpda

COLLABORATOR(S)
Cassie Klingler, designer at Studio Matthews. And the client Joyce Pisnanont was great in collecting lots of responses from the local community for the 'IDEA' wall.

TECHNOLOGY
Title sign ('IDEA') is made up of wood blocks laser-etched with written replies that were collected using photocopied response cards. The rest of the interior was a combo of wood and caster structures, IKEA curtain rails used for the display system, paper posters and some yellow vinyl graphics. The oversize flipable map is printed direct to substrate, two-sided on an eco corrugated board.

TIME SPENT
Start to finish, about six months for the whole space. (Several long months trying to figure out what the client needed the space to be and to do; another month to work out the design for the space, including collecting the responses for the IDEA title; then high-speed build-out in a few weeks to meet with their grant deadline!)

TYPEFACE
Various handwriting for block signage. Helvetica throughout space (the client needed to be able to use templates of ours to create new posters, etc., but they work on PCs with a bare-bones font list. So Helvetica/ Arial was the safest bet).

WHY DO YOU LIKE THIS PROJECT?
It was one of those nice situations where the client has been pummelled into low expectations by previous projects. They are used to working in poor facilities without much of a public 'face'. The Idea Space gives them a showpiece. We did it for a pittance, but their gratitude and excitement makes all the difference. I went in the other day to see how it's faring over a year later and they had updated posters up and it was neat as a pin. Very gratifying.

OUTCOMES
See answer opposite (then).

FEEDBACK
Positive: The client loved it and we got great feedback from the community at the opening. Who can resist having their ideas burned into wood?

DO YOU TEACH?
I am an Assistant Professor in Visual Communication Design at the University of Washington, Seattle (USA) and teach Exhibition Design, Design Foundations, Graduate Seminars, Visualizations, etc.

IS IT POSSIBLE TO TEACH DESIGN?
I think you can certainly teach the basic tenets of design; good typog- raphy, what makes a photograph compelling, blah blah. But though I am a university design professor (aside from my studio), I am still uncomfortable in the role of saying what is 'right' and what is 'wrong' in design. Who am I to say? This probably makes me not as strong a teacher as I should be. I prefer showing my own design work and leaving it for the audience to decide whether it is 'good' in their book.

FAVOURITE FOOD NOW
Pasta

YOUR MOST VALUED POSSESSION NOW
My children Finn and Nell

Project Now

BLUSH, STAMMER, SAY "HI MOM." ASK
LAURA TO CALL ME, AND TELL
THE WORLD I'M LOOKING FOR A JOB.
A GOOD ONE. BOW IN THANKS.

I would try to explain with a few pictures,
that people should learn and try to see and feel
not only with their own eyes but they should try
to replace theirselves in as many positions of people
and even things around them. And then, with all
this different states, positions, sights, feelings, and values
they should try to react, (to do things) in balance
every day, every minute and be ready to
change their doings (or work/reactions) if necessary
(not subjectively but objectively in dialogue with
environment)

Look at me. With no clothes on.
Do you know me? How am I just like you?
How am I different from you?
think of nothing but the answer to that
question for two minutes.

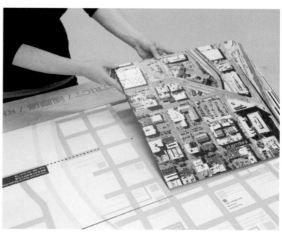

GERMAN

Lars Harmsen

A PIECE OF SOUND ADVICE + A SINGLE WARNING TO A DESIGN STUDENT

Work awake + Get out of the dogma house

YEAR OF PROJECT
1992

STUDENT PROJECT BRIEF
Self-initiated diploma thesis: creating experimental typography with the help of self-built printing machines

COLLEGE
Hochschule Pforzheim (Germany)

TUTOR(S)
Prof. Manfred Schmalriede and Prof. Thomas Ochs

TECHNOLOGY
The printing machines were built out of wood and steel. The typesetting was done on a Macintosh SE and printed on a 300 dpi laser printer. Photography and typography were then collaged page by page and colour-copied on a Canon colour copy machine. A book documents the process, the machines and the final prints.

TIME SPENT
4 months

TYPEFACE
Chicago, DIN and a bunch of custom-made fonts

WHY DO YOU LIKE THIS PROJECT?
Was done during the time of transition between analogue and digital. It was a very intense project done in a very short time, completed with no diversions.

OUTCOMES
Great satisfaction and the love of working on both self-commissioned projects and assigned ones.

FEEDBACK
'Best Graphic Design diploma thesis of the year'.

FAVOURITE FOOD THEN
Pasta

YOUR MOST VALUED POSSESSION THEN
My camera and my first computer

Project Then

PROJECT SIMILARITIES THEN AND NOW
Both are self-commissioned work and have handmade as well as digital elements.

Lars Harmsen (MAGMA Brand Design)

Curiosity + Intelligence

YEAR OF PROJECT
2010

PROFESSIONAL PROJECT BRIEF
Design an exhibition
about identity at the
Goethe Institute in Dakar,
Senegal

CLIENT
Goethe-Institut Dakar,
Senegal

COLLABORATOR(S)
André Rösler (illustration),
Christian Ernst (photog-
raphy) and a local sign-
painter using stencils

TECHNOLOGY
Black-and-white laser
prints on wood board, oil
on canvas, photo prints,
wall paintings

TIME SPENT
2 weeks

TYPEFACE
Helvetica and custom-
made fonts (e.g. stencil
typefaces from the sign-
painter we worked with)

WHY DO YOU LIKE THIS PROJECT?
It was a great opportunity to
visit Senegal and meet
extraordinary people. It was
a very intense project carried
out in a very short time,
with no diversions.

WHAT DO YOU DISLIKE ABOUT IT?
A few more weeks would
have been good to work with
more local artists.

OUTCOMES
Inspiration. And a small book
presenting text from Muhsana
Ali and Amadou Kane-Sy,
both from Senegal ('A cause
de mon histoire personnelle,
je n'ai pas d'attachement
à une seule identité') and
showing our work.

FEEDBACK
The ambassador of Germany
in Dakar bought four pieces
of work.

DO YOU TEACH?
Professor of Typography
and Design at
Fachhochschule
Dortmund (Germany).

IS IT POSSIBLE TO
TEACH DESIGN?
Design is about seeing
and putting together,
organizing. I encourage
students to check all
kinds of path. They have
to discover the world
and themselves.
Nowadays a lot of
students are imprisoned
in a shelter of wealth.
Everything seems to
be accessible, easy,
cool. I hate that. I want
them to jump off the
cliff and learn to fall,
not to be perfect,
not to be safe, not to
think it's over before it
starts. They have to
walk on glass. New is
dead, long live new.
The happy accident is
a hook. To teach design
you have to bring
people to reflect on
what they are doing and
why they are doing it.
Design is not about
making things nice.
A designer is not a
hairdresser. A designer
should be able to see,
hear, smell and taste
more than others in
order to reflect and act.

FAVOURITE FOOD NOW
Home-cooking and good
restaurants. There is a
great Lebanese restaurant
here in Karlsruhe that
I love to go to

YOUR MOST VALUED
POSSESSION NOW
It's not a 'valued
possession', but my family
is something very
important to me now,
more than anything else

Project Now

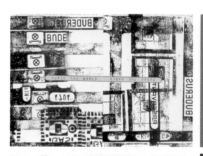

Laurent Lacour

A PIECE OF SOUND ADVICE + A SINGLE WARNING TO A DESIGN STUDENT

Think big + Don't think small

YEAR OF PROJECT
2000

STUDENT PROJECT BRIEF
**1: Development of art/design projects to establish an identity for Südraum, a region south of Leipzig (Germany).
2: Photographic (visual) and contextual research on the development (history and heritage) of Südraum with interviews, etc.**

COLLEGE
Hochschule für Gestaltung Offenbach am Main (Germany)

TUTOR(S)
Prof. Ruedi Baur

COLLABORATOR(S)
Many people from the region: politicians, landscape architects, cultural organizations, etc.

TECHNOLOGY
Digital imaging, video, photography, graphic design, sound recordings, product design, modelling (mixed materials), etc.

TIME SPENT
1 year

TYPEFACE
Not relevant

WHY DO YOU LIKE THIS PROJECT?
The deep and thorough research we conducted into Südraum meant that the project was relevant to and was well received by the local population and official bodies. The aesthetic decisions we made on the project were also informed by the research we had carried out. The implementation of the project was based on a multi-disciplinary communication design approach, and drew on other areas of expertise as well (see Collaborators).

OUTCOMES
Knowledge.

FEEDBACK
Very positive feedback and reactions, especially in the local press.

FAVOURITE FOOD THEN
Tafelspitz

YOUR MOST VALUED POSSESSION THEN
-

PROJECT SIMILARITIES
THEN AND NOW
The interdisciplinary approach and the depth of research.

Project Then

Laurent Lacour (Hauser Lacour)

A VALUABLE QUALITY FOR A DESIGN STUDENT + A DESIGN PROFESSIONAL

Good conceptual thinking, quick in bringing ideas to paper (or any other media) and open to any kind of culture + See above, plus very good at managing discourse with clients

YEAR OF PROJECT
2009

PROFESSIONAL PROJECT BRIEF
Development of a fair (consumer electronics and home appliances – IFA 2009) identity for Siemens

CLIENT
Siemens Elektrogeräte GmbH, Ulrich Twiehaus

COLLABORATOR(S)
Meso: digital imaging; Franken Architekten: architecture, exhibition stand construction, etc.

TECHNOLOGY
Digital imaging, video, photography, graphic design, sound recordings, architectural design, interactive design and programming

TIME SPENT
6 months

TYPEFACE
Not relevant

WHY DO YOU LIKE THIS PROJECT?
It was an exciting inter-disciplinary project with the focus on teamwork. Very interesting interactive exhibits and a good symbiosis between architecture and design.

WHAT DO YOU DISLIKE ABOUT IT?
The client, who didn't stick with us afterwards despite our good work.

FEEDBACK
Very positive feedback/reaction, awards, etc.

DO YOU TEACH?
Professor of Corporate Design at Fachhoch-schule Düsseldorf (Germany).

IS IT POSSIBLE TO TEACH DESIGN?
Yes it is: but it is more about teaching a kind of thinking and discourse than teaching visual skills.

FAVOURITE FOOD NOW
Tafelspitz

YOUR MOST VALUED POSSESSION NOW
My kids (but – oh – I don't possess them)

Project Now

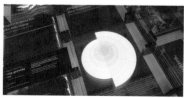

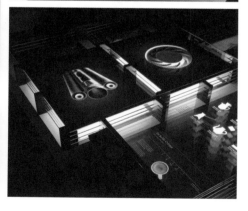

Liza Enebeis

Whatever you do, explore the extremes, and don't lose your sense of humour + If there is something else you want to do apart from design then do something else

YEAR OF PROJECT
1996

STUDENT PROJECT BRIEF
The project was specifically designed for the Work in Progress Show just before our graduation

COLLEGE
Royal College of Art, London (United Kingdom)

TUTOR(S)
Liz Leyland

TECHNOLOGY
A mix between hand-drawing and a typewriter

TIME SPENT
2 months

TYPEFACE
Typewriter

WHY DO YOU LIKE THIS PROJECT?
Because of its roughness. The project was mapping points of view on the definition of the book.

WHAT DO YOU DISLIKE ABOUT IT?
I wish I hadn't sliced it into 15 pieces – I am still not sure what I was thinking.

OUTCOMES
An insight about the nature of the book.

FEEDBACK
It was generally liked, with comments such as 'it's typically Dutch' (which I found strange at the time).

FAVOURITE FOOD THEN
Marmite

YOUR MOST VALUED POSSESSION THEN
My books

Project Then

PROJECT SIMILARITIES THEN AND NOW
There are more similarities in the concepts than in the visual style. Both projects map information, one in words and the other with images, although the starting point to both was the same: in-depth research.

ROTTERDAM, THE NETHERLANDS

Liza Enebeis (Studio Dumbar)

A VALUABLE QUALITY FOR A DESIGN STUDENT + A DESIGN PROFESSIONAL

Curiosity + A sense of humour

YEAR OF PROJECT
2010

PROFESSIONAL PROJECT BRIEF
Redesign the identity for the University of Twente (The Netherlands)

CLIENT
University of Twente (The Netherlands)

COLLABORATOR(S)
For this particular project we were a fixed team of three at Studio Dumbar and another eight people on and off depending on the phase

TECHNOLOGY
Hand-drawings redrawn in Illustrator

TIME SPENT
1 year

TYPEFACE
Univers

WHY DO YOU LIKE THIS PROJECT?
I like the concept of creating a universe for a University, and enjoyed collaborating with the designers in the studio to create the map that was the basis for the identity.

WHAT DO YOU DISLIKE ABOUT IT?
Nothing yet.

OUTCOMES
Everything is possible.

FEEDBACK
The project received a lot of reactions as it was not the usual approach for a university identity.

DO YOU TEACH?
No.

IS IT POSSIBLE TO TEACH DESIGN?
I think it's possible to teach design. At college I learned my most important lesson: 'staying foreign'. The more comfortable you are in a situation, the more likely you are to let things go by unnoticed. Travel to a foreign country, and suddenly you notice different sounds, smells, colours, temperatures, structures, behaviours... For the locals these things go by unnoticed; locals are immune to their surroundings. As designers, photographers and creatives, we are constantly seeking to be in a non-immunized state, to be able to look at the same question and always solve it in a different way. Immunity is our worst enemy. If we learn to remain foreign we will always see what goes by unnoticed. This is what I would like to teach.

FAVOURITE FOOD NOW
Marmite

YOUR MOST VALUED POSSESSION NOW
My books

Project Now

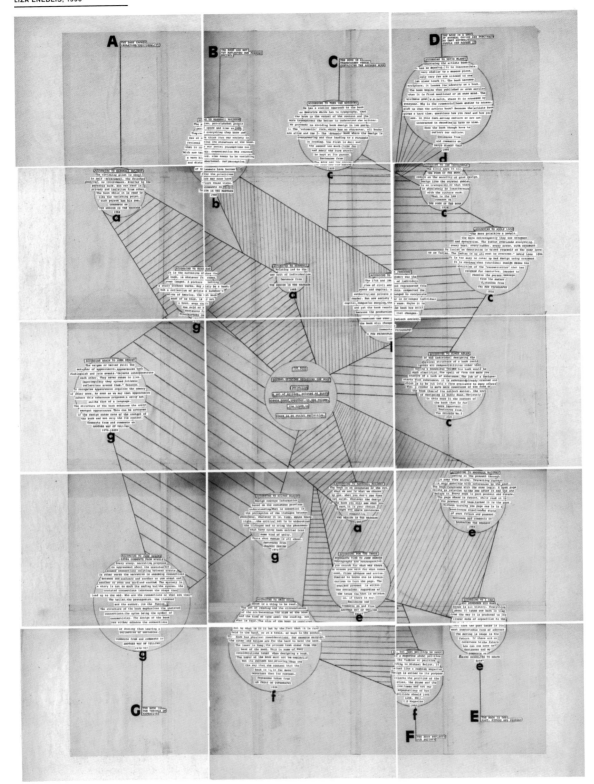

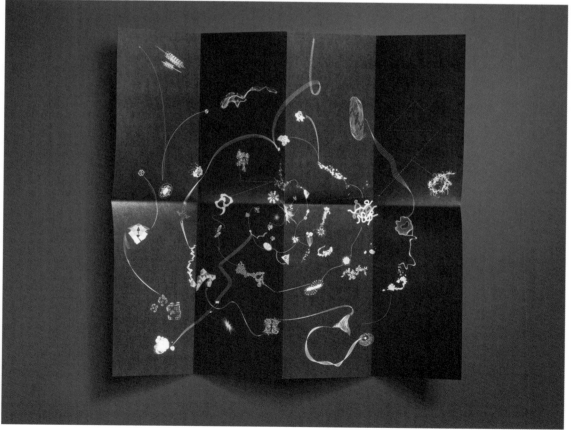

Lucinda Noble

Make the most of your time, facilities and access to people and resources. And enjoy! + Foresee the challenges in the professional world and start considering how you will incorporate them into your design vision

YEAR OF PROJECT
1999

STUDENT PROJECT BRIEF
Self-initiated project.
A series of wall-mounted relief pieces based on a collection of original pieces of polystyrene packaging.

COLLEGE
Royal College of Art, London (United Kingdom)

TUTOR(S)
Richard Bonner-Morgan, Margaret Calvert (see also pp. 150–153), Lol Sargent

TECHNOLOGY
Scalpel knife, ruler, foam board and paint – the pieces were constructed by eye

TIME SPENT
1 week

WHY DO YOU LIKE THIS PROJECT?
I loved making something three-dimensional by hand, and I'm surprised to find that I still think they're beautiful objects! At the time, I mounted them around the Stevens Building at the Royal College of Art and they blended in beautifully with the moulding on the walls, which I loved.

WHAT DO YOU DISLIKE ABOUT IT?
I would have liked to cast them in plaster.

OUTCOMES
Apart from slicing my finger with my scalpel blade working late one night(!), I got a lot of satisfaction out of constructing something with my hands. It was a 'seed' project that led to many other ideas.

FEEDBACK
I think the pieces went pretty much unnoticed!

ANYTHING ELSE
The polystyrene relief piece is perhaps a strange example from my student work. It was a small, insignificant project (in terms of my overall portfolio), but having thought about it, it emphasizes to me how important those sketchy little pieces can be, and how important I still find it to make time simply to follow an inspired creative urge to make something out of those seemingly meaningless little ideas that pop into my head!

PROJECT SIMILARITIES THEN AND NOW
I am still very much following my own lead. From my experience, my strongest work comes from those projects that are self-initiated or that I have most freedom to play around with. I am still fascinated by detail, bringing attention to the everyday, and the juxtaposition of function and beauty. Also, I continue to enjoy how things can be interpreted by the viewer/user in multiple ways.

FAVOURITE FOOD THEN
Probably pasta

YOUR MOST VALUED POSSESSION THEN
My family, my photos, my Mac (sad but true), my ability to see things in a certain way

Project Then

Lucinda Newton-Dunn (space-to-think)

A VALUABLE QUALITY FOR A DESIGN STUDENT + A DESIGN PROFESSIONAL

To be self-motivated, passionate and proactive + To be passionate, believe in your approach but remain open to changes – communicate clearly

YEAR OF PROJECT
2010/11

PROFESSIONAL PROJECT BRIEF
Design a print for a furoshiki (Japanese wrapping cloth) 90×90cm based on the concept of folding and wrapping. This project also involved developing the identity of the brand and marketing it.

CLIENT
Link, Tokyo

COLLABORATOR(S)
Kyoko Bowskill, Hennie Haworth

TECHNOLOGY
Artwork produced from a process involving photography, drawing by hand, and finally output in Illustrator on the Mac. Printed on 100% cotton by a traditional Japanese furoshiki printer in Tokyo – a type of screenprinting process.

TIME SPENT
A year (from conceptualizing to production and sales, etc.)

TYPEFACE
Handwritten

WHY DO YOU LIKE THIS PROJECT?
It is something tangible, useful, beautiful and sustainable.

WHAT DO YOU DISLIKE ABOUT IT?
I would have produced it at less expense and got someone else to do the marketing!

OUTCOMES
I learned a lot about working long-distance and about many aspects of business in the product world.

FEEDBACK
There has been some bewilderment over what this product is! People are amazingly intimidated by the introduction of a very simple but 'new' concept into the Western market. However, we are discovering ways to make it more accessible and there have been many great reviews on the blogosphere and in particular, compliments on the quality of the product (high Japanese production quality).

FAVOURITE FOOD NOW
Japanese food of various kinds

YOUR MOST VALUED POSSESSION NOW
Same as then

Project Now

DO YOU TEACH?
No.

IS IT POSSIBLE TO TEACH DESIGN?
I think you can certainly teach aspects of design. I wish I had been taught more of the fundamentals in terms of layout, colour theory, typography, business, etc. In the British design education system (at least where I studied) it seems that most focus is put on concept development. At the time I was happy developing the conceptual side of things but being young and inexperienced (I came straight through the school and college system), I didn't have the foresight personally to pursue an adequate amount of research in the more technical and business-orientated side of design. Tutors didn't really push that either. So I came away from college conceptually strong, but lacking the more structural, workmanship skills of design. It's quite hard as a student to know what to focus on during your time at college and guidance can be quite vague. Time is limited and it is the opportune moment to experiment with ideas and media, but it is also a great time to learn some of the nitty-gritty. More design theory should be encouraged and internships should be made a compulsory part of a design course.

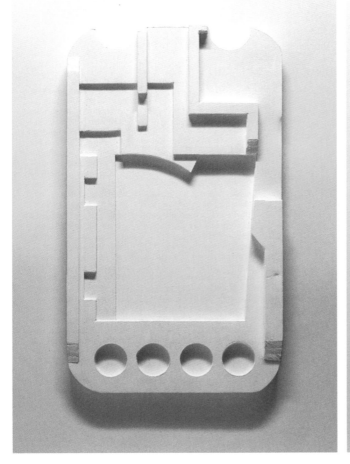

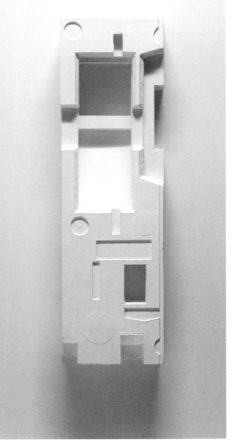

Maki Suzuki

A PIECE OF SOUND ADVICE + A SINGLE WARNING TO A DESIGN STUDENT

Try everything + Don't read, watch, look at design compilation books or blogs

YEAR OF PROJECT
1998

STUDENT PROJECT BRIEF
Express your given colour in a way that makes us see it as if for the first time. Nicole Udry got purple and I got turquoise.

COLLEGE
Royal College of Art, London (United Kingdom)

TUTOR(S)
Margaret Calvert (see also pp.150–153)

COLLABORATOR(S)
Nicole Udry, classmate

TECHNOLOGY
Digital inkjet printout, wood and foam board

TIME SPENT
1 week, among other projects

WHY DO YOU LIKE THIS PROJECT?
It is very difficult to remember the whole process, but the idea was that Nicole had chosen red and I, blue. To design a compromise of our collaboration, we printed out a very ugly drawing of the same dog in red on one side and blue on the other on a wooden stick. On the day of the presentation we turned the stick in our hands so the dog would somehow be purple. I like my own uncertainty of such a work. It somehow made sense (why a dog at all? why that dog?). What is perhaps most likely is that it gave me the hope that I could work towards something not only that people could find challenging but that I also would consider an eyesore. At the time Nicole was also on a similar quest, perhaps even more so as she did study graphics in Switzerland.

WHAT DO YOU DISLIKE ABOUT IT?
Too late. Definitely the ugliest thing.

OUTCOMES
Mixed feelings about disappointing a teacher I admired (see Feedback) and feeling guilty that I should have tried to please her. This has followed me since. A client, a commissioner or a collaborator is not someone to please or 'service'.

FEEDBACK
Margaret Calvert:
'I am so disappointed'.

PROJECT SIMILARITIES THEN AND NOW
In both projects we acknowledge they are not logical-conceptual, a tautological idea leading to one, often single, 'solution'. The design decisions are rather convoluted and spiral out of our own comfort zone. Of course once we get there we need to go further as comfort installs itself almost immediately. They also have in common that they force handlers, readers, receivers to wonder about them as performative objects. Obviously a book is always also an object, but in this case, I remember the slight shame at spinning the dog in front of the class or seeing people discard the book as a piece of trash they cannot throw away but would never put next to a 'real' publication.

FAVOURITE FOOD THEN
Being French and being a vegetarian was a national joke… Studying at the Royal College of Art (London, UK), where many cosmopolitan truths collide, I met Glaswegian and Swedish non-meat eaters who proved me wrong and I have been pescetarian since

YOUR MOST VALUED POSSESSION THEN
Comic books collection

Project Then

Maki Suzuki (Åbäke)

For both: Try everything

YEAR OF PROJECT
2010

PROFESSIONAL PROJECT BRIEF
Design a short text by
artist Eline McGeorge

CLIENT
Hollybush Gardens
(gallery)

COLLABORATOR(S)
Åbäke members

TECHNOLOGY
Offset printing,
staple-binding

TIME SPENT
3 weeks from idea
to production

TYPEFACE
Chicago, New York
and Arial

WHY DO YOU LIKE THIS PROJECT?
The text was a meta-fiction
of a person who could possibly
try to contact someone in a
democratic country. To design
it, we felt it needed to bring out
the world in which it would
have been written, namely
a fictitious totalitarian regime.
This led us to design a whole
'computer manual' around the
text to camouflage it from 'the
thought police'. There is an
overall fascination for vernacular
design, but it usually is in the
safe area of the just-vintage.
For this publication, we used
the most contemporary
manuals as models, resulting
in a rather revolting result in
terms of our own tastes.

WHAT DO YOU DISLIKE ABOUT IT?
Too late. Definitely the
ugliest thing.

OUTCOMES
A client, a commissioner or
a collaborator is not someone
to please or 'service'.

FEEDBACK
Eline McGeorge on her return
from an exhibition in Oslo,
where the booklets were
stacked as a sculpture people
could take parts from: 'Nobody
took one; they thought it was
a computer manual'.

DO YOU TEACH?
Tutor at the Royal
College of Art,
London (UK) from
2004 to 2010.

**IS IT POSSIBLE TO
TEACH DESIGN?**
Yes, education is part
of our practice. We
have never given the
same brief twice,
which makes it difficult
to test the validity of a
method, but we believe
in experimentation as
a principle of education,
which implies lots of
errors lived together
with students. We have
never taught at BA
level regularly, so it is
difficult to say.

FAVOURITE FOOD NOW
Fish, still

**YOUR MOST VALUED
POSSESSION NOW**
A copy of Steal This Book
by Abbie Hoffman

Project Now

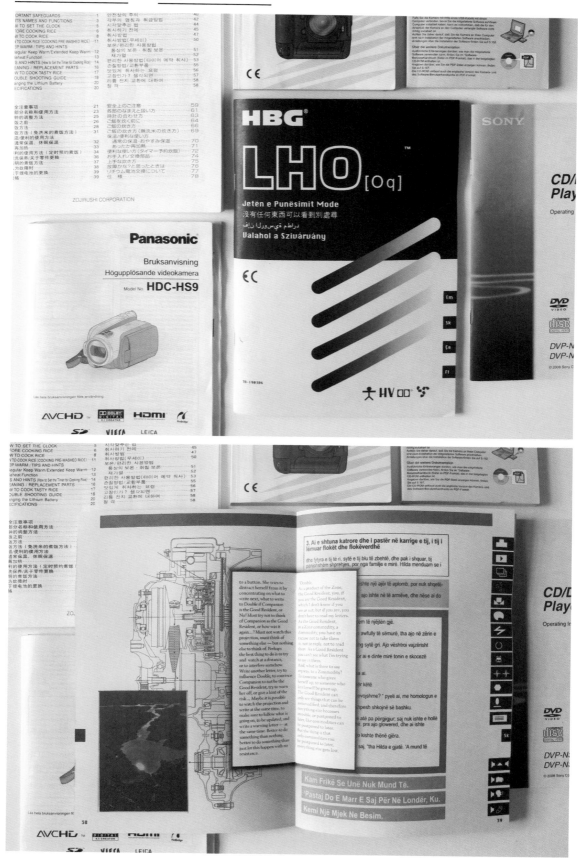

Marc van der Heijde

A PIECE OF SOUND ADVICE + A SINGLE WARNING TO A DESIGN STUDENT

Search for your personal quality, the strength that defines you – and develop that further + No tutor knows the answer

YEAR OF PROJECT
1993

STUDENT PROJECT BRIEF
Self-initiated project: six images for three classical music pieces. On the following spread is sketch material for one of the six images only; a design to fit a Renaissance piece called Spem In Alium by Thomas Tallis. It is a very particular piece, composed for 40 singers without accompaniment. At places, all 40 singers simultaneously have their own part; texts are interwoven at the cost of audibility to form something extremely complex and beautiful.

COLLEGE
Academy of Art and Design St. Joost, Breda (The Netherlands)

TUTOR(S)
Team of tutors, among them Henk Cornelissen, Hartmut Kowalke and Jaap van Triest

TECHNOLOGY
Staged photography, no use of the computer

TIME SPENT
6 months

TYPEFACE
Gill

WHY DO YOU LIKE THIS PROJECT?
I have selected one of the sketches for Spem In Alium, because I find it more interesting than the final piece. I didn't crop or manipulate it; it shows the honest set-up, which I like. In the end, the design used limited elements; text in colour foil, two light sources and a camera. But the way they come together visualizes to my mind exactly the aural essence of the piece as I heard it.

WHAT DO YOU DISLIKE ABOUT IT?
Looking back, I dislike some of the images because they just feel too random. Although not a necessity, I now think it could have been interesting to make them into more of a collection; that the images dealing with music from various periods still share something, or make a collection. Logically, I now see many more possibilities than back then.

OUTCOMES
Another six months at the academy to try something else!

FEEDBACK
I can't remember any particular reactions from that time, but I am sure my mother liked them.

PROJECT SIMILARITIES THEN AND NOW
It was Eric Gill who said: 'I think that if you look after goodness and truth, beauty will take care of itself.' I like the idea of a restraint on elements, interesting enough for the process to lead to strong images that feel right. The truth in both projects is the fact that you take the essence of a piece (interwoven texts) or an organization (singing texts) and stay close to it. Although 'right' seems to be a subjective connotation, the reception of the Dutch Chamber Choir's identity validates the approach. The challenge is to get your client to recognize himself – but in a way that surprises him and others.

FAVOURITE FOOD THEN
Pasta

YOUR MOST VALUED POSSESSION THEN
A German Perzina piano from the 1920s

Project Then

16

Marc van der Heijde (Studio Dumbar)

A VALUABLE QUALITY FOR A DESIGN STUDENT + A DESIGN PROFESSIONAL

Curiosity + Curiosity (hey, I used to be a design student too)

YEAR OF PROJECT
2006/2007

PROFESSIONAL PROJECT BRIEF
A new visual identity for the Dutch Chamber Choir (Nederlands Kamerkoor) to suit the world-renowned ensemble

CLIENT
Nederlands Kamerkoor; Leo Samama (general manager) and Anne Douqué (business manager)

COLLABORATOR(S)
Daniel Markides, Ties Alfrink (graphic designers), Simon Scheiber (motion designer), Paul van der Laan (type designer)

TECHNOLOGY
Graphic design and type design, with ubiquitous use of the computer

TIME SPENT
6 months

TYPEFACE
Franklin Gothic (as basis for NKK Gothic) and Eureka

WHY DO YOU LIKE THIS PROJECT?
The choir always performs text-based material. That is, let's say, the tangible part. But music is ephemeral; the moment the text is sung and music made, it is gone. We set out to do something paradoxical: to capture in form this fleeting character of music.

FAVOURITE FOOD NOW
Thai food

YOUR MOST VALUED POSSESSION NOW
A Japanese Yamaha grand piano from the 1990s

Starting with the textual content, we adjusted letterforms by breaking open their closed shapes. This led to a unique typeface that is the core of the identity: any text set in that font immediately refers to the choir, both visually and in the character of their 'product'.

WHAT DO YOU DISLIKE ABOUT IT?
We made one series of posters. We had to work with an overload of information that greatly diminished their impact. The graphic style's relative lightness does require clear choices.

OUTCOMES
The identity won a Red Dot Award and the corporate animation was awarded a European Design Merit. Over time, it hasn't lost its initial appeal at all; I still respond to the freshness of this unique and fitting design. The animation can be seen online: http://vimeo.com/studiodumbar

FEEDBACK
It was a genuine pleasure getting feedback from the members of the choir when they saw the end result. These people are very committed to the group and their work, and so were critical and demanding. We presented the concept of the identity

through animation and the response was overwhelming. Choir members even suggested using the techniques in every single performance. And we still get very good reactions whenever the identity and animation are shown to students, designers and potential clients.

ANYTHING ELSE
This project gave me a chance to work with Paul van der Laan, a Dutch type designer educated at the Royal Academy in The Hague. The orginal typeface, Franklin Gothic, was adapted for the purpose of opening up letterforms, and the resultant NKK Gothic font was designed in three different weights. Great care has also been given to the typography of the programme listings, at the top of the right pages. Single text lines almost always bring together the composer's name, when he lived, the name of the piece and when it was written. The Eureka typeface has some very sharp characteristics and we spent quite some time looking for the right font size, spacing, etc. to bring harmony to its appearance.

DO YOU TEACH?
No.

IS IT POSSIBLE TO TEACH DESIGN?
The most important thing I learned at the Academy was to look. Drawing is a fundamental stage; it releases you from what you (think you) know, and forces you to concentrate on what you actually see. The next step is interpretation, but now in a conscious manner. If I were a tutor, I would teach typography. That requires the same kind of looking. I like the idea of studying 'historic' examples, principles, etc. and then letting the students think to what extent they want to get away from that.

Project Now

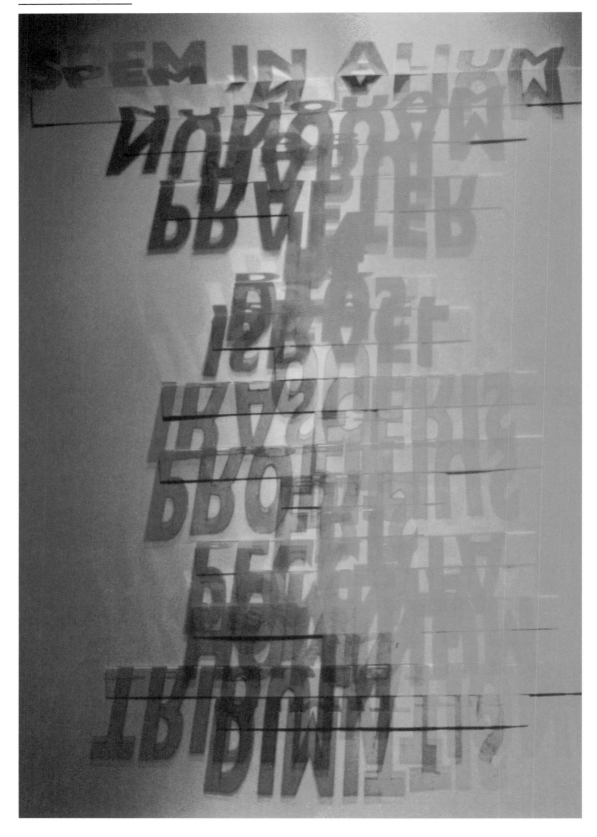

William Byrd 1540-1623 — *Responses uit The Great Service*
David Lang 1957 — *Again (after ecclesiastes)*
Willam Byrd 1540-1623 — *Psalm*
Howard Skempton 1947 — *Rise up, my love 2002*
William Byrd 1540-1623 — *Te Deum*
Jack Body 1944 — *Five Lullabies 1988*
William Byrd 1540-1623 — *Magnificat*
Gavin Bryars 1943 — *And so ended Kant's travelling in this world 1997*
William Byrd 1540-1623 — *Nunc dimittis*

Paul Hillier *dirigent*
Abonnementsconcerten in Amersfoort, Amsterdam (Concertgebouw),
Arnhem, Den Haag, Leeuwarden en Utrecht

William Byrd componeerde zijn *Great Service* waarschijnlijk aan het einde van de zestiende eeuw (de eerste editie ervan dateert van 1606 en is een handschrift van Byrds collega John Baldwin). Het werd pas in het begin van de twintigste eeuw ontdekt in Durham Cathedral en heeft sedertdien een snelle zegetocht gemaakt als een van de mooiste voorbeelden van Elizabethaanse Katholieke religieuze muziek. Immers, ondanks alle religieuze stormen in het Engeland van Elizabeth I en Jacobus I, bleef Byrd zijn levenlang een overtuigd Rooms-Katholiek. Met dit magistrale tienstemmige werk van Byrd komt de internationaal vermaarde koordirigent Paul Hillier na lange tijd weer terug bij het Nederlands Kamerkoor (voor het eerst en laatst stond hij in 1995 voor het koor). De verschillende delen van *The Great Service* worden afgewisseld met vier hedendaagse werken, waarin de sfeer van de Engelse polyfonie en het intense geloof dat uit Byrds muziek spreekt sterk op de voorgrond staan. De werken van de Amerikaan David Lang, de Britten Howard Skempton en Gavin Bryars, en de Nieuw-Zeelandse componist Jack Body passen wonderwel in dit bijzonder rijke vocale kader. Kortom, een bijzonder programma onder leiding van een bijzondere dirigent.

14

15

Willem Ceuleers 1964 — *Twee Madrigalen op teksten van Francesco Petrarca*
Raymond Schroyens 1933 — *Door de nevel'n van de avond*
Saskia Macris 1964 — *Soleil, coeur du monde*
Mateus de Perusio 2e helft 14e eeuw-vóór 1418 — *Puisque la mort*
Jacobus Clemens non Papa 1510-1555/56 — *Qui consolabatur*
Pieter Maessins ca. 1505-1555 — *Venant de Lyon, Tota pulchra es*
Bertrandus Vaqueras ca. 1450-1507 — *Agnus Dei uit de Missa 'Baysiez Moy'*
Thomas Ashewell ca. 1478-na 1513 — *Agnus Dei uit de Missa 'Ave Maria'*
Michelangelo Rossi 1601-1656 — *O Miseria d'amante*
Matheus de Sancte Johanne fl. ca. 1380, Avignon — *Science na nul annemi*

Paul Van Nevel *dirigent*
Abonnementsconcerten in Amsterdam (Muziekgebouw aan 't IJ),
Arnhem, Den Haag, Leeuwarden en Utrecht

Paul Van Nevel heeft voor het Nederlands Kamerkoor ook dit seizoen weer een zeer bijzonder programma samengesteld, met ditmaal hoogtepunten uit de vocale polyfonie: *Visages de la polyphonie*. Vanuit de Ars Subtilior van Matheus de Sancte Johanne uit Avignon en de vijftiende-eeuwse Gotiek van Mateus de Perusio, Bertrandus Vaqueras en Thomas Ashewell wordt de luisteraar via de Vlaamse en Nederlandse Renaissance van Pieter Maessins en Clemens non Papa meegenomen naar het laat zestiende-eeuwse Humanisme van Michelangelo Rossi en bovendien de hedendaagse polyfone werk van Willem Ceuleers, Raymond Schroyens en Saskia Macris. Maar dan met het hedendaagse werk voor de pauze en de oude meesters erna. Zowel Ceuleers als Macris laten zich in hun koorwerken inspireren door de vocale polyfonie van de zestiende eeuw. Dit programma is hiermee een kolfje naar de hand van Paul Van Nevel en naar de kelen van de zangers van het Nederlands Kamerkoor!

6

7

Margaret Calvert

Enjoy + Don't waste time

YEAR OF PROJECT
1956

STUDENT PROJECT BRIEF
**Life drawing in pen
and ink**

COLLEGE
**Chelsea College of Art,
London (United Kingdom)**

TUTOR(S)
Leonard Rosoman

TECHNOLOGY
Pen and ink

TIME SPENT
A morning

WHY DO YOU LIKE THIS PROJECT?
Discovering that I could draw.

OUTCOMES
**An ability to be totally
obsessed with the project
in hand.**

FAVOURITE FOOD THEN
Pasta

YOUR MOST VALUED
POSSESSION THEN
My work

Project Then

PROJECT SIMILARITIES
THEN AND NOW
**Appropriating the
discipline of drawing for
a particular purpose.**

Margaret Calvert

Energy, enthusiasm and imagination + An ability to communicate and initiate great ideas

YEAR OF PROJECT
2008

PROFESSIONAL PROJECT BRIEF
Painting depicting Woman at Work for the Royal Academy of Art 2008 Summer Exhibition

CLIENT
Humphrey Ocean, Curator of the Royal Academy of Art 2008 Summer Exhibition

TECHNOLOGY
Acrylic paint on top of a metal Roadworks sign that I designed in the 1960s.

TIME SPENT
4 days

WHY DO YOU LIKE THIS PROJECT?
Simply because it is unique (almost a self-portrait), in that it relates to the Man at Work roadworks pictogram that I designed in the 1960s. I liked the idea of substituting the image of a woman for the workman, in the context of work usually considered appropriate only for men. I also was attracted to the idea of painting over a slightly rusted old sign found lying abandoned in the street; thus giving it an added value once exhibited in the Royal Academy.

FEEDBACK
Someone wanted to buy the painting.

DO YOU TEACH?
Initially invited to teach Royal College of Art, London (UK) Industrial Design students typography. Taught part-time in the Graphic Design Department from 1966. Eventually retired as a senior tutor in 2001. Head of Graphic Design from 1987 to 1991.

IS IT POSSIBLE TO TEACH DESIGN?
Yes. It's possible to teach an ability to draw and communication.

FAVOURITE FOOD NOW
Pasta

YOUR MOST VALUED POSSESSION NOW
My work

Project Now

Marion Fink

Keep it simple + Don't mix ideas

YEAR OF PROJECT
1999

STUDENT PROJECT BRIEF
**Self-initiated moving-
image studies**

COLLEGE
**Royal College of Art,
London (United Kingdom)**

TUTOR(S)
**Margaret Calvert
(see pp. 150–153)**

COLLABORATOR(S)
Ben Duckett

TECHNOLOGY
Sony Mini DV handycam

TIME SPENT
1 month

WHY DO YOU LIKE THIS PROJECT?
**The simplicity of framing a
space, leading the viewer's
eye and adding iconic value.**

OUTCOMES
Learning by doing.

ANYTHING ELSE
**Ideas come more easily
without a concrete brief in
your mind.**

FAVOURITE FOOD THEN
**Hummus, and the soups
and spicy sauces of my
Korean flatmate**

YOUR MOST VALUED
POSSESSION THEN
Computer + Sony camera

Project Then

PROJECT SIMILARITIES
THEN AND NOW
**The conceptual and
formal approach of the
frame (as described
above) as a cultural
symbol for giving
something a meaning or
even calling it art.**

Marion Fink (at the time of this project in 2004: KMS Team, Munich)

A VALUABLE QUALITY FOR A DESIGN STUDENT + A DESIGN PROFESSIONAL

Curiosity and persistence + Curiosity and persistence plus using your resources in a sustainable way

YEAR OF PROJECT
2004

PROFESSIONAL PROJECT BRIEF
Indentity and opening
campaign for the Museum
of Modern Art Munich
(Pinakothek der Moderne)

CLIENT
Pinakothek der Moderne,
Munich

COLLABORATOR(S)
KMS Team (Marc Ziegler,
Xuyen Dam)

TECHNOLOGY
Super 8, 35mm slides
(Nikon), 6×4.5cm
(Hasselblad), the usual
Mac software: Adobe
Photoshop, Adobe
Illustrator...

TIME SPENT
2 years

TYPEFACE
FF DIN

WHY DO YOU LIKE THIS PROJECT?
Same answer as
opposite (then).

WHAT DO YOU DISLIKE ABOUT IT?
The font!

OUTCOMES
Doing and still learning.

ANYTHING ELSE
Same answer as
opposite (then).

DO YOU TEACH?
Professor of typography
and information design
at Hochschule für
Gestaltung und Kunst,
Basel (Switzerland).

IS IT POSSIBLE TO
TEACH DESIGN?
I learned at college to
bounce ideas around,
but often I felt the
tutors/school wanted
to force a certain style
upon the students.
In teaching today,
I try to strengthen the
students' strong points
and weaken their weak
points. They should
find their own voice
and attitude rather
than copying someone
else's.

FAVOURITE FOOD NOW
Pasta and good wine

YOUR MOST VALUED
POSSESSION NOW
My flat

Project Now

SAMMLUNG MODERNE KUNST

KUNST IN DER
PINAKOTHEK DER MODERNE

EIN JAHR

PINAKOTHEK DER
MODERNE

Martin Lorenz

A PIECE OF SOUND ADVICE + A SINGLE WARNING TO A DESIGN STUDENT

Learn to learn +
Don't be arrogant

YEAR OF PROJECT
1997

STUDENT PROJECT BRIEF
Draw the animals in the zoo

COLLEGE
Hochschule Darmstadt (Germany)

TUTOR(S)
Prof. Osterwalder

TECHNOLOGY
Charcoal

TIME SPENT
1 afternoon

WHY DO YOU LIKE THIS PROJECT?
I like the strength of the drawing. As the animals were constantly moving, one only had the time to draw the most essential things, but this makes you think about what is important to draw and what isn't. You need to memorize the shades and forms you have seen because in the next second the animals will have moved to a different position. It was fun, because I wasn't doing anything else than drawing in those years and my hand was fluent. I draw much worse these days.

OUTCOMES
It made me grow.

FEEDBACK
Prof. Osterwalder: 'Man erkennt die Schweizer Schule' (One does recognise the Swiss school).

FAVOURITE FOOD THEN
All kinds

YOUR MOST VALUED POSSESSION THEN
Comic collection

Project Then

PROJECT SIMILARITIES THEN AND NOW
Both projects only use what is needed, not more, not less. Even though they appear visually playful, they are highly minimalistic.

Martin Lorenz (TwoPoints.Net)

A VALUABLE QUALITY FOR A DESIGN STUDENT + A DESIGN PROFESSIONAL

For both: Be autodidactic

YEAR OF PROJECT
2010

PROFESSIONAL PROJECT BRIEF
Develop a visual identity for the Helsinki Design Lab, which defines itself as follows: 'We believe that the scale and complexity of today's challenges are more effectively addressed when design is a leading voice co-ordinating many, rather than a service applied to pre-defined problems. With a specialized ability to bring synthesis to complex problems, to work from conception to implementation, and to visualize complex relationships, the strategic designer plays a lead role in addressing the issues faced by contemporary society. Helsinki Design Lab (HDL), a project initiated by Sitra – the Finnish Innovation Fund – fosters state-of-the-art knowledge, capability and achievement in the area of strategic design in order to improve global supply of this essential 21st-century problem-solving skill.'

FAVOURITE FOOD NOW
All kinds

YOUR MOST VALUED
POSSESSION NOW
Book collection

CLIENT
Sitra, the Finnish Innovation Fund

COLLABORATOR(S)
Lupi Asensio

TECHNOLOGY
Acrylic paint and computer

TIME SPENT
2 months

TYPEFACE
Univers & Minion

WHY DO YOU LIKE THIS PROJECT?
The driving idea of the visual identity is drawn from the 'space' occupied by the strategic framework of the HDL, which draws together a diverse group of actors and entities from various fields. These actors, each one a specialist in his field, contributes a unique point of view within a group that can offer a more holistic definition of the problem, thereby creating the opportunity for a more effective range of solutions. The Strategic Designer acts as an enzyme, co-ordinating the process. The visual identity is coherent with the idea of the institution. It is highly flexible without losing recognizability.

Project Now

OUTCOMES
It made me grow.

FEEDBACK
'The work from Two Points for our Helsinki Design Lab visual identity captures the spirit of our endeavour: it's systematic, nimble, and founded in really sharp thinking about the various mediums that the identity needs to suit. In this way, the visual identity of our Helsinki Design Lab is similar to how Sitra sees a role for strategic design operating as part of the solution to today's large-scale challenges: a reflexive capability responding intelligently to real-world needs. We at Sitra are very pleased with the work from Two Points and are constantly receiving compliments on the uniqueness and attention to detail that our visual identity embodies.' (Bryan Boyer, Design Lead at Sitra, the Finnish Innovation Fund.)

DO YOU TEACH?
I am co-director of the Postgraduate Degree of Applied Typography at the private design school ELISAVA in Barcelona (Spain). I teach mostly flexible visual systems.

IS IT POSSIBLE TO
TEACH DESIGN?
No, design cannot be taught, but a teacher can help the student to develop rational and emotional design methodology and train his eye for visual communication, which involves studying design history as well.

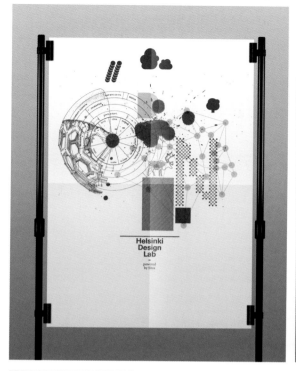

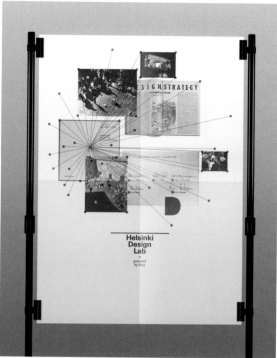

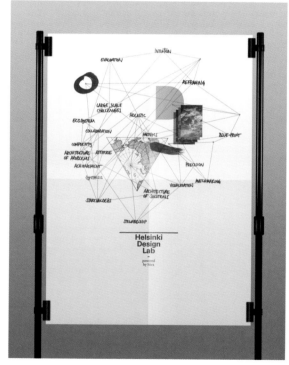

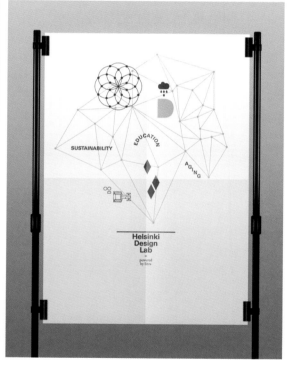

Matthias Görlich

A PIECE OF SOUND ADVICE + A SINGLE WARNING TO A DESIGN STUDENT

Find it out for yourself + There are easier ways to earn money, honestly

YEAR OF PROJECT
2000

STUDENT PROJECT BRIEF
Design a series of posters and a programme for an imaginary theatre

COLLEGE
Hochschule Darmstadt (Germany)

TUTOR(S)
Prof. Sandra Hoffmann (see also pp. 194–197)

COLLABORATOR(S)
Florian Walzel

TECHNOLOGY
Silkscreen-printing and stamps on existing surfaces (posters, the street, houses, etc.) and for the programme we used Xerox machines

TIME SPENT
6 months

TYPEFACE
Trade Gothic

WHY DO YOU LIKE THIS PROJECT?
What I like most about the project is that the original briefing was quite strict but that we found some flexible parts in it. So in the end we were not designing posters to announce a play for an imaginative theatre, but we took the play directly onto the streets by the means of posters.

WHAT DO YOU DISLIKE ABOUT IT?
This project was one of the most physically exhausting projects I ever did; this came out of a great lack of experience paired with a lot of ambition. Looking back, this physical/psychological 'borderline' experience turned out to be a key ingredient in all the projects I really like. Paradoxically, now, running a design studio, I try to avoid those moments of total exhaustion as much as possible.

FEEDBACK
Our posters got destroyed after the presentation (don't know whether that's a positive or negative sign); maybe it was pure coincidence. In general, we received a positive reaction, I think mainly because we were 'rethinking the brief' a bit more drastically than expected and the project was executed in the city. I once received a drastic (but very honest and true) reply from one of the Swiss superstar designers, saying that the choice of the form and technique was purely a formal one. Things would have been a lot easier to produce in a different technique, which would have led to a different visual outcome. He was right.

PROJECT SIMILARITIES THEN AND NOW
One of the links between both projects might be the strategy of 'rethinking the brief'. With the Cologne project, we tried to look at a spatial strategy differently (at least for me as a graphic designer and most certainly also for the audience, who were expecting an architectural proposal for a new building). With the other project we did this by not designing posters that announce theatre plays but by using the posters to start the play on the street. The other aspect that links both projects is that they both deal with our physical environment. The places we live in were objects of design, of interventions by simple means.

FAVOURITE FOOD THEN
Whatever was available within a limited budget

YOUR MOST VALUED POSSESSION THEN
-

Project Then

Matthias Görlich (Studio Matthias Görlich)

A VALUABLE QUALITY FOR A DESIGN STUDENT + A DESIGN PROFESSIONAL

Curiosity and being excitable + Curiosity and scepticism, in constant conflict with one another

YEAR OF PROJECT
2007

PROFESSIONAL PROJECT BRIEF
To come up with a proposal for a spatial strategy for an art institution that (at that time) did not have a physical presence.
In this case, one of the concepts was applied to an exhibition in the city of Cologne.

CLIENT
Curator Nicolaus Schafhausen and Vanessa Joan Müller of European Kunsthalle Cologne. They commissioned a research project titled Spaces of Production from architects Nikolaus Hirsch, Philipp Misselwitz, Markus Miessen and me.

COLLABORATOR(S)
Architects Nikolaus Hirsch, Philipp Misselwitz and Markus Miessen. The design was done in collaboration with Miriam Rösch.

TECHNOLOGY
A guide was produced in offset printing (2c), which was distributed as part of a local magazine. Sites of interventions were marked with little stickers. The works by the artists were done using very diverse techniques.

TIME SPENT
3 months

TYPEFACE
Modified version of Schulbuch Grotesk

WHY DO YOU LIKE THIS PROJECT?
I think re-reading the city by the means of graphic design and maps played an important role in the project. And maps and diagrams became a major interest for me for the following projects. I think there is some power within the visualization of space, and this can be an interesting domain for graphic design.

FEEDBACK
I think in general the project was well received, although it was part of a bigger project that was seriously discussed within Cologne's cultural scene. In the end we delivered the framework and the works by the artists were up for discussion.

DO YOU TEACH?
I taught at Hochschule Wiesbaden (Germany), Hochschule Darmstadt (Germany) and in Zurich (Switzerland). I often conduct workshops and do lectures in various cities e.g. Paris, Aachen, Mumbai and Lucerne. Currently I am working as a researcher at Universität Stuttgart (Germany), Institute for Urban Planning, concentrating on the visual representation of urban space and at the Institute for Design research, Design2-context, in Zurich (Switzerland).

IS IT POSSIBLE TO TEACH DESIGN?
To answer this question one might first need to define the word 'design' a bit more. If we are talking about teaching the invention of visual form, then I think certain aspects of this can be taught (such as cognition theory, certain aspects of typography, etc.). But what I think can't be taught (or at least has to be taught a lot earlier) is the ability to walk with open eyes; to identify visual phenomena that can then be transformed into new things.

FAVOURITE FOOD NOW
Whatever is available

YOUR MOST VALUED POSSESSION NOW
-

Project Now

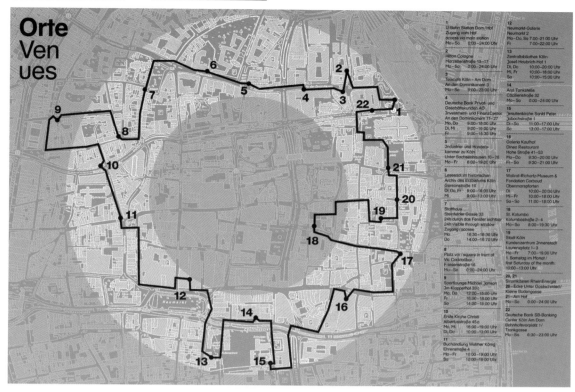

Michael Georgiou

Do as much research as you can + Never copy, only get influenced

YEAR OF PROJECT
1984

STUDENT PROJECT BRIEF
Design a poster for a circus

COLLEGE
Vakalo College of Art and Design, Athens (Greece)

TUTOR(S)
George Pavlopoulos (visual artist)

TECHNOLOGY
Paper, colour markers, self-adhesive film

TIME SPENT
2 weeks

TYPEFACE
Trade Gothic Condensed

WHY DO YOU LIKE THIS PROJECT?
Because of the process.

OUTCOMES
Through this student project I realized that in order to visualize a concept by hand a great deal of effort was needed.

FAVOURITE FOOD THEN
Spaghetti bolognese

YOUR MOST VALUED POSSESSION THEN
A watch

Project Then

PROJECT SIMILARITIES
THEN AND NOW
Simplicity.

Michael Georgiou (G Design Studio)

A VALUABLE QUALITY FOR A DESIGN STUDENT + A DESIGN PROFESSIONAL

A diverse background +
Integrity

YEAR OF PROJECT
2008

PROFESSIONAL PROJECT BRIEF
**Design a poster for the
exhibition Mapping
(Europe), a co-production
of Apeiron Photos and
the photography agency
Corbis**

CLIENT
Apeiron-Corbis

COLLABORATOR(S)
Alexandros Gavrilakis

TECHNOLOGY
**Laser-cut Forex® and
digital print**

TIME SPENT
3 days

TYPEFACE
Helvetica

WHY DO YOU LIKE THIS PROJECT?
Because of the concept.

OUTCOMES
**A strong concept was
visualized easily due to
technology.**

FAVOURITE FOOD NOW
Spaghetti bolognese

YOUR MOST VALUED
POSSESSION NOW
My art collection

DO YOU TEACH?
**Vakalo College of Art
and Design (Greece),
Graphic Design.**

IS IT POSSIBLE TO
TEACH DESIGN?
**I have been a graphic
design tutor since 1992.
The thing I try to pass on
is the importance of
conducting research
before starting to
design.**

Project Now

THIS IS AN E48 SIZE POSTER

A SIZES		B SIZES		E SIZE
A0	841 × 1189	B0	1000 × 1414	48 EUROPEAN COUNTRIES
A1	594 × 841	B1	707 × 1000	
A2	420 × 594	B2	500 × 707	ALBANIA
A3	297 × 420	B3	353 × 500	ARMENIA
A4	210 × 297	B4	250 × 353	AUSTRIA
A5	148 × 210	B5	176 × 250	AZERBAIJAN
A6	105 × 148	B6	125 × 176	BULGARIA
A7	74 × 105	B7	88 × 125	BELARUS
A8	52 × 74	B8	62 × 88	BELGIUM
A9	37 × 52	B9	44 × 62	BOSNIA & HERZEGOVINA
A10	26 × 37	B10	31 × 44	GEORGIA
				CROATIA
				CYPRUS
				CZECH REPUBLIC
				DENMARK
				ESTONIA
				FINLAND
				FRANCE
				FYROM
				GERMANY
				GREECE
				HUNGARY
				IRELAND
				ISLAND
				ITALY
				LATVIA
				LIECHTENSTEIN
				LITHUANIA
				LUXEMBOURG
				MALTA
				MOLDOVA
				MONACO
				MONTENEGRO
				NETHERLANDS
				NORWAY
				POLAND
				PORTUGAL
				ROMANIA
				RUSSIA
				SAN MARINO
				SERBIA
				SLOVAKIA
				SLOVENIA
				SPAIN
				SWEDEN
				SWITZERLAND
				TURKEY
				UKRAINE
				UNITED KINGDOM
				VATICAN CITY

Nikki Gonnissen

Set some goals and try to reach them + No warnings

YEAR OF PROJECT
1993

STUDENT PROJECT BRIEF
The Knee was my final exam project. It was a self-initiated project

COLLEGE
Hogeschool voor de Kunsten Utrecht (The Netherlands)

TUTOR(S)
Wim Wal

TECHNOLOGY
Silkscreen printing

TIME SPENT
6 months

TYPEFACE
Joanna

WHY DO YOU LIKE THIS PROJECT?
It was a private project, and I therefore created my own private world.

WHAT DO YOU DISLIKE ABOUT IT?
Certain spreads didn't come out so well.

OUTCOMES
It was very difficult to get my own thoughts clear.

FEEDBACK
I got my diploma.

PROJECT SIMILARITIES
THEN AND NOW
I think it starts with ambition. Both projects are very ambitious. In 1993 there were no colour printers, and I wanted to make a real publication, not one with sticky Letraset type. So I made a big effort to silkscreen the book. I found a publisher who sponsored the project. Like all students, I wanted to show my complete self within this book. I would never try this again; it was horrible. Now when I look back at the project I think I already identified with social issues. The whole 'knee' book is about falling, being overthrown, being a failure. It's about hierarchy, and I had a deep sympathy for the fallen person and the lower social classes. I used pictures and texts from books and newspapers, and made some myself, of workmen on their knees, praying men, pilgrims, a shot-down man, wounded people, etc.

The nrc (professional) project was ambitious because we approached it from a designer's and not an advertisement agency's perspective. The brief was
to make a new advertising campaign, and we did, but for us it was important also to rebrand all forms of communication – business cards, commercials, the newspaper itself, radio spots, the Internet, etc.

There is a similarity in content between the two projects also. I have read this newspaper for years now, so I was already personally engaged. It publishes news in an independent but critical way, it is forward-looking, it approaches people not as consumers but as citizens with their own opinions. Its subjects are social and political. We decided to use the news in order to advertise the newspaper itself. So, for example, we featured a photo of the pope and accompanied it with the word: 'truth?' So nrc is announcing and commenting on the news of the day through an advertisement in its own newspaper. So another similarity is the engagement within the approach.

Also important is changing the context, and therefore also changing the form or altering the content. Stylistically there are similarities too, such as the use of pictures and contrasting simple signs. In the case of the 'knee' book, a hinge above a pilgrim woman kneeling. In the case of nrc, the 'guillemet' alongside a picture of the pope.

FAVOURITE FOOD THEN
Indonesian (my mother comes from Indonesia)

YOUR MOST VALUED POSSESSION THEN
If family is a possession, my family

Project Then

Nikki Gonnissen (Thonik)

Being able to focus and collaborate, being ambitious, interested, communicative + Being able to focus and collaborate, being ambitious, interested, practical, realistic, communicative but also having an experimental attitude

YEAR OF PROJECT
2010

PROFESSIONAL PROJECT BRIEF
To create a new advertising campaign for Holland's most intellectual newspaper company

CLIENT
nrc Media

COLLABORATOR(S)
Thonik studio staff

TECHNOLOGY
Cross media

TIME SPENT
6 months

TYPEFACE
Lexicon

WHY DO YOU LIKE THIS PROJECT?
This is a project in the midst of society. We developed a new brand: nrc, along with a new theme, 'ik denk nrc' (I think nrc). nrc now has different products: nrc Handelsblad, nrc next and nrc.nl. In the design for the brand, the 'guillemet' (angle quote) has the lead.

OUTCOMES
It was very exciting to work for a newspaper that I had been reading myself for years. We shared many values.

FEEDBACK
The project was very successful; we had a lot of positive reactions. But we also had some negative ones – those came from the advertising scene, mostly on blogs. I think we came, as graphic designers, too close to their area of expertise.

FAVOURITE FOOD NOW
Indonesian, Japanese, French

YOUR MOST VALUED POSSESSION NOW
Family, books, shields, ceremonial outfits, bis poles from the Asmat

Project Now

DO YOU TEACH?
At the moment I teach on the Masters course in Graphic Design at the Academy of Art and Design, St. Joost, Breda (The Netherlands).

IS IT POSSIBLE TO TEACH DESIGN?
It is very hard for students to focus.

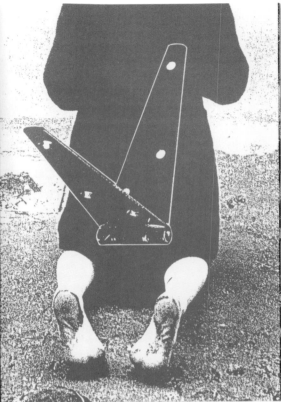

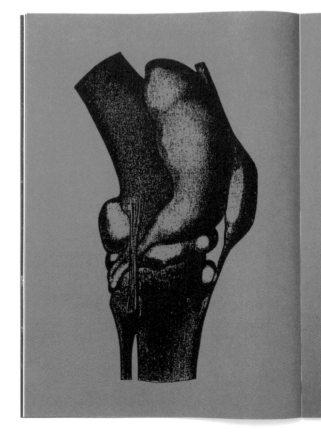

Een knie loopt eenzaam over
straat. Het is een knie, niet meer!
Het is geen boom, is geen granaat.
Het is een knie, niet meer!
In de oorlog werd een man aan het
slot van top tot teen doorzeefd.
Alleen een knie bleef buiten schot,
vandaar dat die nog leeft. En
eenzaam voortgaat over straat.
Het is een knie, niet meer! Het is
geen boom, is geen granaat. Het is

waarheid
ik denk **nrc**

lees **nrc**handelsblad›
nu 4 weken 15 euro
ga naar nrc.nl

Oliver Klimpel

More courage –
who dares wins +
Think about it

YEAR OF PROJECT
1996

STUDENT PROJECT BRIEF
Design posters for a series
of student exhibitions for
one class in the photo-
graphy department of
the Leipzig art college.
Title: Fin Sans

COLLEGE
Hochschule für Grafik und
Buchkunst Leipzig
(Germany)

TUTOR(S)
Prof. Rolf Felix Müller
(Klasse Illustration)

COLLABORATOR(S)
The photography students
involved

TECHNOLOGY
Inkjet and laser printout,
manual cropping

TYPEFACE
Molli, a display typeface
by Typoart, the former
type foundry of East
Germany, and Helvetica
Extended

WHY DO YOU LIKE THIS PROJECT?
Its design was very much at
odds with what was taught at
the college and what graphics
looked like in Leipzig. It was
fun – and looked nice inside
the college building on the neo-
classical columns. I enjoyed
using Molli, the typeface,
because it seemed such
a weird/'vernacular' choice
at the time…

WHAT DO YOU DISLIKE ABOUT IT?
It is very much of its time and
doesn't look that special today.
It might have only worked in
the very specific context of the
college. I had the idea at the
time to have the diagonal line
going back and forth like a
metronome from one show to
the next to the next. There
were not enough shows to
make that clear…

OUTCOMES
It was nice to bring a different
idea of visual communication
to the announcement for a
college show. I've done more
projects with that photography
class and am working, as we
speak, on a book for the
photographer who ran that unit
at the time, Timm Rautert.

FEEDBACK
'Not legible, too confusing,
not respectful enough…'

FAVOURITE FOOD THEN
Cheap

**YOUR MOST VALUED
POSSESSION THEN**
-

Project Then

**PROJECT SIMILARITIES
THEN AND NOW**
I basically selected
the pieces because
they are quite different.
But they share a
leaning towards the
typographic.

Oliver Klimpel (Büro International)

Being self-motivated and brave, cheeky, not risk-averse + Able to foresee the consequences and results of processes plus generosity

YEAR OF PROJECT
2003

PROFESSIONAL PROJECT BRIEF
Design of promotional/
recruitment poster for the
newly started Masters
course at Central Saint
Martins College of Art &
Design: MA Creative
Practice for Narrative
Environments. To be sent
out to other colleges and
other institutions.

CLIENT
Tricia Austin, Course
Leader, MA Creative
Practice for Narrative
Environments at Central
Saint Martins College
of Art & Design

TECHNOLOGY
Offset litho, 2 colours

TYPEFACE
Times New Roman

WHY DO YOU LIKE THIS PROJECT?
I like it for its proportional pun
and deadpan fun. However,
I like to think there's a chance
of profundity in it. But I selected
this poster because of its quite
different idea of a poster to
the one done in 1996.

WHAT DO YOU DISLIKE ABOUT IT?
The weak spot of the project is
probably the distribution of the
posters and the dependence
on people of putting the
posters up on message boards
where there is stiff competition
for space. I do know from
friends, though, that posters
did hang at least in some
UK colleges.

OUTCOMES
I did more work for the course
and came in as a visiting tutor
a few times.

FEEDBACK
'Not catchy enough, no image,
too discreet.' 'Nice and simple.'

FAVOURITE FOOD NOW
Japanese

**YOUR MOST VALUED
POSSESSION NOW**
Currently my new sofa,
otherwise a painting by
Peter McDonald and
a few books

Project Now

DO YOU TEACH?
I am a Professor for
System-Design at the
Hochschule für Grafik
und Buchkunst Leipzig
(Germany).

**IS IT POSSIBLE TO
TEACH DESIGN?**
Yes: Craft. Techniques
and camaraderie.
Fairness. Thoroughness
and being critical.
'Doubt, Delight and
Change' (Cedric Price).

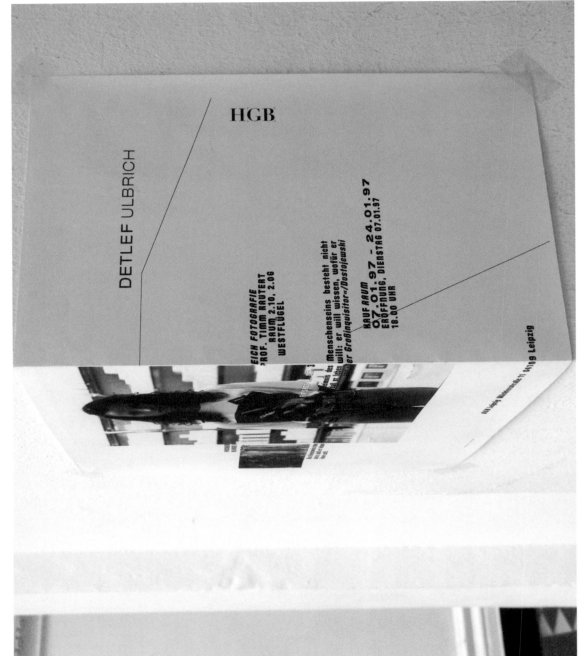

MA Creative Practice for Narrative Environments
Central Saint Martins College of Art and Design

NEW COURSE

- pioneers collaborative practice between architects, designers, curators and writers
- work in museums, visitor centres, speciality stores, themed entertainment venues, corporate HQs
- introduces you to an international industry network
- integrates film, objects, text, sound and image
- 2 year course; 3-days per week Subject to validation

apply now to start in October

For further information call +44 (0)20 7514 7022, e-mail: info@csm.linst.ac.uk or visit: www.csm.linst.ac.uk

THE LONDON
INSTITUTE CENTRAL SAINT MARTINS
COLLEGE OF ART AND DESIGN CAMBERWELL
COLLEGE OF ARTS CHELSEA COLLEGE OF
ART AND DESIGN LONDON COLLEGE OF FASHION
LONDON COLLEGE OF PRINTING

Paul Barnes

Look at the books in the library + Don't expect to get your way at all times

YEAR OF PROJECT
1992

STUDENT PROJECT BRIEF
A type specimen made at the University of Reading

COLLEGE
University of Reading (United Kingdom)

TUTOR(S)
Paul Stiff

TECHNOLOGY
Hand rendering, letterpress type, photocopying (B&W/colour), painting, laser-printed type from Apple Macintosh using Pagemaker software

TIME SPENT
3 weeks

TYPEFACE
Akzidenz Grotesk, Bauer Bodoni, Kuenstler Schrift, Caslon, Caslon Black, Futura Black, Futura, Monotype Garamond, Wilhelm Klingspor Schrift, Caslon Ornaments, Kilmer, Optima, Palace, Univers, Van Dijck, Venus

WHY DO YOU LIKE THIS PROJECT?
For the enjoyment of manufacturing something using all the technology; from working by hand, to hand-setting, to using the Macintosh and creating something physical from many materials.

OUTCOMES
It crystallized a way of thinking and aesthetic I had been practising when at college; it reached its end conclusion in this project. It was the end of being a student.

FEEDBACK
It seemed well received.

ANYTHING ELSE
In most of the work you do, you almost always feel it could be better or done differently. With both of these projects (student and professional shown overleaf) they are exactly as I envisaged them and I am proud of them.

FAVOURITE FOOD THEN
Pasta

YOUR MOST VALUED POSSESSION THEN
-

Project Then

PROJECT SIMILARITIES THEN AND NOW
Both have their roots in the handmade and the past and how the past can inform the future.

Paul Barnes

Curiosity + Curiosity and patience

YEAR OF PROJECT
1997–2010

PROFESSIONAL PROJECT BRIEF
Self-initiated typeface
design (Dala Floda)

CLIENT
Self-initiated

COLLABORATOR(S)
Commercial Type
(Christian Schwartz and
Berton Hasebe)

TECHNOLOGY
Apple Macintosh,
Illustrator, Fontographer
and Fontlab software

TIME SPENT
13 years on and off

TYPEFACE
It is a font – Dala Floda

WHY DO YOU LIKE THIS PROJECT?
Having an idea and taking
it to its conclusion and doing
it to the best of one's level
of craft.

WHAT DO YOU DISLIKE ABOUT IT?
The length of time it took
to design.

OUTCOMES
Finally learning and understanding how to make
a typeface from an idea.

FEEDBACK
It seemed to be well
received.

DO YOU TEACH?
No

**IS IT POSSIBLE TO
TEACH DESIGN?**
I think if we accept that
design is in part
technical or craft, then
it's possible to teach
people the craft and
technics of design.
The problem is how we
teach the 'creative' part
of design. That seems
to be more elusive.
I think also that the
history of design is also
teachable, and probably
in my opinion a vital
thing for design
education. Certainly
at the University of
Reading, I learned the
technical, craft and
historical aspects
of typography.

FAVOURITE FOOD NOW
Sushi and home-
made bread

**YOUR MOST VALUED
POSSESSION NOW**
–

Project Now

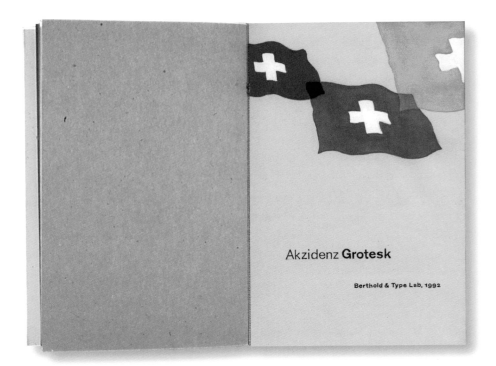

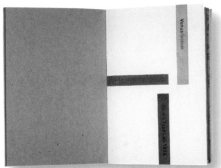

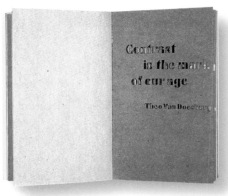

Dala Floda

Dala Floda has its roots in the typefaces of the Renaissance but adds the twist of being a stencil letterform. Originally inspired by worn gravestone lettering and lettering on shipping crates, the elegance of the forms belies their everyday origins.

PUBLISHED
2010

DESIGNED BY
PAUL BARNES

16 STYLES
8 WEIGHTS W/ ITALICS

FEATURES
PROPORTIONAL OLDSTYLE FIGURES
PROPORTIONAL LINING FIGURES
SMALL CAPS (ROMAN)
FRACTIONS
SWASH CAPITALS
DISCRETIONARY LIGATURES

First designed in 1997 for a logotype, Dala Floda eventually became the headline typeface for the art magazine *frieze* in 2005. Since then the family has grown considerably, with the addition of an italic and a range of heavier weights, all the way up to a fat weight. Its stencil form makes it well suited for headline use and especially for logotypes.

Dala Floda Roman
Dala Floda Italic
Dala Floda Roman No. 2
Dala Floda Italic No. 2
Dala Floda Medium
Dala Floda Medium Italic
Dala Floda Bold
Dala Floda Bold Italic
Dala Floda Black
Dala Floda Black Italic
Dala Floda Fat
Dala Floda Fat Italic

Sesquicentennials
DALA FLODA ROMAN, 60 PT

Autobiographical
DALA FLODA ROMAN NO. 2, 60 PT

Photojournalism
DALA FLODA MEDIUM, 60 PT

Grindavíkurbær
DALA FLODA BOLD, 60 PT [SWASH r]

Decompensates
DALA FLODA BLACK, 60 PT

Setzmaschinen
DALA FLODA FAT, 60 PT

Officiation
KVITSØY
Distinctive
DALA FLODA ROMAN, 100 PT [ALTERNATE Y, DISCRETIONARY ct LIGATURE]

Contributes
ANTIQUE
Bichromatic
DALA FLODA ITALIC, 100 PT [SWASH A Q]

Prem Krishnamurthy

Pay close attention to the things you like and why + Don't be lazy in your work, thinking or actions in the world. Always seek to overperform

YEAR OF PROJECT
1998

STUDENT PROJECT BRIEF
Create a series of movie posters for screenings of three films by a single filmmaker (who was assigned randomly)

COLLEGE
Yale College, New Haven (USA)

TUTOR(S)
Michael Rock

TECHNOLOGY
Illustrator, Nikon 35 mm camera, Photoshop

TIME SPENT
2–3 weeks

TYPEFACE
Agenda

FAVOURITE FOOD THEN
Taco Bell bean burritos

YOUR MOST VALUED
POSSESSION THEN
My 4×5 camera

WHY DO YOU LIKE THIS PROJECT?
First, one major outcome of the project was that I received the assignment at random to watch at least three films by David Lynch. Having barely seen his work before, I took the opportunity to watch nearly all of his films before deciding which ones to make posters for. His films made a great impression on me then, in the way that they uniformly found pockets of deep strangeness and uncanny activity within the contours of everyday American life. So the brief itself proved to be a learning experience. Over the course of developing the poster concept, I came to the solution of actually creating three posters (in one case, a still image on a DVD), which I would insert into locations that possessed the weirdness intrinsic to Lynch's films; the final step would be photographing them to create the finished posters. This approach seemed natural enough to me, as it combined my existing interest in photographing interiors with a self-referential approach to design. And it turned out, back then, to be the perfect method of making a set of graphic posters for these very particular films.

WHAT DO YOU DISLIKE ABOUT IT?
The typography and design of the posters within the posters.

OUTCOMES
This was the first time that I had tried to combine my interests in photography and design in a conscious and compact manner. I also realized that graphic design could become spatialized and inhabit real contexts; this interest in the particularities and specificity of spaces continued to grow over the years.

FEEDBACK
When these posters were shown in an undergraduate end-of-semester art show, a graduate design student remarked that they were the best pieces in the show, which was quite flattering.

PROJECT SIMILARITIES
THEN AND NOW
Although I see the two projects as quite different in essential approach, I find them to have a common interest in situating graphic design within real spaces and also allowing design to spread in unusual ways. Both projects collapse representation and presentation in different ways. Also, for me, the earlier project presages my later deep engagement with exhibitions and physical spaces that nevertheless demonstrate a certain self-awareness.

Project Then

NEW YORK, USA

Prem Krishnamurthy (Project Projects)

A VALUABLE QUALITY FOR A DESIGN STUDENT + A DESIGN PROFESSIONAL

Desire + Resolve

YEAR OF PROJECT
2008

PROFESSIONAL PROJECT BRIEF
**Design an exhibition
on the city planning and
radical thinking on
urbanism and space
of Otto Neurath**

CLIENT
**Stroom Den Haag
(The Netherlands)
(Curator: Nader
Vossoughian)**

COLLABORATOR(S)
**Adam Michaels,
Chris Wu**

TECHNOLOGY
**Adobe InDesign,
Illustrator, Photoshop**

TIME SPENT
2 months

TYPEFACE
**Neutraface 2 Display,
FF Bau, Plantin**

WHY DO YOU LIKE THIS PROJECT?
**After Neurath: The Global Polis
was an exhibition in The Hague,
The Netherlands, in 2008.
Without delving too much into
the content of the show [more
information on the show is
here: http://bit.ly/hWVGZ6],
the exhibition served as an
interesting opportunity to test
out several ideas in exhibition
design, which again came
directly from the subject matter
itself. Given Otto Neurath's
forward-thinking ideas about
'mass-produced exhibitions',
we decided to create a set of
posters for the show that
would present the wall texts
within the exhibition while also
functioning as take-aways that
could serve as a secondary,
portable mini-exhibition in
the home of the visitor or in
other contexts.**

WHAT DO YOU DISLIKE ABOUT IT?
**The typography of the posters,
perhaps.**

OUTCOMES
**This was the first exhibition
I had designed where I had not
visited the exhibition space
previously; as such, this was
a useful learning experience
in visualizing a space through
virtual models only, and then
adjusting the installation to
match the actual space.**

FEEDBACK
**The exhibition was very well
received in the architecture
and design press, and in
general by the public. The
take-away posters ran out
before the show's end –
also a good sign.**

DO YOU TEACH?
**Generally yes, though
currently no. Past
teaching includes:
University of
Connecticut (USA),
advanced design, senior
thesis. Parsons The
New School for Design
(USA), senior thesis.
Rhode Island School of
Design (USA), graduate
elective course.
University of the Arts
Bremen (Germany),
visiting designer
workshop.**

IS IT POSSIBLE TO
TEACH DESIGN?
**Yes, otherwise I wouldn't
teach! Though in college,
I actually learned not so
much about design –
apart from good typog-
raphy, which is one
thing you can teach that
is essential! – but,
rather, about how to
think about design.
And I happened to have
enough self-awareness
to know what things
I was very weak in,
and to work very hard
to get better at them.**

FAVOURITE FOOD NOW
Chicken shawarma

YOUR MOST VALUED
POSSESSION NOW
**My notebooks from
the past years**

Project Now

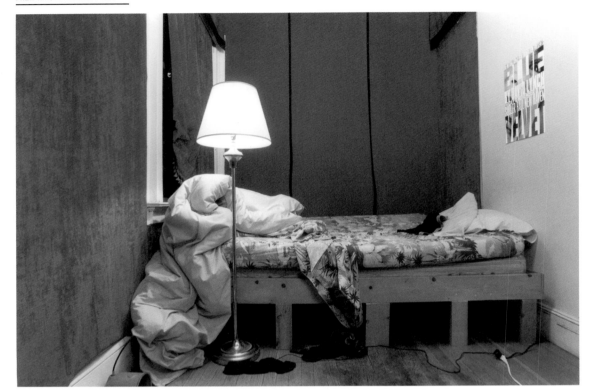

BRAZILIAN/AMERICAN

Renata Graw

A PIECE OF SOUND ADVICE + A SINGLE WARNING TO A DESIGN STUDENT

One can never say something won't work until they have done it + Don't be afraid to fail

YEAR OF PROJECT
2008

STUDENT PROJECT BRIEF
Café 4102: Our friend and colleague Phillip Matesic approached us during our final thesis semester as he had decided to change the format of his thesis paper from a theoretical paper to a small book. The book would capture the essence and 'dialogue' of his café project and remain as a document of an ephemeral installation. As Phillip said, 'I have one week to develop a sample version and have no skills with a layout program. I have been working in Word just to get a feel for the image + text relationship and will now work with real photos and cut-out text. Would you or anyone you know in the Graphic Design programme be willing to help me lay out the book?' Though it was an intense time for all of us, we gladly accepted the project.

COLLEGE
University of Illinois at Chicago (USA)

TUTOR(S)
Phillip Matesic (client and friend)

COLLABORATOR(S)
Jeremiah Chiu, Phillip Matesic

TECHNOLOGY
Hands, photography, computers

TIME SPENT
1 week

TYPEFACE
Nimbus Condensed Rounded and Scala Serif

WHY DO YOU LIKE THIS PROJECT?
This project was really the first in-school, but self-initiated, project Jeremiah and I (now Plural) collaborated on fully from start to finish. We enjoyed the opportunity to create a real, tangible piece, we liked the fact that it felt like a real, client-based project, where we were in charge of all aspects from designing and editing to printing and producing.

OUTCOMES
Besides the tangible product, both Café 4102 and Lumpen Magazine served as platforms to explore and experiment with what we knew, skills and otherwise, and what we were interested in/studying at the time. I think we were fortunate in both projects to work with great collaborators who really allowed us and the projects to realize their full potential (well, as full as could happen within one week). With Café 4102 we gained the experience of working together outside of a school assignment, which, in a way, led to us starting our own studio practice.

FEEDBACK
Phillip and his colleagues were pleased with the outcome and we like to think it served as a successful documentation of his project.

FAVOURITE FOOD THEN
I love all things food, but...
(Cont. opposite – now)

YOUR MOST VALUED POSSESSION THEN
My camera

Project Then

PROJECT SIMILARITIES THEN AND NOW
Both projects were fun; labours of love. The opportunity to collaborate with artists and makers to explore and experiment with new ways of experiencing the world is why we do what we do.

Renata Graw (Plural)

For both: Curiosity, experimentation, patience

YEAR OF PROJECT
2010

PROFESSIONAL PROJECT BRIEF
Lumpen Magazine:
Ed Marszewski, founder
and overlord of Public
Media Institute, contacted
us about redesigning
Lumpen Magazine to
begin its 18th year. As
the scheduling had been
revised, there was very
little time left before the
issue was to be released
to print. With only one
week ahead of us, we
were to rethink every
aspect of the magazine
from the logo/masthead
and format to the
typesetting and layout.

CLIENT
Ed Marszewski (Public
Media Institute)

COLLABORATOR(S)
Jeremiah Chiu,
Ed Marszewski

TECHNOLOGY
Hands, photography,
computers

TIME SPENT
1 week (a very
intense week)

TYPEFACE
Golden Type, Bodoni,
Univers among others –
a lot of drawn type too

FAVOURITE FOOD NOW
…I am addicted to just
one: coffee

**YOUR MOST VALUED
POSSESSION NOW**
My hands

WHY DO YOU LIKE THIS PROJECT?
We took this project on as
a challenge, but also to create
a piece that would showcase
what we were capable of,
as we were, and still are,
interested in creating/
designing publications.
We liked the challenge of
creating something that tested
our limits, both in time and
skill, resulting in something
meaningful. What we liked
the most was working with
Ed, who really understood the
relationship between client
and designer, and valued our
insight and research, which
ultimately allowed us to push
ourselves further and try out
things we had never tried
before.

WHAT DO YOU DISLIKE ABOUT IT?
Nothing. Design decisions are
made with the knowledge and
experience you have at the
time. Lumpen is an ongoing
project, it has been evolving
from one issue to the next.
We enjoy that. For us, it serves
as a document of the time;
one that we can go back to and
remember the decisions,
preferences, ideas, revolutions
of that moment.

OUTCOMES
With Lumpen Magazine,
we received quite a bit of
recogni-tion from our peers
and the professional field
alike (see feedback).
With the recognition, we
have been fortunate to gain
a few new clients who are
interested in collaborating on
meaningful projects. Lumpen
continues to serve as a project
where we can explore our
current ideas and constantly
collaborate with a variety
of artists, writers, etc.…

FEEDBACK
Ed and his readers/community
were thrilled with the new
redesign, as it created a
new experience that was
bold, fresh and engaging.
Since then, Lumpen has
received recognition from
Communication Arts, PRINT
Magazine, Taiwan DPI and
the Type Directors Club.

ANYTHING ELSE
Because this project now and
the project then were very fast
projects, we didn't have time
to doubt our decisions. There
was time to develop only one
idea, so we had to focus on
the task at hand.

DO YOU TEACH?
University of Illinois at
Chicago (USA), Graphic
Design and Typography.

**IS IT POSSIBLE TO
TEACH DESIGN?**
Yes. I believe it is
possible to teach design
technique. It is important
to learn the rules so you
can break them, and to
learn the history so you
can understand your
role in it. More important
is to teach how to see
and think critically and
creatively.

Project Now

Café 4102

con·viv·i·al (kan-viv'ē-al) adj.
Fond of feasting, drinking, and good
company; sociable.

COFFEE $1
TEA $1
SODA $1
IF YOU FORGOT $2
YOUR MUG

HELP YOURSELF

PAY WHAT YOU
THINK ITS WORTH

FREE

"What does it mean, to live in a room? Is
to live in a place to take possession
of it? What does taking possession of a
place mean? As from when does
somewhere become truly yours?"

CAFÉ 4102 /

SPECIAL THANKS TO /

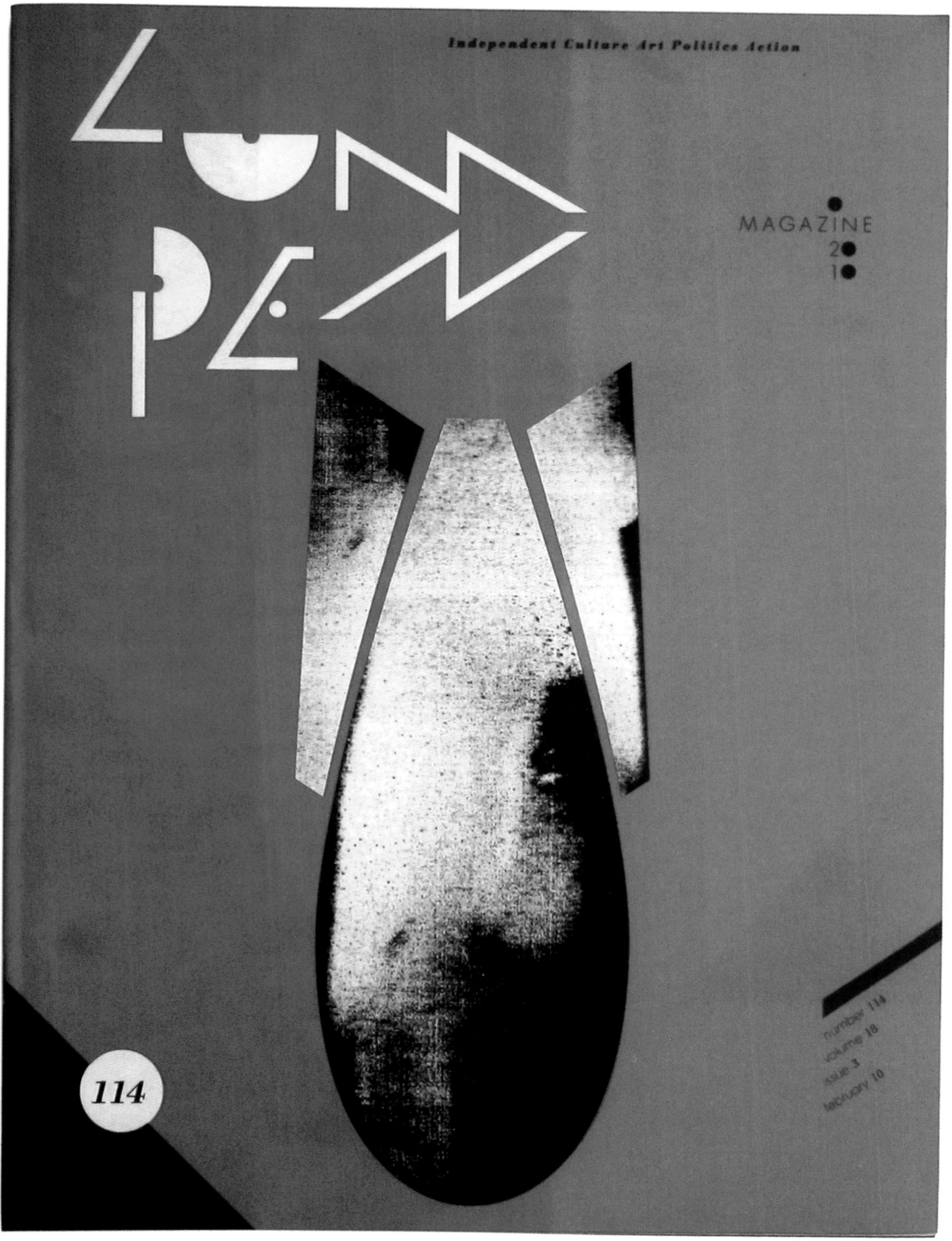

Independent Culture Art Politics Action

MAGAZINE
2
1

114

number 114
volume 18
issue 3
february 10

Richard Walker

Always finish your work + Don't feel obliged to have an opinion on everything. If you don't know, say you don't know

YEAR OF PROJECT
1996

STUDENT PROJECT BRIEF
I think the college brief was a one-day project run by Scott King. Something about 'breaking the rules of communication'.

COLLEGE
Camberwell College of Arts, London (United Kingdom)

TUTOR(S)
Scott King

COLLABORATOR(S)
Stewart, the printmaking technician at Camberwell College of Arts

TECHNOLOGY
Silkscreen

TIME SPENT
1 day

TYPEFACE
Looks like Gill Sans extra bold

WHY DO YOU LIKE THIS PROJECT?
I liked the sense of urgency. I liked the fact you could make an attention-grabbing poster with a lot of words.

WHAT DO YOU DISLIKE ABOUT IT?
I was going for a 'Pushpin' look, but got it a bit wrong.

FEEDBACK
Scott King dismissed the work as 'a bit old', but was impressed I managed to finish it in one day.

ANYTHING ELSE
The rule, 'Too many words are counter-productive if you want to grab public attention' is from a list of rules written by Bill Drummond in the manual How to Have a Number One the Easy Way by The KLF. It was a rule they applied to making pop records. I was seeing if the same rule applied visually. I thought I was being clever at the time, but looking at it again I think it's a bit naff.

PROJECT SIMILARITIES THEN AND NOW
They were both made at Camberwell College of Arts. I know someone who knows someone who works in the letterpress room, and he did me a favour.
They are both playing with words and type. They both state the literal obvious and are a bit ironic. They both used traditional techniques – silkscreen and letterpress. They both took a similar amount of time to make. They both have similar influences from 1960s collectives – namely Pushpin and Fluxus.

FAVOURITE FOOD THEN
Indian food

YOUR MOST VALUED POSSESSION THEN
I had an original copy of How to Have a Number One the Easy Way by the KLF

Project Then

Richard Walker (KK Outlet / KesselsKramer)

A VALUABLE QUALITY FOR A DESIGN STUDENT + A DESIGN PROFESSIONAL

Develop a thick skin +
Be punctual and polite

YEAR OF PROJECT
2010

PROFESSIONAL PROJECT BRIEF
Poster for an exhibition at KK Outlet. The exhibition was called We're All Art Directors. Erik Kessels asked all the art directors from KesselsKramer to show their personal work. I was just asked to make something to go on a sandwich board outside the gallery.

CLIENT
KK Outlet/KesselsKramer, London (United Kingdom)

COLLABORATOR(S)
The letterpress technician at Camberwell College of Arts

TECHNOLOGY
Letterpress

TIME SPENT
1 day

TYPEFACE
Grot something or other (it was the biggest font they had)

WHY DO YOU LIKE THIS PROJECT?
I've always liked the finger-pointing icon; I think it's quite rude.

WHAT DO YOU DISLIKE ABOUT IT?
I like it as it is.

OUTCOMES
A sense of completion. Jobs tend to drag on in advertising. I've worked on campaigns that have literally taken two years to make four posters.

FEEDBACK
The finger-pointing poster is the biggest-selling poster in our shop at KK Outlet.

ANYTHING ELSE
I think I prefer the finger-pointing poster in relation to the work then.

FAVOURITE FOOD NOW
Cheese

YOUR MOST VALUED POSSESSION NOW
I have an original May '68 poster. It's the one with the riot policeman holding a baton. I love it, but it has a big SS symbol on the shield. My wife won't have it in the house. I've tried explaining that it's actually very anti-fascist, but I see her point

Project Now

DO YOU TEACH?
No.

IS IT POSSIBLE TO TEACH DESIGN?
My tutor used to point me in the direction of what books to have a look at, what exhibitions to go and see and let me get on with it and then hassle me to finish what I'd started. There is an art to being a teacher; just because you work as a designer does not mean you have the ability to teach, and vice versa – I'm not going to pretend I have the ability to teach a class of 30 art students.

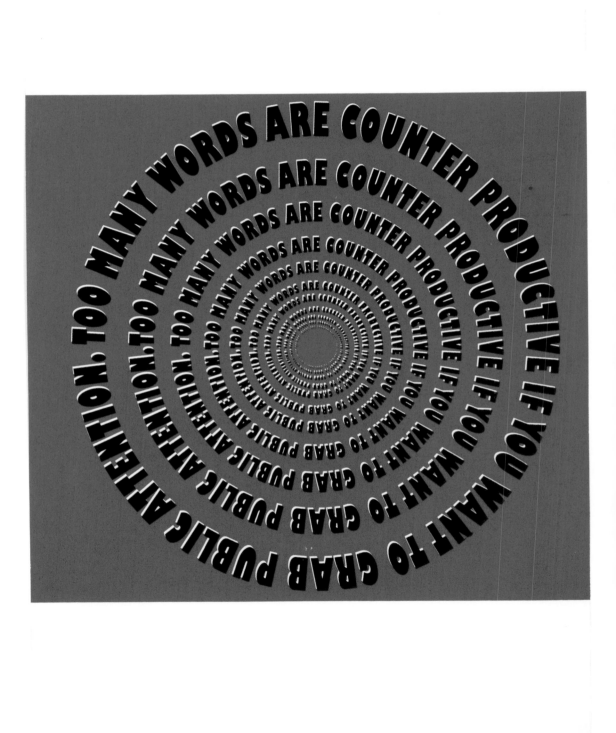

THIS
WAY

TO THE

FINGER
POINTING
CONVENTION

CANADIAN/SWISS

Sandra Hoffmann

A PIECE OF SOUND ADVICE + A SINGLE WARNING TO A DESIGN STUDENT

Difficult to answer here

YEAR OF PROJECT
1990

STUDENT PROJECT BRIEF
Colour class: Colour compositions of 'my coloured days – 7 from 126 compositions'. Visualization exploration searching for the corresponding colour combination of my mental imagery of the words 'Monday to Sunday'.

COLLEGE
Schule für Gestaltung, Basel (Switzerland)

FAVOURITE FOOD THEN
Canadian

YOUR MOST VALUED POSSESSION THEN
A toolbox with instruments (Swann-Morton scalpel, marble, roller, Caran d'Ache pens and pencils, Racher typometre, calculating scale, Falzbein, Cementit, Kern compasses, mink paintbrushes, loupe, Juwel stapler, Prismacolor pencil crayons, Gedess pencil sharpener, bulldog clips, magnets, Omega Reiss-nagel drawing-pins, hole punch, stamp pad and letter stamps, technograph 777 pencils, gyro compass, burnisher, green masking tape, brown paper tape, Post-its, Minox, coloured stones, Klebeband from EPA, Pelikan plaka, sketchbooks from Rebetez, Knetgummi, Ilford canisters…)

TUTOR(S)
Moritz Zwimpfer (project initiated in a class with Armin Hofmann, Brissago 1986)

TECHNOLOGY
Plaka, water, paper, paintbrush

TIME SPENT
1 year of Friday afternoons

WHY DO YOU LIKE THIS PROJECT?
For the investigation between the interaction of colour and form. Colours in relationship to other colours through change in proportions. Refinement and enrichment of a personal colour vocabulary (SfG-Basics). 'Making' the colour compositions was very satisfying, as well as the joy of 'seeing' my day colours come to life.

WHAT DO YOU DISLIKE ABOUT IT?
I was not aware that 'my coloured days' are slightly different depending on the language. I would have to make variations in English and in German.

OUTCOMES
Lovely painting moments overlooking the Rhine. It was often sunny. Interesting dialogue with the instructor.

FEEDBACK
It was difficult to exactly pin-point the colours of the days. Although they were in my mind, getting them on the paper was not easy. I didn't know then that not everyone has specific colour correspondences for their days of the week.

PROJECT SIMILARITIES THEN AND NOW
The similarity between the projects lies in the content, the topic of synaesthesia. At the time of the intitial project, it was unknown to me that not everyone experiences this way of 'seeing', or possibly is not aware of it. I am convinced that this way of 'seeing' influences not only everyday life, but also the way of designing and decision-making.

Project Then

Sandra Hoffmann Robbiani
(Visual Studies)

A VALUABLE QUALITY FOR A DESIGN STUDENT + A DESIGN PROFESSIONAL

Sight and insight, self-initiative +
As above plus the ability
to focus, persistence, vigorousness,
a thick skin, boldness

YEAR OF PROJECT
2011

PROFESSIONAL PROJECT BRIEF
**Designerly research:
Compendium of
Typographic Synaesthesia.
Inventory of Aspects.
A booklet accompanying
a workshop to increase
the awareness of
synaesthesia. The aim
of this study is to initiate
visual evidence of the
synaesthetic phenomenon
that has recently been
made verifiable through
neuroscientific research.
The investigation develops
a design-specific metho-
dology for synaesthetic
research, which will
provide insight into
synaesthesia from a
designer's point of view.**

CLIENT
**Hessische Hochschulen
research grant**

TECHNOLOGY
Computer-generated

TIME SPENT
3 months

TYPEFACE
**Times New Roman,
Letter Gothic**

WHY DO YOU LIKE THIS PROJECT?
**Through the interaction
between design and science,
new knowledge can be gained
about the phenomenon of
synaesthesia.**

WHAT DO YOU DISLIKE ABOUT IT?
**The terminology is diffuse.
I am trying to define and
develop a precise vocabulary
to accompany the topic.
The rendering skills could
be better.**

OUTCOMES
**This small piece accompanies
a larger theoretical
investigation. A productive
balance between 'making' and
'thinking and writing'.**

FEEDBACK
**This research project
investigates the phenomenon,
but the reaction of disbelief
or astonishment still
accompanies the work.**

FAVOURITE FOOD NOW
Italian, Ticinese

YOUR MOST VALUED
POSSESSION NOW
**The diamond necklace
from my husband**

Project Now

DO YOU TEACH?
**Professor at the
Hochschule Darmstadt,
Faculty of Design,
Darmstadt (Germany).**

IS IT POSSIBLE TO
TEACH DESIGN?
I try.

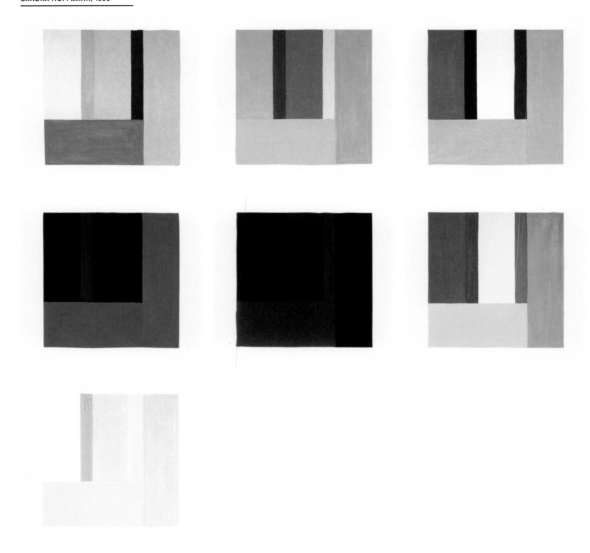

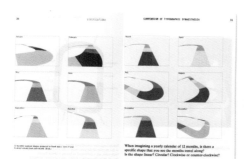

Sascha Lobe

Be fast, but don't trip over your own feet + Never stop!

YEAR OF PROJECT
1990–97

STUDENT PROJECT BRIEF
**Development of an open
flexible corporate image
that continues to work
over a longer period
and that always offers
new solutions for posters
and flyers**

COLLEGE
**Hochschule Pforzheim
(Germany)**

TUTOR(S)
**Self-initiated project for
Kupferdächle Pforzheim,
a youth club. The project
began before I was a
student, and I worked
on it until after I had
graduated.**

TECHNOLOGY
**Apple Macintosh,
Photoshop, QuarkXPress,
offset printing, silkscreen
printing**

TIME SPENT
**I always spent the time that
I felt was necessary for each
particular job and that it
took until I was satisfied –
despite tight deadlines.**

TYPEFACE
**Over the course of time, I have
experimented with various
fonts, starting with Kabel.
Interestingly, it was created
by Rudolf Koch, who worked
at HfG Offenbach from 1921,
the school where I teach
typography – which is a nice
coincidence. Later I used
Metro (William Addison
Dwiggins) and various fronts
by Emigre (e.g. Base).**

WHY DO YOU LIKE THIS PROJECT?
**Both projects (then and now)
are pieces of work in which
a visual image evolved over
a period of several years and
that had to (and was allowed
to) do without any set rules –
that's great fun and lets us
experiment and try things out.
Of course, you learn most from
this kind of work. Unfortunately,
these are small projects,
both in terms of budget and
print run, etc.**

FEEDBACK
**The works for Kupferdächle
mostly met with positive
reactions. As a student, of
course, it was great that the
works were also published
by various specialist
magazines.**

FAVOURITE FOOD THEN
Italian cuisine

YOUR MOST VALUED
POSSESSION THEN
Books

Project Then

PROJECT SIMILARITIES
THEN AND NOW
**Both projects work
with typographical
modifications and with
layering; those are
probably the stylistic
devices that suit
me best.**

Sascha Lobe (L2M3)

A VALUABLE QUALITY FOR A DESIGN STUDENT + A DESIGN PROFESSIONAL

An open mind towards the world.
Self-confidence; recognizing one's own
skills and weaknesses. Good communication.
The ability to distinguish between and
to integrate concept and styling +
Professionals need to be a bit better at figures
perhaps, but, besides that, all as above

YEAR OF PROJECT
2006 – ongoing

PROFESSIONAL PROJECT BRIEF
Development of an open
flexible corporate image
that continues to work
over a longer period and
that always offers new
solutions for posters
and flyers

CLIENT
Württembergischer
Kunstverein, Stuttgart
(Germany)

COLLABORATOR(S)
Ina Bauer, a staff member
at L2M3

TECHNOLOGY
Apple Macintosh,
Photoshop, InDesign,
offset printing

TIME SPENT
We usually work between
three and five days on a poster
for the Württembergischer
Kunstverein. Often, this is very
difficult due to lack of time.
Nevertheless, the yardstick
is generally not time but the
quality achieved and
satisfaction with it.

TYPEFACE
I have stuck to sans serif
fonts, and I still switch fonts,
too – at least in this project.
From poster to poster,
Monotype Grotesque is
accompanied by a font that
suits the particular topic.

WHY DO YOU LIKE THIS PROJECT?
See answer opposite (then).

FEEDBACK
We generally get very positive
feedback from graphic artists
and designers (and from
Iris Dressler and Hans Christ
at Württembergischer
Kunstverein, the client, too,
thank goodness). With artists,
it varies a lot; some accept the
fact that the designer is an
author himself; others would
rather do their own posters.

DO YOU TEACH?
I have been Professor
of Typography at the
Hochschule für
Gestaltung Offenbach
(Germany) since 2010
and taught at various
colleges before that.

IS IT POSSIBLE TO
TEACH DESIGN?
That's a very difficult
question. I think you
can create a certain
atmosphere in which
students work and you
can ask the right or
wrong questions. And
you can offer them a
sphere that deals with
technical aspects and
reflection on the media.
The rest is hope…

FAVOURITE FOOD NOW
Japanese cuisine

YOUR MOST VALUED
POSSESSION NOW
Books

Project Now

ROCK FOR SKATES!
FLO + DIE SCHANDE
CHRIS LEONHARDT
SODA
SA 4.4.20 UHR
KUPFERDAECHLE
PFORZHEIM
DM 15/10

Di, Do – So: 11 – 18 Uhr, Mi: 11 – 20 Uhr
www.wkv-stuttgart.de

Württembergischer Kunstverein Stuttgart
Schlossplatz 2, D – 70173 Stuttgart

||||||||IICCCCCCCDDDiDie
||||||||<<<<<<<CCCChronolog(
|||||||<<<cccccdddd der
——————TTTTTTTTTeTeresa
||||||||IIEEEEBBBBBBuBurga
|||||IIEEEEEEBBBBBB(BeBerichte,
|||||IICCCCCCCDDDDiDiagramme,
|||||||||||I|I|I|I|rInIntIntervalle /
||||||||<<<<<2222222229;29.9.11

Die Chronologie der Teresa Burga
Berichte, Diagramme, Intervalle / 29.9.11
30. September 2011 – 8. Januar 2012
Württembergischer Kunstverein Stuttgart

Stefan Sagmeister

A PIECE OF SOUND ADVICE + A SINGLE WARNING TO A DESIGN STUDENT

Work your ass off +
Don't be an asshole

YEAR OF PROJECT
1984

STUDENT PROJECT BRIEF
**To save a historic
theatre from destruction
by bringing it back to
the attention of the
Viennese public**

COLLEGE
**Universität für angewandte
Kunst Wien (Austria)**

TUTOR(S)
Prof. Kurt Schwarz

COLLABORATOR(S)
**Thomas Sandri
(manufacturer)**

TECHNOLOGY
Various media

TIME SPENT
6 months

TYPEFACE
Custom font

WHY DO YOU LIKE THIS PROJECT?
**It was a fun process to be able
to come up with 20 different
posters for the same theatre,
and, as a student, it was such
a thrill that the project was
'real', i.e., that parts of it
got produced and were hung
all over Vienna.**

WHAT DO YOU DISLIKE ABOUT IT?
**I would take the form more
seriously.**

OUTCOMES
**That was one of only two 'real'
projects in my portfolio that
I was happy with at the time.**

FEEDBACK
**It worked; the theatre was
saved, and is now one of the
leading theatres in Vienna.**

FAVOURITE FOOD THEN
**Zürich veal with cream
sauce and mushrooms**

YOUR MOST VALUED
POSSESSION THEN
Silkscreen equipment

Project Then

PROJECT SIMILARITIES
THEN AND NOW
Variatons on a theme.

Stefan Sagmeister (Sagmeister Inc.)

Tenacity + Curiosity

YEAR OF PROJECT
2008

PROFESSIONAL PROJECT BRIEF
To create a visual identity for a music centre in Portugal

CLIENT
Guta Muera Guedes, Casa da Musica

COLLABORATOR(S)
Matthias Ernstberger, Quentin Walesh, Ralph Ammer

TECHNOLOGY
Various media

TIME SPENT
10 months

TYPEFACE
Custom font

WHY DO YOU LIKE THIS PROJECT?
It's a good example of a changing identity really working for the client's interest. Our goal was to show the many different kinds of music performed in one house. Depending on the music it is filled with, the house changes its character and works dice-like by displaying different views and facets of music. A Casa da Musica logo generator was developed – a custom piece of software connected to a scanner that turns any image into an animated and still image Casa da Musica logo within a fraction of a second.

WHAT DO YOU DISLIKE ABOUT IT?
I would stay involved longer than two years.

OUTCOMES
We receive many client calls about identities, saying that they saw Casa da Musica.

FEEDBACK
The identity received a lot of press in design circles and is still properly used even after the marketing director changed.

FAVOURITE FOOD NOW
Tiny bow Shanghainese soup dumplings

YOUR MOST VALUED POSSESSION NOW
My dad's watch

DO YOU TEACH?
Graduate Design, School of Visual Arts, New York (USA). Course name: Is it possible to touch someone's heart with design?

IS IT POSSIBLE TO TEACH DESIGN?
I learned the most from my classmates.

Project Now

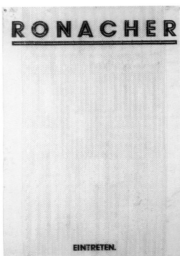

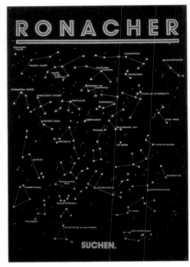

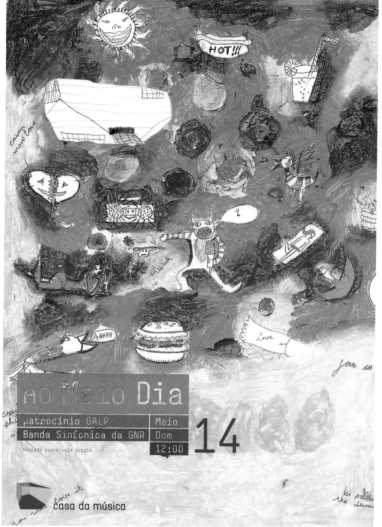

Sven Voelker

The years of studying are nice but afterwards it gets even better – it's worth it to finish + If it's at all possible, don't work so much in bars or driving taxis; use the time for studying – it's better brief but intense

YEAR OF PROJECT
1998

STUDENT PROJECT BRIEF
Self-initiated project –
programme for a Profile
Intermedia conference at
the Hochschule für
Künste Bremen

COLLEGE
Hochschule für Künste
Bremen (Germany)

COLLABORATOR(S)
Peter Rea (tutor),
Thomas Weiling and
Dorthe Meinhardt
(fellow students)

TIME SPENT
18 months

TYPEFACE
Helvetica

WHY DO YOU LIKE THIS PROJECT?
It was a mad idea in the
first place. That was long
before design conferences
were a common thing at art
schools. Back then, designers
went to professional
conferences like the Typo
Berlin. We wanted to offer an
alternative, a Woodstock sort
of thing. It was a wonderful
thing to see how we, a small
group of students, were able
to accomplish a huge
conference with 1,300 visitors.

WHAT DO YOU DISLIKE ABOUT IT?
I wouldn't change anything.

OUTCOMES
This project was very important
to me. I met many people
during this project who I am
still friends with today: John
Warwicker (Tomato, UK), Laurie
Makela (Los Angeles, USA),
Michael Schirner (Germany)
but also a lot of journalists and
other people within our small
world of graphic design.

FEEDBACK
The Profile Intermedia
developed into a wonderful
conference series over the
years. Many other students
have worked in the organizing
teams together with Peter Rea
over the years. There was
much positive feedback,
but I have to say that the
credits go to a very big group
of individuals. Though I must
say, nobody after us probably
ever had the chance to walk
with Peter Greenaway and
Laurie Makela through heavy
snow at midnight.

**PROJECT SIMILARITIES
THEN AND NOW**
I think the two projects
are very similiar. In
terms of concept, they
are nearly identical.
I like to set up a surface
on which many people
can place something.
You can call it a platform
or a project, but it is
always something that
involves others. This
was my way of studying
and it is the way I teach.
Besides this conceptual
similarity, both are also
very similar in their look.
I like Grotesk typefaces
and I find it difficult to
decide whether I prefer
Helvetica, Arial or,
now, Francois Rappo's
Theinhardt. I am not
good at making 'rich'
layouts; I prefer it if
everything is simple and
honest. Sometimes that
looks boring, but then
you have to make
the story even more
exciting.

FAVOURITE FOOD THEN
Käsespätzle (thimble
dumplings made with
cheese)

**YOUR MOST VALUED
POSSESSION THEN**
My most expensive asset
at the time was a Paul
Smith suit. Actually, not
right – it was the first G3
PowerBook for approx.
£4,000

Project Then

Sven Voelker (Sven Voelker Studio)

A VALUABLE QUALITY FOR A DESIGN STUDENT + A DESIGN PROFESSIONAL

A student should learn to develop his own projects – seminars are OK, self-initiated projects are better + A designer should learn to develop his own projects – clients are OK, self-initiated projects are better

YEAR OF PROJECT
2010

PROFESSIONAL PROJECT BRIEF
Self-initiated project –
the concept, research and
design of a magazine
made by students at the
Burg Giebichenstein
Kunsthochschule Halle
(Germany)

CLIENT
Burg Giebichenstein
Kunsthochschule Halle

COLLABORATOR(S)
A group of students
(Juliane Hohlbaum,
Rafaela Lorenz,
Ulrike Schuckmann)

TIME SPENT
1 semester

TYPEFACE
Various

FAVOURITE FOOD NOW
Käsespätzle (thimble
dumplings made with
cheese)

YOUR MOST VALUED
POSSESSION NOW
My most beautiful material
thing is a 40-year-old
Porsche

WHY DO YOU LIKE THIS PROJECT?
The students put together
a great new magazine in an
amazingly short period of
time. While doing that, maybe
without intention, they created
an exceptional platform for all
our activities. The magazine
is not the final product; it is the
beginning of new things. We
are able to involve companies
like smart or ABSOLUT,
artists like Lawrence Weiner,
Apparatjik and Luc Tuymans
or journalists like Hendrik
Lakeberg and Max Dax in
our work at the art school.

WHAT DO YOU DISLIKE ABOUT IT?
It is a lot of work. Making
a magazine looks easy in the
first place, but if you are not
a professional journalist,
everything is very hard work
(except the graphic design
at the end).

OUTCOMES
It is the motor of all my
activities at the art school.
But it is only a motor; what is
really interesting is where it
can take us. Again it has made
clear that graphic design is
nice, but a good story is much
more. I want designers to
work like artists and authors.
I don't want them to talk about
type sizes, but about words
and sentences. A designer
who talks about typefaces all
the time is like a photographer
who talks and talks about
his Nikon or a drummer who
keeps throwing his mind
and money at the latest gear.
A good camera has never
made a good photographer,
a good drum kit never made a
good drummer, and using
a good typeface will not make
you a good designer.

FEEDBACK
It is a good project and it has
received good feedback.
But because being successful
is not the most important thing
at art schools, we have to
make it more risky. The theme
of our next issue will be 'error'.
Hopefully we will be able to
make mistakes.

DO YOU TEACH?
Professor at the
Hochschule für
Gestaltung Karlsruhe
(Germany) from 2004
to 2010 and since 2010
Professor at the Burg
Giebichenstein
Kunsthochschule
Halle (Germany).

IS IT POSSIBLE TO
TEACH DESIGN?
It's definitely possible
to teach design. In my
experience, this is only
possible if the studies
are based on a series of
projects. A college is a
relatively free space
for students to develop
their own projects, with
enough people around
who help, advise,
criticize and eventually
compliment them on
their work. If you do
this throughout the five
years of studies, they
learn enough to main-
tain this outside college
too. I disagree with a
more school-based
approach, as I don't
think that works. I think
I have done a good job
as a professor if my
students recognize and
set their own targets
and reach them. I am
looking to educate
strong personalities
who understand
themselves as design
entrepreneurs.

Project Now

Some Magazine, Repair

A Magazine between Design and Art
Issue #0 Autumn 2010
www.somemag.com
9 Euro

Tim Brauns: Der Sammler, Otto von Busch: Fashion Repair, Roland Roos: Free Repair,
John Zabrucky: Modern Times, The Arial Press and more.

BRITISH

Tim Balaam

A PIECE OF SOUND ADVICE + A SINGLE WARNING TO A DESIGN STUDENT

Personally experience as much art, design and architecture as possible + Having considered this question for some time, I don't have any

YEAR OF PROJECT
1998

STUDENT PROJECT BRIEF
Self-initiated project for graduation show

COLLEGE
Camberwell College of Arts, London (United Kingdom)

TUTOR(S)
Darren Lago

COLLABORATOR(S)
Photographic processing lab

TECHNOLOGY
SLR camera

TIME SPENT
4 weeks

WHY DO YOU LIKE THIS PROJECT?
The simplicity of the project process.

OUTCOMES
It was the first time I outsourced the production of a project.

FEEDBACK
It had a positive impact on my final grade.

ANYTHING ELSE
It was enjoyable to work on at the time.

FAVOURITE FOOD THEN
Bread

YOUR MOST VALUED POSSESSION THEN
Sepak takraw ball

Project Then

PROJECT SIMILARITIES THEN AND NOW
Both projects simply tell a story.

Tim Balaam (Hyperkit)

Open-mindedness +
Have an understanding of
how things are made

YEAR OF PROJECT
2010

PROFESSIONAL PROJECT BRIEF
Identity and interior for
contemporary men's
barbershop.

CLIENT
Joe and Co.

COLLABORATOR(S)
Four other studio
members, client, furniture-
maker, lighting contractor,
lithographic printer,
website developer,
signmaker, enameller

TECHNOLOGY
Apple iMac

TIME SPENT
1 year

TYPEFACE
Custom typeface and
Akkurat

WHY DO YOU LIKE THIS PROJECT?
The opportunity to consider
something in its entirety.

WHAT DO YOU DISLIKE ABOUT IT?
I think that there are always
things that you would like
to change about a project once
the dust has settled. In this
particular instance, we would
change the front of the shop
so that it could be opened/
rolled up like a garage door,
so that in the summer months
it would become more
connected to its urban
surroundings.

OUTCOMES
Pleasure in seeing designs
realized on a larger scale.

FEEDBACK
To date, there have been
no negative reactions, only
really positive feedback, which
I hope will only grow with
time as the shop and services
establish themselves.

ANYTHING ELSE
It was enjoyable to work
on at the time.

DO YOU TEACH?
I taught Graphic Design
2001–04 at the Kent
Institute of Art and
Design (UK) and the
University of
Portsmouth (UK).

IS IT POSSIBLE TO
TEACH DESIGN?
Yes, I believe the
technical skills required
of a designer can be
taught to anyone, but
whether those skills are
applied successfully or
not depends upon the
individual's creative
instinct, something that
cannot be taught.

FAVOURITE FOOD NOW
Bread

YOUR MOST VALUED
POSSESSION NOW
Sepak takraw ball

Project Now

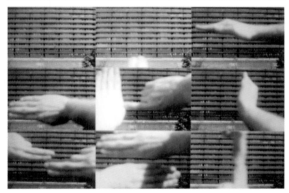

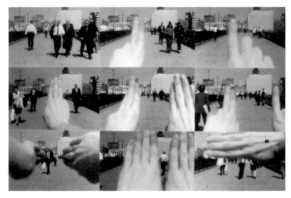

Urs Lehni

'Design is a lot of work' (Cornel Windlin) + Don't be late (again)

YEAR OF PROJECT
1999

STUDENT PROJECT BRIEF
Self-initiated diploma project – Transport

COLLEGE
Hochschule Luzern (Switzerland)

COLLABORATOR(S)
Rafael Koch, Markus Wohlhüter, Peter Körner

TECHNOLOGY
Running a public space

TIME SPENT
Approx. 5 months

TYPEFACE
Various

WHY DO YOU LIKE THIS PROJECT?
See answer opposite (now).

OUTCOMES
As Transport was conceived in the context of college diploma work, the project reached a much smaller public than Corner College (project opposite) does now. Conceptually though, the outcome is the same in both cases: a public space.

FEEDBACK
Feedback mostly came from fellow students and some teachers. It was entirely positive, but maybe more based on the fact that we had done something different than for the actual outcome.

PROJECT SIMILARITIES THEN AND NOW
Both projects are basically the same; Transport (1999) could be considered as something like a preliminary version of Corner College. Both projects involve the conception, management and production of a public space that is somewhat focusing on the topic of design in the broadest sense. Transport did this in a rather naive way as, back then, we knew little about both the form and the content of such a venture. Corner College now tries to take on the same idea in a more serious way. Also, it's somewhat more professionally led; it receives funding and provides a more ordered programme.

FAVOURITE FOOD THEN
-

YOUR MOST VALUED POSSESSION THEN
Self-restored Vespa Tourist 150 (1960)

Then

Urs Lehni (Lehni-Trüb, Rollo Press, Corner College)

A VALUABLE QUALITY FOR A DESIGN STUDENT + A DESIGN PROFESSIONAL

For both: Curiosity

YEAR OF PROJECT
2008 – ongoing

PROFESSIONAL PROJECT BRIEF
**Self-initiated project –
Corner College**

CLIENT
Self-initiated

COLLABORATOR(S)
**http://www.corner-college.
com/Kollaborateure**

TECHNOLOGY
Running a public space

TIME SPENT
2¾ years so far…

TYPEFACE
Various

WHY DO YOU LIKE THIS PROJECT?
I didn't think much more about Transport (1999) until I started to show Corner College in some of my talks. Then I realized that Transport was a kind of beta version or study for Corner College. All the essential components were already there. It just took me some years to realize that this is something that I really enjoy doing.

OUTCOMES
Same as then (see opposite).

FEEDBACK
In Zürich there's a big crowd of art-and-design-savvy people, so the feedback is delivered on a more objective level. One thing we hear a lot in Zürich is that people really appreciate the intimacy and the simplicity of both our space and the events.

DO YOU TEACH?
I teach in the Communications Design department at the Staatliche Hochschule für Gestaltung Karlsruhe (Germany).

IS IT POSSIBLE TO TEACH DESIGN?
I think it's possible as a teacher to trigger some kind of thinking that is related to design in the broadest sense. During my education, this impulse came mainly through frustration with the lack of any curriculum whatsoever, which resulted in us taking the initiative and coming up with our own projects.

FAVOURITE FOOD NOW
-

YOUR MOST VALUED
POSSESSION NOW
Wedding ring

Now

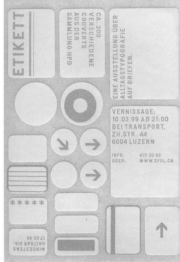

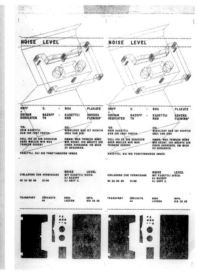

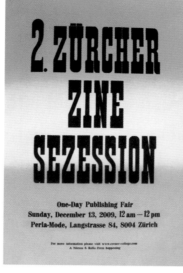

Yasmin Khan

A PIECE OF SOUND ADVICE + A SINGLE WARNING TO A DESIGN STUDENT

Follow your ideas beyond what you know how to assess + Don't rush to get out into the 'real world' – you're already in it

YEAR OF PROJECT
2004

STUDENT PROJECT BRIEF
**MFA thesis project –
a study in speculative
design: artefacts of
national identity were
designed for three
imaginary nation-states
(stamps, currency, flag
and travel poster). The
character of each nation-
state was based on
current social, economic
and scientific trends.**

COLLEGE
**California Institute of the
Arts, CalArts (USA)**

TUTOR(S)
**Lorraine Wild, Michael
Worthington, Ed Fella,
Jeff Keedy**

TECHNOLOGY
**Adobe CS3 + various
imagemaking techniques
including hand-drawing,
photography, digital
collage**

TYPEFACE
OCR

WHY DO YOU LIKE THIS PROJECT?
**I entered graduate school with
an interest and background in
typography and publication
design. I didn't have much skill
or experience as an image-
maker. This is because I have
questionable taste, and at the
time, I had no clue how to
turn that into an asset.**

WHAT DO YOU DISLIKE ABOUT IT?
**I would make things stranger,
less familiar, less polite.**

OUTCOMES
**A space to explore my interest
in speculative design: what
it looks like, what its role is,
how it might live in a
professional practice.**

FEEDBACK
**I was too exhausted to
remember much about thesis
presentation... Although I do
remember someone said the
work was beautiful...**

PROJECT SIMILARITIES
THEN AND NOW
**There was a similar
interest in representing
imaginary worlds.
The thesis project did
it literally, and the
Bulletin metaphorically
through student
portraits that depicted
the student's internal
world. There's also a
similar interest in
experimenting with
materials and collage,
and a consistent
interest in and heavy
use of bright colour.**

FAVOURITE FOOD THEN
**Anything that wasn't
dehydrated**

YOUR MOST VALUED
POSSESSION THEN
Not sure

Project Then

Yasmin Khan (Counterspace)

For both: Scepticism

YEAR OF PROJECT
2009

PROFESSIONAL PROJECT BRIEF
CalArts Bulletin 2009–2011 – design a catalogue for CalArts that visually distinguishes it from peer institutions. The Bulletin must be comprised of one overview booklet and a set of individual booklets to be used by each of the schools within the Institute. A limited edition of all books stitched together was also produced.

CLIENT
California Institute of the Arts, CalArts (USA)

COLLABORATOR(S)
Michael Worthington (Counterspace), Erin Hauber, Randy Nakamura, Cassandra Chae. Photography: Scott Groller, Steven Gunther

TECHNOLOGY
Adobe CS5 and various imagemaking techniques, including photography and digital collage

TYPEFACE
Rolleta

WHY DO YOU LIKE THIS PROJECT?
I think the Bulletin represents the fullness and intensity and exuberance of the programme at CalArts, as well as the bohemian spirit that still pervades the Institute. I think it is beautiful and fussy and loud, and most importantly, it feels committed.

WHAT DO YOU DISLIKE ABOUT IT?
I would make things subtly stranger, less familiar, less polite.

OUTCOMES
A space to make a print object that was full and dense and detailed, and to play out my interests in imaginary worlds, trompe l'oeil and other forms of fake 3D. Also provided a way to explore print 'special effects' – use of speciality bindings, inks, materials and formats that distinguish print from screen experience.

FEEDBACK
Feedback was mixed. Designers responded positively. Evidently some people found it confusing.

DO YOU TEACH?
Yes. Senior Lecturer, Otis College of Art and Design, Los Angeles (USA). BFA programme: curriculum co-ordinator for graphic design + instructor for typography, senior project studio, visual language. MFA programme: course in Social Responsibility.

IS IT POSSIBLE TO TEACH DESIGN?
It better be. That's my day job. What I learned at college and what I teach now: I learned to trust the process, to be curious and sceptical, and how to view my deficiencies (bad taste) as an asset (a particular sensibility). I learned that the difference between nerdy and badass is level of commitment. I learned to like working from a place that is uncomfortable and unfamiliar. I also developed a very thick skin. I teach the same thing.

FAVOURITE FOOD NOW
Peaches in pie, in cobbler, in anything or just by themselves

YOUR MOST VALUED POSSESSION NOW
Not sure

Now

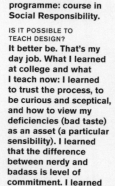

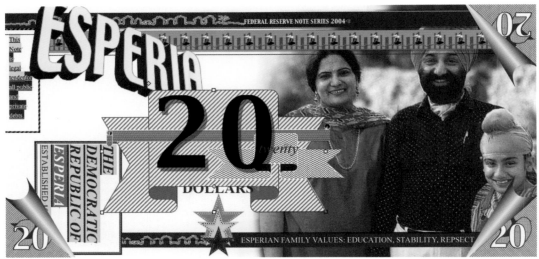

SWISS/SPANISH

Yves Fidalgo

Work hard + Don't work too much

YEAR OF PROJECT
2000

STUDENT PROJECT BRIEF
Design the annual poster presenting our school (competition)

COLLEGE
Ecole cantonale d'art de Lausanne (ECAL) (Switzerland)

TUTOR(S)
On my own for this project

TECHNOLOGY
Photography (Ekta), computer vector design, offset printing

TIME SPENT
1 week

TYPEFACE
Akzidenz Grotesk

WHY DO YOU LIKE THIS PROJECT?
The process (going to Spain with my father, following him on a hunting day).

WHAT DO YOU DISLIKE ABOUT IT?
The vector drawings.

OUTCOMES
No money.

FEEDBACK
Vector drawings on the pictures weren't necessary.

FAVOURITE FOOD THEN
Pasta

YOUR MOST VALUED POSSESSION THEN
My comics collection

Project Then

PROJECT SIMILARITIES THEN AND NOW
The process.

Yves Fidalgo (Fulguro)

For both: be hard-working

YEAR OF PROJECT
2010

PROFESSIONAL PROJECT BRIEF
Design the communication for a charitable exhibition about breast cancer

CLIENT
Ligue Vaudoise contre le Cancer

COLLABORATOR(S)
Cédric Decroux, my colleague at Fulguro

TECHNOLOGY
Photography (digital), paper, pens, computer, offset printing

TIME SPENT
6 months

TYPEFACE
Futura

WHY DO YOU LIKE THIS PROJECT?
The process (going to 20 artists' studios to take their picture, meeting them, getting to know them).

OUTCOMES
Money.

FEEDBACK
Good feedback in general.

FAVOURITE FOOD NOW
Pasta

YOUR MOST VALUED POSSESSION NOW
My bike

DO YOU TEACH?
Workshops in France (Lyon) for graphic and product design students.

IS IT POSSIBLE TO TEACH DESIGN?
If such things as design schools exist, it must be that design is taught in them. But if I remember correctly, you don't learn to be a designer at school.

Project Now

Ecole cantonale d'art de Lausanne

ANDREAS GNASS
(U9 VISUELLE ALLIANZ)

EDUCATION: Darmstadt (D), Hochschule Darmstadt, Diplom (Dipl.-Des. FH), Kommunikations-Design ARE YOU EMPLOYED OR SELF-EMPLOYED?: Self-employed PREVIOUS EMPLOYMENT: None ARCHITECTS/BUILDINGS THAT INFLUENCED YOU THEN/NOW: Mies van der Rohe / Hanns Malte Meyer MUSICIANS/ALBUMS THAT INFLUENCED YOU THEN/NOW: Uncountable ANY OTHER INFLUENCES THEN/NOW: Travelling DID YOU OWN ANY SORT OF COLLECTION THEN/NOW?: Vinyl / Vinyl and some pieces of art

ANDREW STEVENS
(GRAPHIC THOUGHT FACILITY)

EDUCATION: Sheffield (UK), Sheffield College, Bachelor of Technology (B.Tech), Graphic Design / Leeds (UK), Leeds Polytechnic, Bachelor of Arts (B.A.), Graphic Design / London (UK), Royal College of Art, Master of Arts (M.A.), Graphic Design ARE YOU EMPLOYED OR SELF-EMPLOYED?: Self-employed in own company PREVIOUS EMPLOYMENT: Always GTF DID YOU OWN ANY SORT OF COLLECTION THEN/NOW?: No

ANNELYS DE VET

EDUCATION: Utrecht (NL), HKU Hoge-school voor de Kunsten, Bachelor of Arts (B.A.), Graphic Design / Amsterdam (NL), Sandberg Instituut, Master of Arts (M.A.), Design and Fine Arts / Melbourne (AU), RMIT, Sculpture department, artist in residence ARE YOU EMPLOYED OR SELF-EMPLOYED?: Self-employed

ANTÓNIO SILVEIRA GOMES
(BARBARA SAYS…PROJECTO PRÓPRIO)

EDUCATION: Lisbon (PT), Faculdade de Belas Artes da Universidade de Lisboa (FBAUL), Communication Design / Lisbon (PT), Faculdade de Arquitectura Universidade Técnica de Lisboa, Post-graduate in Design, Communication Design ARE YOU EMPLOYED OR SELF-EMPLOYED?: Self-employed ARCHITECTS/BUILDINGS THAT INFLUENCED YOU THEN/NOW: Superstudio (Continuous Monument), Archizoom (mostly sci-fi architecture) / R. Buckminster Fuller (Dymaxion House and 'Bucky Balls'), Didier Fiuza Faustino (One Square Meter House and Stairway to Heaven) MUSICIANS/ALBUMS THAT INFLUENCED YOU THEN/NOW: John Zorn, Sprung aus den Wolken, His Name is Alive / John Cage, Gyorgy Ligeti, Karlheinz Stockhausen, Memorize The Sky, Les Troubadours du roi Baudouin – Missa Luba, The Books – The Lemon of Pink ANY OTHER INFLUENCES THEN/NOW: Robin Fior (Graphic designer, teacher and critic of Portuguese graphic design), Rigo 23 (Portuguese-born American artist), Paulo Ramalho (graphic designer and colleague teacher) DID YOU OWN ANY SORT OF COLLECTION THEN/NOW?: No / Rare books, encyclopedias and dictionaries of all sorts

BEN BRANAGAN

EDUCATION: Kingston (UK), Kingston University, Foundation Studies, Art & Design / Brighton (UK), University of Brighton, Bachelor of Arts (B.A. Hons) Graphic Design / London (UK), Royal College of Art, Master of Arts (M.A.), Communication Art & Design ARE YOU EMPLOYED OR SELF-EMPLOYED?: Self-employed PREVIOUS EMPLOYMENT:

Sea Design, Thomas.Matthews MUSICIANS/ALBUMS THAT INFLUENCED YOU THEN/NOW: Can (Tago Mago) / Robert Waytt, Bill Drummond (45) ANY OTHER INFLUENCES THEN/NOW: Idle afternoons with my friends Owen and Dan, Tutors: Frank Philipin (see also p. 256), Daniel Eatock (see also pp. 58–61), David Crowley, Andrzej Klimowski / Going to the park DID YOU OWN ANY SORT OF COLLECTION THEN/NOW?: Records / Books

BERND HILPERT
(UNIT-DESIGN)

EDUCATION: Darmstadt (D), Hochschule Darmstadt, Diplom (Dipl.-Des. FH) / Paris (F), ENSCI Les Ateliers, year studying abroad ARE YOU EMPLOYED OR SELF-EMPLOYED?: Managing director/partner in my own limited company PREVIOUS EMPLOYMENT: One employment and different engagements as freelancer ARCHITECTS/BUILDINGS THAT INFLUENCED YOU THEN/NOW: Architecture always inspired me most. Archigram, Jean Nouvel, Frei Otto, Dominique Perrault, Bernard Tschumi, Herzog & de Meuron, Ingenhoven, OMA (Rem Koolhaas), MVRDV, Sanaa, Wandel Hoefer Lorch, Meixner Schlüter Wendt and many others. MUSICIANS/ALBUMS THAT INFLUENCED YOU THEN/NOW: Electronic music, still ANY OTHER INFLUENCES THEN/NOW: I admire the perfection and clearness I find in nature's work DID YOU OWN ANY SORT OF COLLECTION THEN/NOW?: A collection of different design pieces / Collections on several issues – my source for research and inspiration PIECES OF DESIGN THAT INFLUENCE YOU NOW: Every day I see designs that have an effect on my projects. Now, I'm influenced by everyday objects, like an old wooden camping table from Romania (which can be packed very small!), a ceramic vase found in a 'brocante' in France, a Japanese lacquer painting, my old Caran d'Ache fixpencil, French tourist maps of the early 1930s (printed as lithography), a stone with a wonderful decor of lichens, …)

BRIAN WEBB
(WEBB & WEBB DESIGN)

EDUCATION: Liverpool (UK), Liverpool College of Art, Intermediate Technical Illustration, Pre Diploma / Canterbury (UK), Canterbury College of Art, Dip.AD ARE YOU EMPLOYED OR SELF-EMPLOYED?: Self-employed PREVIOUS EMPLOYMENT: Trickett and Webb 1971–2003, Derek Forsyth Partnership 1969–71, Michael Tucker4 and Associates 1967–69 ARCHITECTS/BUILDINGS THAT INFLUENCED YOU THEN/NOW: Frank Lloyd Wright, I. K. Brunel MUSICIANS/ALBUMS THAT INFLUENCED YOU THEN/NOW: 1930s Blues singers, Bob Dylan ANY OTHER INFLUENCES THEN/NOW: Edward Hughes at Canterbury, who introduced design as a problem-solving process / Lynn Trickett, we worked and argued together for 30 years DID YOU OWN ANY SORT OF COLLECTION THEN/NOW?: Ephemera, printed stuff, books / More expensive versions of the same

CHRISTIAN HEUSSER
(EQUIPO)

EDUCATION: Basel (CH), Hochschule für Gestaltung und Kunst Basel, Visual Communication, Visueller Gestalter FH

(Visual Designer FH) ARE YOU EMPLOYED OR SELF-EMPLOYED?: Self-employed in my own design studio with my partners Roman Schnyder and Dirk Koy PREVIOUS EMPLOYMENT: Büro für Kommunikationsdesign, Basel ARCHITECTS/BUILDINGS THAT INFLUENCED YOU THEN/NOW: Mies van der Rohe / Ted Mosby MUSICIANS/ALBUMS THAT INFLUENCED YOU THEN/NOW: Massive Attack (Unfinished Sympathy) / Idris Muhammad (Could Heaven Ever Be Like This) ANY OTHER INFLUENCES THEN/NOW: Gregory Vines, one of the best teachers I ever had / Other designers around me, in my own studio or from different small studios in Basel DID YOU OWN ANY SORT OF COLLECTION THEN/NOW?: Records (vinyl) / Many more records WHAT DO YOU DISLIKE ABOUT WORKING AS A DESIGNER?: That my own ego still gets in the way when dealing with clients – it is difficult not to consider the project as one's own artistic expression, instead having to put the clients' considerations first – the problem of sometimes being more of an artist than a provider of services

DANIEL EATOCK

EDUCATION: Ravensbourne (UK), Ravensbourne College of Design and Communication, Bachelor of Arts (B.A.), Graphic Design / London (UK), Royal College of Art, Master of Arts (M.A.), Graphic Design ARE YOU EMPLOYED OR SELF-EMPLOYED?: Self-employed PREVIOUS EMPLOYMENT: Walker Art Center, Minneapolis (USA) ARCHITECTS/BUILDINGS THAT INFLUENCED YOU THEN/NOW: Bedsit flat / Lacaton & Vassal MUSICIANS/ALBUMS THAT INFLUENCED YOU THEN/NOW: Nirvana, Camper Van Beethoven ANY OTHER INFLUENCES THEN/NOW: Rupert Bassett / Richard Torchia DID YOU OWN ANY SORT OF COLLECTION THEN/NOW?: Books / Books

DANIJELA DJOKIC
(PROJEKTTRIANGLE)

EDUCATION: Schwäbisch Gmünd (D), Hochschule für Gestaltung, Diplom-Designer (Dipl.-Des), Communication Design ARE YOU EMPLOYED OR SELF-EMPLOYED?: Self-employed and employed (Professor at Fachhochschule Potsdam (D)) ARCHITECTS/BUILDINGS THAT INFLUENCED YOU THEN/NOW: Tadao Ando / Erhardt+Bottega, Peter Zumthor MUSICIANS/ALBUMS THAT INFLUENCED YOU THEN/NOW: Grandmaster Flash, Prince, George Clinton, etc. / The same now ANY OTHER INFLUENCES THEN/NOW: Prof. Peter Vogt, Prof. Frank Zebner / Prof. Boris Müller, Prof. Frank Heidmann DID YOU OWN ANY SORT OF COLLECTION THEN/NOW?: No / Colors magazine

EMMI SALONEN
(STUDIO EMMI)

EDUCATION: Brighton (UK), University of Brighton, Bachelor of Arts (B.A.), Graphic Design ARE YOU EMPLOYED OR SELF-EMPLOYED?: Self-employed PREVIOUS EMPLOYMENT: None ARCHITECTS/BUILDINGS THAT INFLUENCED YOU THEN/NOW: Tadao Ando MUSICIANS/ALBUMS THAT INFLUENCED YOU THEN/NOW: Le Tigre, Gossip & The Locust / Gladiators, Gyptian & others DID YOU OWN ANY SORT OF COLLECTION THEN/NOW?: Notebooks

ÉRIC & MARIE GASPAR
(ÉRICANDMARIE)

EDUCATION: Lyon (F) (both), Martinière-Terreaux, BTS (Brevet de Technicien Supérieur), Visual Communication / Paris (F) (Marie only), ESAG (Ecole supérieure de design, d'art graphique et d'architecture intérieure), Foundation / Paris (F) (Eric only), Olivier de Serres, DSAA (Diplôme Supérieur en Arts Appliqués) / London (UK) (both), Central Saint Martins College of Art & Design, Bachelor of Arts (B.A.), Graphic Design / London (UK) (both), Royal College of Art, Master of Arts (M.A.), Communication Art & Design ARE YOU EMPLOYED OR SELF-EMPLOYED?: Self-employed PREVIOUS EMPLOYMENT: None ARCHITECTS/BUILDINGS THAT INFLUENCED YOU THEN/NOW: Herzog & de Meuron / Alvaro Siza MUSICIANS/ALBUMS THAT INFLUENCED YOU THEN/NOW: The American minimalists of the 1970s (Philip Glass, Meredith Monk, John Cage…) / Late 19th-century French composers (Debussy, Ravel, Satie…) ANY OTHER INFLUENCES THEN: Geoff Fowle, Al Rees

FONS HICKMANN
(FONS HICKMANN M23)

EDUCATION: Düsseldorf (D), Fachhochschule Düsseldorf, Photography and Communication Design / Wuppertal (D), Heinrich Heine Universität, Aesthetics and Media Theory ARE YOU EMPLOYED OR SELF-EMPLOYED?: Self-employed and employed (Professor at Universität der Künste Berlin, (D)) ARCHITECTS/BUILDINGS THAT INFLUENCED YOU THEN/NOW: Football pitches / Parking lots MUSICIANS/ALBUMS THAT INFLUENCED YOU THEN/NOW: Beatles (White Album) / Archives DID YOU OWN ANY SORT OF COLLECTION THEN/NOW?: Slips / Eggcups

HANS DIETER REICHERT
(HDR VISUAL COMMUNICATION)

EDUCATION: Iserlohn Letmathe (D), apprenticeship as a compositor / Dortmund (D), Fachhochschule für Gestaltung / Essen (D), Universität-Gesamthochschule Essen and Wuppertal, Communication Design, Vor-Diplom / Basel (CH), Allgemeine Gewerbeschule Basel, Grafik Design / London (UK), University of the Arts, London College of Communication, Media and Production Design, Bachelor of Arts (B.A.) / London (UK), University for the Creative Arts (UCA), Visual Communication, Master of Arts (M.A. Honorary Degree) ARE YOU EMPLOYED OR SELF-EMPLOYED?: Self-employed PREVIOUS EMPLOYMENT: Total Design bv. (Amsterdam), BRS maatschap van vormgevers bv (Amsterdam), Banks and Miles (London, Hamburg, Brussels), Consultant to UCA (University for the Creative Arts) ARCHITECTS/BUILDINGS THAT INFLUENCED YOU THEN/NOW: Walter Gropius, Mart Stam, Max Bill, Frank Lloyd Wright, Alvar Aalto, Mies van der Rohe, Le Corbusier / Norman Foster, Renzo Piano, Shigeru Ban, Tony Fretton, Michael Hopkins, Peter Zumthor, Bernard Tschumi, Will Alsop, Herzog & de Meuron MUSICIANS/ALBUMS THAT INFLUENCED YOU THEN/NOW: Hannes Wader, Konstantin Wecker, Marius Müller-Westernhagen, Santana, Randy Crawford, Eric Clapton, Leonard Cohen, Neil Young, Bob Dylan, Bob Marley, Deep Purple, Black Sabbath, Kraftwerk, UFO / Coldplay, Lonnie

Donegan, Keith Jarrett, Lee Morgan, Ry Cooder, Gorillaz, Jackson Browne, James Taylor, Company Segundo, Sarod Maestro Amjad Ali Khan, Al di Meola, George Benson, Weather Report, Joni Mitchell, Astrud Gilberto, Stan Getz, Ali Farka Touré, B. B. King, Thelonious Monk, John Coltrane, Charlie Parker, Louis Armstrong, Youssou N'Dour, Tinariwen, Errol Garner, Lou Reed, Capercaillie (Scottish Gaelic folk music), Dubliners ANY OTHER INFLUENCES THEN/NOW: Music, nature, Dutch and English design, Willy Fleckhaus, fellow students, Brian Grimbley, Anthony Froshaug, Günter Gerhard Lange, Adrain Frutiger, 8vo / Nature, music, film, environment, Internet, Michael Twyman, Alan Fletcher DID YOU OWN YOUR SORT OF COLLECTION THEN/NOW?: Magazines, music tapes and records / Music CDs, books, printed ephemera, posters, prints, tools DESIGNERS THAT INFLUENCE YOU NOW: Jan Tschichold, Dieter Rams, Anthony Froshaug, Otl Aicher, Helmut Schmid, Derek Birdsall, Irma Boom, North, Harry Beck, Paul Lohse, Wolfgang Schmidt, Paul Rand, Jost Hochuli

HOLGER JACOBS
(MIND DESIGN)

EDUCATION: Cologne (D), Universität Köln, Linguistics and Philosophy / Essen (D), University of Essen, Pre-Diploma, Communication Design / London (UK), Central Saint Martins College of Art & Design, Bachelor of Arts (B.A. Hons), Graphic Design / London (UK), Royal College of Art, Master of Arts (M.A.), Graphic Design ARE YOU EMPLOYED OR SELF-EMPLOYED?: Self-employed and employed (Visiting Professor of Typography at the Fachhochschule Düsseldorf (D)) PREVIOUS EMPLOY-MENT: Art director at a publishing company in Tokyo (JP) ARCHITECTS/BUILDINGS THAT INFLUENCED YOU THEN/NOW: Modernist buildings / Art Deco buildings MUSICIANS/ALBUMS THAT INFLUENCED YOU THEN/NOW: Sex Pistols ANY OTHER INFLUENCES THEN/NOW: I was reading a lot about linguistics and post-structuralism. Japan, the culture and the writing system became a big influence even though I did not visit the country until after graduation / Our client Tom Dixon inspired me to explore different materials and to consider the production process as an essential part of the design DID YOU OWN ANY SORT OF COLLECTION THEN/NOW?: Fonts (I printed a specs sheet for every font I had on my computer), cassette tapes from the 1980s / Still fonts (but I lost the overview), ridiculously cute Japanese stationery, rare bicycle parts HOW DO/DID YOU DEVELOP/RESEARCH AN IDEA THEN/NOW?: I spent a lot of time in the library while in college. Projects were long and complex and research was everything. I even got my first (and only) job when I met the publisher of one of the books I used a lot in my research / I still do research but more sporadically and there is no systematic approach or strategy behind it. I learned to trust sudden inspiration that can come from anywhere. Usually I walk around with the brief in my head for a while and see what happens. I do not believe that there is only one best 'solution' to a brief that evolves as a logical conclusion from research.

A more personal and random approach may scare the client, but often produces more original results

HOON KIM
(WHY NOT SMILE)

EDUCATION: Providence (USA), Rhode Island School of Design, Master of Fine Arts (M.F.A), Graphic Design / Seoul (KR), Seoul National University, Bachelor of Fine Arts (B.F.A.), Visual Communication Design / Providence (USA), Brown University, Teaching Certificate ARE YOU EMPLOYED OR SELF-EMPLOYED?: Self-employed PREVIOUS EMPLOYMENT: Museum of Modern Art – MoMA (New York, USA), Practise (London, UK) (see also pp. 98–101), Crosspoint (Seoul, KR), Imagedome (Seoul, KR), Samsung Design Membership (Seoul, KR) ARCHITECTS/BUILDINGS THAT INFLUENCED YOU THEN/NOW: Maya Lin / Yoshiharu Tsukamoto and Momoyo Kaijima (Atelier Bow-Wow), Brooklyn Bridge DID YOU OWN ANY SORT OF COLLECTION THEN/NOW?: I collected flight sick bags and still do / I like to pick up random small pieces of paper making patterns on the street HOW DID/DO YOU DEVELOP/RESEARCH AN IDEA THEN/NOW?:I used to research related fields to gain a good understanding between those and graphic design. In addition, both the positive and negative feedback of colleagues and teachers was always helpful to keep on the right track. How to screen a lot of information is up to the student's ability – I have learned that through various projects / Basically, clients and co-workers develop an idea together. I still study related disciplines by reading books and Googling to avoid assumptions that might lead to nonsense outcomes

HYOUN YOUL JOE
(HEY JOE)

EDUCATION: Seoul (KR), Dankook University, B.F.A. Visual Communication Design / New Haven (USA), Yale University, M.F.A., Graphic Design ARE YOU EMPLOYED OR SELF-EMPLOYED?: Self-employed PREVIOUS EMPLOYMENT: None DID YOU OWN ANY SORT OF COLLECTION THEN/NOW?: Graphic designers' works / Flyers, cards, product packages, and lots of graphic design stuff that I found on the street. WOULD YOU STILL HAVE BECOME A DESIGNER IF YOU KNEW WHAT YOU KNOW NOW?: Yes, I am enjoying what I am doing now. Actually, I wanted to be an artist and still have a desire to be an artist since artists have their own voice, while most of a graphic designer's job focuses on form and creating the container for contents than on creating their own voice. Nonetheless, I feel that I enjoy making form, no matter what the form is for DESIGNERS THAT INFLUENCED YOU THEN/NOW: Anh Graphics, Doosup Kim, Helmut Schmid, Hong Design, Image & Imagination, Kohei Sugiura, Matsuda Yukimasa, Sangsoo Ahn, S/O Project, Strike-Communication, Sulki & Min, Vi-nyl, Wolfgang Weingart, Workroom / Antoni Muntadas, Daniel Eatock (see pp. 58–61), Daniel Harding + Tomas Celizna, Daniel van der Velden, Experimental Jetset, Hans Gremmen, Helmut Smits, Lehni-Trüb (see pp. 214–217), Mevis en Van Deursen, Na Kim, Min Oh, Julia Born, Karel Martens, Paul Elliman, Sara De Bondt, Sheila Levrant de Bretteville, Sulki & Min, Roel Wouters, Workroom

ISABELLE SWIDERSKI
(SEVEN25)

EDUCATION: Ottawa (CA), La Cité Collégiale, Foundation, Graphic Design / Vancouver (CA), Emily Carr Institute of Art + Design, Bachelor of Arts (B.A.), Communication Design / London (UK), Royal College of Art, Master of Arts (M.A.), Communication Design ARE YOU EMPLOYED OR SELF-EMPLOYED?: Employed by my own studio (with two other employees) ARCHITECTS/BUILDINGS THAT INFLUENCED YOU THEN/NOW: Not so much / Rem Koolhaas, Zaha Hadid MUSICIANS/ALBUMS THAT INFLUENCED YOU THEN/NOW: ABBA to Yazz, Madonna to Danny Tenaglia with a dash of jazz / Armin Van Buuren to Beethoven, 2Pac to The Script to Gaga ANY OTHER INFLUENCES THEN/NOW: My somewhat culturally mixed childhood (Canada and France) / Teaching design & studying film DID YOU OWN ANY SORT OF COLLECTION THEN/NOW?: Music CDs / Cameras (analogue)

JAMES GOGGIN
(PRACTISE)

EDUCATION: Pontypridd (UK), Mid Glamorgan Centre for Art & Design, Diploma in Foundation Studies, Art & Design) / London (UK), Ravensbourne College of Design & Communication, Bachelor of Arts (B.A. Hons), Visual Communication / London (UK), Royal College of Art, Master of Arts (M.A.), Graphic Design ARE YOU EMPLOYED OR SELF-EMPLOYED?: Self-employed (1999–2010), employed (2009–2012). Currently Design Director at Museum of Contemporary Art, Chicago (USA) PREVIOUS EMPLOYMENT: Werkplaats Typografie (Arnhem, NL), ECAL – Ecole cantonale d'art de Lausanne (CH) ARCHITECTS/BUILDINGS THAT INFLUENCED YOU THEN/NOW: Rem Koolhaas (OMA), Foreign Office Architects, Caruso St. John, Archigram / Louis Kahn, Alison & Peter Smithson, Denys Lasdun, James Stirling, David Kohn, Cedric Price, 6a Architects, SANAA, Walter Netsch, Tony Fretton, Sergison Bates MUSICIANS/ALBUMS THAT INFLUENCED YOU THEN/NOW: Kraftwerk, Yo La Tengo, Pavement, St. Etienne, Wu-Tang Clan, Pan Sonic, Carsten Nicolai, Ryoji Ikeda, The Pastels, among others / The above, plus labels more than specific musicians: Stones Throw, Häpna, Kranky, Rune Grammofon, Geographic, Hyperdub, R&S, Wax Trax, among others ANY OTHER INFLUENCES THEN/NOW: Cultural studies, anthropology, Japan, colour theory, cartography / Politics, critical theory, environmentalism DID YOU OWN ANY SORT OF COLLECTION THEN/NOW: Stencils, snowglobes / Stencils, books, art WHAT WOULD YOU DO TODAY IF YOU STOPPED DESIGNING?: I would just read all day. I don't think I'll stop designing, but I often think about finding a different system in which to operate as a designer, outside of the studio/client/designer model. My move to a museum is one step in this quest. DESIGNERS WHO INFLUENCED YOU THEN: Charles & Ray Eames, Michael Marriott, Karel Martens, Graphic Thought Facility (see also pp. 30–33), Ettore Sottsass, Mevis & Van Deursen, Ikko Tanaka, Scott King ARTISTS/WORKS OF ART THAT INFLUENCE YOU NOW: See then (p. 242), plus a seemingly infinite list that could include Nathan Coley, Dora García, Leonor Antunes,

Tauba Auerbach, Simon Starling, Martin Boyce, Goshka Macuga, John Baldessari, Wallace Berman, Michelangelo Pistoletto

JAN WILKER
(KARLSSONWILKER)

EDUCATION: Stuttgart (D), Staatliche Akademie der Bildenen Künste, Diplom, Graphic-Design ARE YOU EMPLOYED OR SELF-EMPLOYED?: Self-employed PREVIOUS EMPLOYMENT: Two internships during design school (Jung von Matt, Sagmeister Inc. (see also pp. 202–205), no other previous employment MUSICIANS/ ALBUMS THAT INFLUENCED YOU THEN/NOW: Putte & Edgar, Queens of the Stone Age / Caribou, DJ Koze ANY OTHER INFLUENCES THEN/NOW: The people who are close to me

JULIE GAYARD
(JUTOJO)

EDUCATION: London (UK), Chelsea College Of Art, Foundation Studies, Art & Design / London (UK), Camberwell College Of Arts, Bachelor of Arts (B.A.), Visual Communication / London (UK), Royal College Of Art, Master of Arts (M.A.), Grapic Design, not completed ARE YOU EMPLOYED OR SELF-EMPLOYED?: Self-employed PREVIOUS EMPLOYMENT: None ARCHITECTS/BUILDINGS THAT INFLUENCED YOU THEN/NOW: Archigram / Treehouses MUSICIANS/ALBUMS THAT INFLUENCED YOU THEN/NOW: Massive Attack, Portishead, Mo' Wax Records, Beastie Boys, Sonic Youth, Stereolab (all for the music AND the artwork) and many more / Sonic Youth, Stereolab, Honest Johns Records (for the music AND the artwork), Moondog and many more ANY OTHER INFLUENCES THEN/ NOW: Friends who were studying with me (Ed Gill, Vassilis Marmatakis, Christina Christoforou, Clare Shilland, Dana Levy, Will Bankhead) and some of their influences (skateboarding and graffiti), my father Patrice Gayard (art director in the 1970s in Paris), tutor Scott King / Still the same as then and some contemporaries and studios in Berlin, London, Holland DID YOU OWN ANY SORT OF COLLECTION THEN/NOW?: Records HOW DO YOU RESEARCH/DEVELOP AN IDEA NOW?: Talking to the client about the product and its context. Writing, drawing in a sketchbook, researching on the Internet. Trying out typefaces. Talking to the printer about unusual ways of making things – within the restrictions of the budget

KAI VON RABENAU
(MONO.GRAPHIE)

EDUCATION: London (UK), Camberwell College of Arts, Foundation / London (UK), Central Saint Martins, Bachelor of Arts (B.A.), Graphic Design / London (UK), Royal College of Art, Master of Arts (M.A.), Communication, Art & Design ARE YOU EMPLOYED OR SELF-EMPLOYED?: Self-employed PREVIOUS EMPLOYMENT: Always self-employed ARCHITECTS/BUILDINGS THAT INFLUENCED YOU THEN/NOW: Herzog & de Meuron, Peter Zumthor MUSICIANS/ALBUMS THAT INFLUENCED YOU THEN/NOW: Autechre, Nine Inch Nails, Radiohead / Carsten Nicolai, Talk Talk, Nine Inch Nails ANY OTHER INFLUENCES THEN/NOW: Travel DID YOU OWN ANY SORT OF COLLECTION THEN/NOW?: No / Magazines and photography books

KEN GARLAND

EDUCATION: London (UK), John Cass College, National Diploma Art & Design (NDAD) / London (UK), Central School of Arts & Crafts, National Diploma Art & Design (NDAD), Central Dipl. ARE YOU EMPLOYED OR SELF-EMPLOYED?: Self-employed PREVIOUS EMPLOYMENT: Too many to list ARCHITECTS/ BUILDINGS THAT INFLUENCED YOU THEN/NOW: Royal Festival Hall MUSICIANS/ALBUMS THAT INFLUENCED YOU THEN/NOW: Rolling Stones ANY OTHER INFLUENCES THEN/NOW: Jesse Collins and Anthony Froshaug

KIRSTY CARTER
(A PRACTICE FOR EVERYDAY LIFE)

EDUCATION: Cambridge (UK), Cambridge Regional College, Foundation Diploma, Art & Design / Brighton (UK), College: University of Brighton, Bachelor of Arts (B.A. Hons), Graphic Design / Nagoya (JP), Nagoya University of Arts (NUA), 6-month scholarship during University of Brighton, Graphic Design / London (UK), Royal College of Art, Master of Arts (M.A.), Communication Art & Design ARE YOU EMPLOYED OR SELF-EMPLOYED?: Self-employed PREVIOUS EMPLOYMENT: Only ever worked for myself, started A Practice for Everyday Life straight after college GENERAL COMMENT ON ALL THE QUESTIONS ABOUT INFLUENCES: Writing down influences is very difficult, as there are so many influences over time and things/people that I read/saw/or listened to many years ago that still influence me now. I tried to choose just one person/thing per question to keep my answers short, but endless books, writers, buildings, artists and musicians influence me ARCHITECTS/BUILDINGS THAT INFLUENCED YOU THEN/NOW: Eames House (Case Study House No. 8) by Charles & Ray Eames / The Hepworth Wakefield by David Chipperfield. It's difficult to think of any other building that has influenced our studio so much (we even drew a typeface for it!); he was a client and is also a fantastic architect MUSICIANS/ALBUMS THAT INFLUENCED YOU THEN/NOW: Blur (The Universal) and Pulp (Common People). I was a teenager growing up in England in the 1990s; these are the two most influential bands of my generation. These two songs would make it into my eight Desert Island Discs (Desert Island Discs is a long-running BBC Radio 4 programme, first broadcast on 29 January 1942. Each week, a guest, or 'castaway', is asked to choose eight pieces of music, a book and a luxury item for their imaginary stay on the island, while discussing their lives and the reasons for their choices. In the studio, the six members of A Practice for Everyday Life prepared their own 'Desert Island Discs'). I spend a lot of time in Gothenburg in Sweden, and Fever Ray's (aka Karin Drejer Andersoon) music is part of this city. I went to see her at a concert in Brixton last year. That might have been the best concert I have ever been to – incredible stage set, lights and odd lyrics. ANY OTHER INFLUENCES THEN/NOW: Emma Thomas (fellow student) at the Royal College / Emma Thomas (my partner in A Practice for Everyday Life) – she is and will always be my biggest influence DID YOU OWN ANY SORT OF COLLECTION THEN/NOW?: I think every designer is a collector; I have lots of collections of sorts tucked away in boxes or on my shelves. Though I must say, I am not a hoarder – the people in my studio get a little annoyed with me, as I am always trying to chuck things out. I don't like mess or chaos and things can eventually weigh you down. I don't own many possessions; what I do own is carefully considered. This has always been the same YOUR FAVOURED MODE OF TRANSPORT THEN: In Brighton, I lived a stone's throw away from the university where I studied, and I walked every morning along the seafront. I couldn't think of a nicer place to study; it was such a perfect place to study and a lot of fun. During my studies at the Royal College, I lived in East London and cycled 6 miles every day across central London, day in, day out, in all weathers; I can't say I enjoyed it. I love cycling and it is always my first chosen form of transport, but that journey was hard WOULD YOU STILL HAVE BECOME A DESIGNER IF YOU KNEW WHAT YOU KNOW NOW?: Yes! I love being a designer; anyway, I am not very good at anything else, other subjects at school were quite a struggle; art and design were subjects I was very good at at school. My parents are not in creative industries, but their interest grew when they realized they had a little aspiring artist as their daughter and took me to museums and galleries from an early age HOURS SPENT DESIGNING PER DAY THEN/NOW: I think about design and our projects all the time, it's an enormous part of my life, which I am sure is the case for most designers. In terms of physical brainstorming, making, meetings and managing the studio, I would say I work 65 hours a week. The way I work hasn't changed since I was a student – I was very dedicated and hard-working, I worked similar hours HOW DID/DO YOU DEVELOP/RESEARCH AN IDEA THEN/NOW?: Research is key to a successful project or idea; we spend a great deal of time doing it, whether it's a trip to the British Library or a visit to the Barbara Hepworth Garden in St. Ives, time and research is absolutely essential. This hasn't changed since I was a student; I feel my design process has been exactly the same for 13 years (since starting my degree); the only thing that has changed is that there is a client now

KRISTINE MATTHEWS
(STUDIO MATTHEWS)

EDUCATION: Seattle (USA), University of Washington, Bachelor of Fine Arts (B.F.A), Graphic Design / London (UK), Royal College of Art, Master of Arts (M.A.), Communication Design ARE YOU EMPLOYED OR SELF-EMPLOYED?: Self-employed and employed (Assistant Professor in Visual Communication Design, University of Washington, Seattle (USA)) PREVIOUS EMPLOYMENT: thomas.matthews (London, UK) – founder and joint-director, Royal College of Art (London, UK), The Traver Company (Seattle, USA), Edquist Design (Seattle USA) ARCHITECTS/ BUILDINGS THAT INFLUENCED YOU THEN/NOW: Charles & Ray Eames, Herzog & de Meuron / Tom Kundig, Alan Kitching (Olson Kundig Architects), Rem Koolhaas, Weiss/Manfredi (landscape architects of Seattle's Olympic Sculpture Park), Oskar Shindler, Neutra MUSICIANS/ALBUMS THAT INFLUENCED YOU THEN/NOW: Liz Phair, Pixies, Cake / Matthew Herbert, The Dodos, and I still listen to Yo La Tengo, Pavement and Bell Helicopter ANY OTHER INFLUENCES THEN/NOW: Living in London, on a course with 25 students from 18 different countries / Teaching design at a university with faculties from all different backgrounds

LARS HARMSEN
(MAGMA BRAND DESIGN)

EDUCATION: Saarbrücken (D), Werbeagentur M&D, Vocational Training in Prepress Repro / Basel (CH), Kunstgewerbeschule Basel, I left the college before the end of the first year / Pforzheim (D), Hochschule Pforzheim, Diplom-Designer (Dipl.-Des.), Graphic Design ARE YOU EMPLOYED OR SELF-EMPLOYED?: Self-employed and employed (Professor at Fachhochschule Dortmund (D)) ARCHITECTS/ BUILDINGS THAT INFLUENCED YOU THEN/NOW: Frank Gehry / Peter Zumthor MUSICIANS/ALBUMS THAT INFLUENCED YOU THEN/NOW: David Bowie, Pavement, Primal Scream, Style Council, Jane's Addiction, Prince, some heavy metal… / Coldplay, Moby, electronic stuff,… and all the music I loved to hear when I was a student ANY OTHER INFLUENCES THEN/NOW: Travelling DID YOU OWN ANY SORT OF COLLECTION THEN/NOW?: Old keys / Passports and identities WHAT DO YOU LIKE ABOUT WORKING AS A DESIGNER?: Working with the people in my studio; I am very happy to have such great partners – Uli Weiß and Florian Gaertner. Making things happen, having ideas and trying to make them work, that's what we do all day WOULD YOU STILL HAVE BECOME A DESIGNER IF YOU KNEW WHAT YOU KNOW NOW?: No, I don't think so. My dream was to be a bush pilot. Seriously. But at that time you had to go into the army to be a pilot. I did my civilian service – I was and am still a militant anti-militarist. Now I am a designer, I love to travel, looking for the unexpected. I hate to make plans when I travel

LAURENT LACOUR
(HAUSER LACOUR)

EDUCATION: Offenbach am Main (D), Hochschule für Gestaltung (HFG), Diploma (Dipl.-Designer), Visual Communication ARE YOU EMPLOYED OR SELF-EMPLOYED?: Self-employed by my own studio and employed (Professor at Fachhochschule Düsseldorf (D)) PREVIOUS EMPLOYMENT: Freelance for Intégral Ruedi Baur (CH/D/F), Heine/Lenz/Zizka (D), Surface (D) ARCHITECTS/ BUILDINGS THAT INFLUENCED YOU THEN/NOW: Herzog & de Meuron / Alvar Aalto MUSICIANS/ALBUMS THAT INFLUENCED YOU THEN/NOW: J. S. Bach / Chilly Gonzales ANY OTHER INFLUENCES THEN/NOW: Brazilian culture / Modern artists like Tobias Rehberger, Thomas Zipp DID YOU OWN ANY SORT OF COLLECTION THEN/NOW?: Stickers, sea shells, gemstones (all then, as a child)

LIZA ENEBEIS
(STUDIO DUMBAR)

EDUCATION: Paris (F), Parsons School of Design, Bachelor of Arts (B.A.), Communication Design / London (UK), Royal College of Art, Master of Arts (M.A.), Graphic Design ARE YOU EMPLOYED OR SELF-EMPLOYED?: Both PREVIOUS EMPLOYMENT: Pentagram (London, UK) ARCHITECTS/BUILDINGS THAT INFLUENCED YOU THEN/NOW: Luis Barragan, Le Corbusier, Zaha Hadid, Rem Koolhaas, Peter Zumthor ANY OTHER INFLUENCES THEN/NOW: Everything and everyone DID YOU OWN ANY SORT OF COLLECTION THEN/NOW?: Yes – I collect books on all sorts of topics: bibles, Snoopy, flower-arranging, street maps, atlases, primitive art, design, photography, etiquette. And I still keep my old discontinued collections from my childhood such as sugar bags, rocks, match boxes, stamps, coins, stationery, napkins, erasers, pencils, stuffed animals

LUCINDA NEWTON-DUNN
(SPACE-TO-THINK)

EDUCATION: London (UK), London Guildhall University, Sir John Cass Faculty of Arts, BTEC Diploma Foundation Studies, Art & Design / London (UK), Camberwell College of Arts, Bachelor of Arts Joint Honours Degree (B.A. Hons), Graphics/Fine Art / London (UK), Royal College of Art, Master of Arts (M.A.), Graphic Design ARE YOU EMPLOYED OR SELF-EMPLOYED?: Self-employed PREVIOUS EMPLOYMENT: I have worked freelance pretty much ever since college, starting at Ralph Appelbaum Associates (London, UK), then continuing to work in graphic design, photography, moving image and printed textiles, for various clients in England, Tokyo and the USA ARCHITECTS/BUILDINGS THAT INFLUENCED YOU THEN/NOW: Tadao Ando / Japanese traditional architecture, modernist and mid-century modern architecture MUSICIANS/ALBUMS THAT INFLUENCED YOU THEN/NOW: Interested in some more experimental ideas from artists such as John Cage. Various classical music and Ninja Tunes, Bjork, The Cardigans / I don't make much time for music these days. I mostly listen to radio programmes on KCRW/public radio, and still enjoy a bit of classical and the choice selection of music I hear my husband play ANY OTHER INFLUENCES THEN/NOW: My family, friends, some tutors, environments, museums / Being a parent, my husband, children's play and toys such as Naef and Galt (1970s) etc., Japanese culture, fashion, design blogs, environments, interiors, mid-century modern furniture DID YOU OWN ANY SORT OF COLLECTION THEN/NOW?: Collections of found objects usually off the street, collections of my photos and small sketchbooks / Collections of paper off-cuts, small plastic objects, fabrics, tenugui (printed Japanese cotton towels), a catalogue of endless photos I shoot from day to day. No art or design collection yet, apart from many art and design books and magazines and a few interesting posters WHAT DO YOU LIKE ABOUT WORKING AS A DESIGNER?: I truly love what I do and it comes from the core, so the fact that I have the opportunity to express myself and make beautiful things is amazing. I love the explorative process and I love that I can take things I notice in everyday life and filter them into my work. I enjoy balancing working within design boundaries and the challenge of answering a brief, with work that retains a certain amount of creative freedom. This is where I sit on the fence between being an artist and being a designer WHAT DO YOU DISLIKE ABOUT WORKING AS A DESIGNER?: I dislike that I cannot easily separate my work from my day-to-day life, which can be an emotional strain. Design is often undervalued and generally badly paid. Also working on the more 'arty' side of design doesn't pay off business-wise! HOW DID/DO YOU DEVELOP/ RESEARCH AN IDEA?: Pretty much the same process creatively then and now – it varies from project to project, but basically I strip a brief down to the basics, look up literal meanings, try to view something from a different angle. Write notes and diagrams, go off on tangents and come back again. Try to move away from the computer and get hands-on with things (recently with drawing and using collage), even when it takes me back to a digital output. I take lots of photos and go through my catalogue of photographs for inspiration, colour and composition references. Now I am more aware of working with the client and their needs and making compromises, so a lot of development comes from dicussion. More research is required now into production – how, where and cost, etc. DESIGNERS THAT INFLUENCED YOU THEN: No particular influences. I've always been inspired by a general mixture of styles and approaches. Names that come to mind: Josef Müller-Brockmann, John Maeda, Graphic Thought Facility (see also pp. 30–33)

MAKI SUZUKI (ÅBÄKE)

EDUCATION: Paris (F), École supérieure d'arts graphiques et d'architecture intérieure (ESAG), Foundation course / Paris (F), École nationale supérieure des Arts Décoratifs (EnsAD), Bachelor of Arts (B. A.) / London (UK), Royal College of Art, Master of Arts (M. A.), Communication Art & Design ARE YOU EMPLOYED OR SELF-EMPLOYED?: Self-employed as part of a partnership of 4 people ARCHITECTS/BUILDINGS THAT INFLUENCED YOU THEN/NOW: Archigram, Tadao Ando / R&sie MUSICIANS/ALBUMS THAT INFLUENCED YOU THEN/NOW: Pretty Hate Machine, Trent Reznor / Kurt Cobain, still ANY OTHER INFLUENCES THEN/NOW: I can't remember / Andy Kaufman, Thor Heyerdahl, Emile Ajar, David Attenborough, Subcomandante Marcos DID YOU OWN ANY SORT OF COLLECTION THEN/NOW?: Records, comics, art ephemera / Tautological objects or things that are errors or aberrations YOUR FAVOURITE FOOD THEN: Being French and being a vegetarian was a national joke… Studying at the Royal College of Art (London, UK) where many cosmopolitan truths collide, I met Glaswegian and Swedish non-meat eaters who proved me wrong and I have been pescetarian since ARTISTS/ WORKS OF ART THAT INFLUENCE YOU: Today the people we work with influence us: Aurélien Froment, Ryan Gander, Benoit Maire, Johanna Billing. Someone we have not worked with but shared a residency with and understood the brilliance of: Jean-Luc Moulène

MARC VAN DER HEIJDE (STUDIO DUMBAR)

EDUCATION: Breda (NL), Academy of Art and Design St. Joost, Bachelor of Arts (B. A.), Graphic Design ARE YOU EMPLOYED OR SELF-EMPLOYED?: Employed PREVIOUS EMPLOYMENT: Barlock (The Hague, NL), Total Design (Brussels, BE), NS Design (Utrecht, NL) ARCHITECTS/BUILDINGS THAT INFLUENCED YOU THEN/NOW: Frank Lloyd Wright, The Jewish Museum in Berlin by Daniel Libeskind MUSICIANS/ ALBUMS THAT INFLUENCED YOU THEN/ NOW: Richard Strauss (Vier letzte Lieder), Jessye Norman, Nick Drake (Five Leaves Left) ANY OTHER INFLUENCES THEN/NOW: Close friends and colleagues have always been the biggest influence on me – logically, as these are the people you spend most of your time with. But also because the things we discuss really matter, they go deep DID YOU OWN ANY SORT OF COLLECTION THEN/NOW?: During my studies, I started a classical music collection that has become quite extensive over the years. It now covers a range of nine centuries of music. I also love books about typography and lettering HOW DID/DO YOU DEVELOP/ RESEARCH AN IDEA?: There is no one way. You might want to approach an idea from a visual angle, or very much from a textual one (to deliberately avoid starting with images). In the end, the way you start is not even the most important issue. Keeping an open mind throughout is much more the key to good development or research. Mind-mapping can provide some structure, without the danger of restrictions PIECES OF DESIGN THAT INFLUENCED YOU: Within the context of the student work (see p. 148) I have selected the typographical posters of Ton Homburg (Opera) for the Apollohuis Eindhoven. Two examples of his work are part of the collection of the Museum of Modern Art, New York. Not his best pieces I think, but it is difficult to find better images from that period. That's a shame, because he made beautiful stuff that captured experimental music in typography

MARGARET CALVERT

EDUCATION: London (UK), Chelsea College of Art, National Design Diploma (NDD), Illustration ARE YOU EMPLOYED OR SELF-EMPLOYED?: Self-employed PREVIOUS EMPLOYMENT: Joined Jock Kinneir (London, UK) immediately after completing my NDD course at Chelsea School of Art, in the late 1950s. Worked on the signing system for Britain's new motorways, soon to be followed by the entire network. The partnership continued through the 1960s, focusing on more signing systems and corporate identities. Kinneir Calvert Tuhill was formed in 1971. Since Jock Kinneir's retirement, I have worked independently ARCHITECTS/BUILDINGS THAT INFLUENCED YOU THEN/NOW: Pirelli Building, Milan, I (Gio Ponti) / St Pancras London, UK (Gilbert Scott) DID YOU OWN ANY SORT OF COLLECTION THEN/NOW?: Only memories and objects relating to them HOW DO YOU DEVELOP/RESEARCH AN IDEA?: I start with the idea, then follow through with research, if applicable; usually within my own head, depending on the project. Eventually however, I check something out; it could be the meaning of a word, an image in a book, or information on the Internet

MARION FINK

EDUCATION: Würzburg (D) Fachhochschule Würzburg, Architecture (1 year) / Schwäbisch Gmünd (D), Hochschule für Gestaltung, Visual Communication, Diploma (Dipl.-Designer) / London (UK), Royal College of Art, Master of Arts (M. A.), Graphic Design ARE YOU EMPLOYED OR SELF-EMPLOYED?: Employed (Professor at Basel School of Design, CH) with temporary additional freelance projects PREVIOUS EMPLOYMENT: Pentagram (London, UK), Meta Design (Berlin, D), KMS Team (Munich, D) MUSICIANS/ALBUMS THAT INFLUENCED YOU THEN/NOW: Philip Glass, Depeche Mode, Nightmares on Wax, Archive, Urbs, Nouvelle Vague, Coco Rosie, Ryuichi Sakamoto

MARTIN LORENZ (TWOPOINTS.NET)

EDUCATION: Darmstadt (D), Hochschule Darmstadt, Diplom-Designer (Dipl.-Des. FH), Visual Communication) / The Hague (NL), Royal Academy of Arts, Bachelor of Arts (B. A.), Graphic- and Typographic Design / Barcelona (ES), Universitat de Barcelona, Master of Arts (M. A.), Design ARE YOU EMPLOYED OR SELF-EMPLOYED?: Self-employed CURRENT AND/OR PREVIOUS EMPLOYMENT: Partner at Constructing Communication (Barcelona, ES), lecturer at Elisava Design School (Barcelona, ES), editor at The One Weekend Book Series (Barcelona, ES), guest lecturer at Hochschule für Künste Bremen (D), guest lecturer at Willem de Kooning Academie (Rotterdam, NL), lecturer at IED Barcelona (ES), lecturer at IDEP Institut Superior de Disseny (Barcelona, ES), creative director at Hort (Berlin, D) GENERAL COMMENT ON ALL THE QUESTIONS WITHIN THE BOOK ABOUT INFLUENCES: I never really thought any designer was THE influence for me, but it would be dumb to say that there aren't any influences. Growing as a designer means a daily struggle with rules and ideas – the rules established by others and yourself. During studying, the strongest influences are teachers and colleagues, who are influenced by others too. In the pre-Internet era, during which I studied, local design tradition still played an important role. So I guess I am pretty much influenced by the post-Ulm, post-Basel and contemporary Dutch design, instead of being influenced by any particular designer, piece of design, book, artist, architect, film, TV, director, musician or album. ARCHITECTS/BUILDINGS THAT INFLUENCED YOU THEN/NOW: Mies van der Rohe / Hannes Meyer MUSICIANS/ALBUMS THAT INFLUENCED YOU THEN/NOW: Camp Lo / Gonja Sufi ANY OTHER INFLUENCES THEN/NOW: Sandra Hoffmann (see pp. 194–197), Christian Pfestorf, Petr van Blokland, Peter Verheul, Michel Hoogervoorst,… I am sure I am forgetting many DID YOU OWN ANY SORT OF COLLECTION THEN/NOW?: Comic and vinyl collection/ Comic, book and vinyl collection WHAT DO YOU LIKE ABOUT WORKING AS A DESIGNER?: There is no clear definition of what a designer does, so everyone can find their own approach, which means one can create his/her own profession within the boundaries of the needs of the market of visual communication WHAT DO YOU DISLIKE ABOUT WORKING AS A DESIGNER?: There is no clear definition of what a designer does, so nearly everyone can work as a designer. Designers selling themselves under what they are worth and offering visual make-up instead of communication mislead about what society generally expects of design and a designer. I often wish designers and society would be more demanding

MATTHIAS GÖRLICH (STUDIO MATTHIAS GÖRLICH)

EDUCATION: Darmstadt (D), Hochschule Darmstadt, Diplom Kommunikations designer (Dipl.-Des. FH), Visual Communication / Zurich (CH), Zürcher Hochschule der Künste (ZHdK), Institute for Design Research (Design2context), Master of Advanced Studies (M. A.), Design Research ARE YOU EMPLOYED OR SELF-EMPLOYED?: Self-employed and employed as a researcher (Design2 context, Zurich (CH)) PREVIOUS EMPLOYMENT: Kram/Weisshaar (Stockholm, SE) and as a freelancer for unit-design (Offenbach, D), Ade Hauser Lacour (Frankfurt am Main, D), Eclat (Zurich, CH) among others. But basically I started my own practice while studying design ARCHITECTS/ BUILDINGS THAT INFLUENCED YOU THEN/NOW: Most of my friends at that time were architecture students and I was influenced by discussions about the contemporary Swiss and Dutch architecture scene. I was especially intrigued by Rem Koolhaas' work with OMA as it pushed the boundaries of architecture and also integrated design / I am very interested in all the DIY building concepts from the 1970s. But also contemporary work by people like Jesko Fezer, Arno Brandlhuber et al. MUSICIANS/ALBUMS THAT INFLUENCED YOU THEN/NOW: I can't really tell if music has any impact or influence on my work. I like listening to music, but very rarely while working. Maybe music is too much of a personal thing for me to escape to, instead of having it around me while working ANY OTHER INFLUENCES THEN/NOW: For me there is no then/now here. People like Prof. Dr. Uli Bohnen, former Professor of Design History at the Hochschule Darmstad, certainly influenced me a lot because he was never talking about 'design history' but always painting a bigger picture where design plays a role in society and where it has responsibilities. Travelling now is a big influence; meeting people with a different cultural background and experience often opens my eyes to new things DID YOU OWN ANY SORT OF COLLECTION THEN/NOW?: Visual stuff I came across when travelling / The collection continued and was enhanced by a collection of historic design books WHAT WOULD YOU DO TODAY IF YOU STOPPED DESIGNING?: I would most probably do something like selling books (although my problem is that I would rather keep them than sell them). But after working with Urban Planners for the last few years, I became really interested in their understanding of design, so maybe I would work in a different field of design instead of stopping designing HOW DID/DO YOU DEVELOP/RESEARCH AN IDEA?: Then and now is pretty much the same process. I like to rethink the process, for example by starting with something purely visual and developing the idea around that, or by doing it the other way around, or I might only work on a project in the evening, or on the road. The tempo of the process is a lot faster now, though DESIGNERS THAT INFLUENCE YOU NOW: There are some designers who I respect for their approach e.g. Urs Lehni for rethinking the idea of a cultural institution or David Reinfurt for extending the field of design and Enzo Mari's approach to do-it-yourself design, etc.

AUTHORS/BOOKS THAT INFLUENCE YOU: Certainly Tomás Maldonado (Umwelt und Revolte) and some other more theoretical books that deal with a broader understanding of design. Strangely, today the books that I really like to flip through are mostly photography books, e.g. Peter Menzel (Material World, The Family of Man) – awfully designed, but the content is extremely interesting

MICHAEL GEORGIOU
(G DESIGN STUDIO)

EDUCATION: Athens (GR), Vakalo College of Art & Design, Graphic Design / London (UK), London College of Printing, Higher National Diploma (HND), Typographic studies ARE YOU EMPLOYED OR SELF-EMPLOYED?: Both self-employed and employed (lecturer at Vakalo College of Art & Design, Athens) ANY OTHER INFLUENCES THEN/NOW: Folk art, Art Deco, Bauhaus / Folk art, MNP, Sara Fanelli, Adrian Shaughnessy DID YOU OWN ANY SORT OF COLLECTION THEN/NOW?: Rubbers / Ducks

NIKKI GONNISSEN
(THONIK)

EDUCATION: Utrecht (NL), Hogeschool voor de Kunsten Utrecht, Bachelor of Art (B.A.), Graphic Design ARE YOU EMPLOYED OR SELF-EMPLOYED?: Self-employed PREVIOUS EMPLOYMENT: None ARCHITECTS/BUILDINGS THAT INFLUENCED YOU THEN/NOW: Le Corbusier: (Ronchamps) / MVRDV: Wozoko's (we commissioned MVRDV to build our studio in 2000), John Kormeling (eccentric and radical) MUSICIANS/ALBUMS THAT INFLUENCED YOU THEN/NOW: I don't know where to start / Different genres ANY OTHER INFLUENCES THEN/NOW: Asmat, Papua New Guinea. I went there for three months in 1996 / Still as then WHAT DO YOU LIKE ABOUT WORKING AS A DESIGNER?: The fact that I can go deeply into a specific subject for a relatively short period of time. The whole proces from listening, analyzing, concepualizing, design, implementation and getting it into the world. To engage with certain projects. It is about sharing values. Content and context are important to me ARTISTS/WORKS OF ART THAT INFLUENCED YOU THEN/NOW: Claes Oldenburg (his giant objects and soft sculptures like hamburgers, but also knees as statues); Wim T. Schippers (Going To The Dogs – a play with only dogs in it; people were watching dogs barking and peeing for two hours); Jan Hoet (Chambres d'Amis – the first exhibition of art in people's homes in Gent (BE)); John Baldessari for his use of photos and signs, playing with context; Yayoi Kusama (1960s, happenings, orgies, performances, comments on society), Sol LeWitt for his conceptional form follows function; Piplotti Rist; Emily Kngwarreye

OLIVER KLIMPEL
(BUERO INTERNATIONAL LONDON)

EDUCATION: Leipzig (D), Hochschule für Grafik und Buchkunst, Diploma (Dipl.-Designer), Graphic & Book-Design / London (UK), Central Saint Martins College of Art & Design, Post-graduate Diploma (PgDip), Graphic Design / London (UK), Royal College of Art, Master of Arts (M.A.), Communication Art and Design ARE YOU EMPLOYED OR SELF-EMPLOYED?: Self-employed and employed (Professor at Hochschule für Grafik und Buchkunst Leipzig (D)) PREVIOUS EMPLOYMENT: None ARCHITECTS/BUILDINGS THAT INFLUENCED YOU THEN/NOW: Coop Himmelblau, John Hejduk, Le Corbusier / Lina Bo Bardi, Cedric Price MUSICIANS/ALBUMS THAT INFLUENCED YOU THEN/NOW: Tortoise, Stereolab, German electronica = music for graphic designers + Flaming Lips, etc. / Music for more mature graphic designer + Brian Ferry + Japan + Animal Collective, etc. ANY OTHER INFLUENCES THEN/NOW: Four teachers I'm very happy to have met. Gabriele Kreutzmann, my German teacher at A-levels (Gymnasium) who brought real thinking and debate to the subject of language, literature and ideas – an eye-opener. Hildegard Korger, tutor for Lettering at Hochschule für Grafik und Buchkunst Leipzig: an amazingly meticulous and inspirational craftswoman! Günter Bose, tutor for Typography at Hochschule für Grafik und Buchkunst Leipzig, who introduced me to the idea of discourse within typography and graphic design. Al Rees, researcher/tutor in Film at the Royal College of Art, London (UK) – not so much of a direct influence as a teacher or confidante but someone who brought a previously unknown world (structural filmmaking) to my attention DID YOU OWN ANY SORT OF COLLECTION THEN/ NOW?: This is touching a nerve: 1) Besides a traditional idea of collecting meaningful finds and inspirational material it has become more common in recent years also for graphic designers to work with a model of the archive as a system for storing their own and foreign material and using it methodically 2) But: all the work I had done throughout my college education and had kept, and many books and magazines, were lost in the severe flooding of 2002 in Dresden (D), since I had stored it in the basement of my parents' house. I tend not to be sentimental, but it is moments like this – when asked about college stuff and collections – that I wish that at least a few things had survived... Therefore I didn't have too many works I had done as a student to choose from... HOW DO YOU DEVELOP/RESEARCH AN IDEA NOW?: I've recently tried to do more speculative work and read more, pursue less result-driven things. That's what my teaching post seems to suggest and allows me to do now. At least I think so. Before it was just project after project. We become victims of our moderate success quickly: you get more work and have more projects to juggle and less time for looking and playing around

PAUL BARNES

EDUCATION: Reading (UK), University of Reading, Bachelor of Arts (B.A. Hons), Typography & Graphic Communication ARE YOU EMPLOYED OR SELF-EMPLOYED?: Self-employed PREVIOUS EMPLOYMENT: Roger Black Inc. (New York, USA), Spin magazine (New York, USA) ARCHITECTS/BUILDINGS THAT INFLUENCED YOU THEN/NOW: Rietveld Schröder House, Utrecht (NL) by Gerrit Rietveld / Georgian architecture and industrial architecture MUSICIANS/ ALBUMS THAT INFLUENCED YOU THEN/ NOW: The Sound of Young Scotland, Kraftwerk, David Bowie, Joy Division and many others DID YOU OWN ANY SORT OF COLLECTION THEN/NOW?: Books / Still books, particularly Insel Verlag (now Suhrkamp Verlag) DESIGNERS THAT INFLUENCED YOU THEN: Jan Tschichold, Charles Collett, Robert and George Stephenson, Isambard Kingdom Brunel, Paul Rand, Max Bill, Hermann Eidenbenz, Peter Saville and my tutor, Paul Stiff. Too many to mention, really

PREM KRISHNAMURTHY
(PROJECT PROJECTS)

EDUCATION: New Haven (USA), Yale College, Bachelor of Arts (B.A.), Fine Arts – concentration on Graphic Design and photography / Berlin (D), Freie Universität, semester abroad, Comparative Literature and Philosophy / Dresden (D), Hochschule für Technik und Wirtschaft Dresden and Technische Universität Dresden, Performance Studies and Industrial Design History, Fulbright Fellowship ARE YOU EMPLOYED OR SELF-EMPLOYED?: Self-employed PREVIOUS EMPLOYMENT: Leonardi.Wollein, Berlin (D), New York Times Magazine, New York (USA), O-R-G, Inc., New York (USA) ARCHITECTS/BUILDINGS THAT INFLUENCED YOU THEN/NOW: Paul Rudolph, Daniel Libeskind, Rem Koolhaas / Peter Zumthor, Herzog & de Meuron, WORKac MUSICIANS/ALBUMS THAT INFLUENCED YOU THEN/NOW: Radiohead, John Coltrane, Tricky, Björk, Bill Evans / Vampire Weekend, Dirty Projectors, Van Morrison, Cookies, Sleigh Bells ANY OTHER INFLUENCES THEN/NOW: Paul Elliman, John Gambell, Matthew Carter, Rita Jules, Randall Hoyt, Tamara Sussman / My business partners (Adam Michaels & Rob Giampietro) and our employees (Chris Wu, Chris McCaddon, Marina Kitchen) DID YOU OWN ANY SORT OF COLLECTION THEN/NOW?: Stamped US pennies from tourist locations / Only my books

RENATA GRAW
(PLURAL)

EDUCATION: Chicago, University of Illinois at Chicago, Master of Fine Arts (M.F.A.), Graphic Design / Rio de Janeiro, Pontifícia Universidade Católica (PUC-RIO), Bachelor of Fine Arts (B.F.A), Industrial Design ARE YOU EMPLOYED OR SELF-EMPLOYED?: Self-employed PREVIOUS EMPLOYMENT: Freelance, Brand Image (Chicago, USA) / McMillan Associates (USA) / Ana Couto Design (BR) ARCHITECTS/BUILDINGS THAT INFLUENCED YOU THEN/NOW: Oscar Niemeyer, Tadao Ando, Renzo Piano, Herzog & de Meuron, OMA, Mies van der Rohe, Eero Saarinen, Buckminster Fuller MUSICIANS/ALBUMS THAT INFLUENCED YOU THEN/NOW: Brazilian music: Jõao Gilberto, Caetano Veloso, Gilberto Gil, Os Mutantes, mixed in with: Jimi Hendrix, Janis Joplin, Miles Davis, Wynton Marsalis, Sonny Rollins and others. Although we pretty much listen to all kinds of music in the studio now, from African beats to classical ANY OTHER INFLUENCES THEN/NOW: My uncle Ricardo Bacha; he was a psychiatrist and amateur photographer in Brazil. He used to show me art books and we discussed art and philosophy during family gatherings DID YOU OWN ANY SORT OF COLLECTION THEN/NOW?: I have never had a collection, although I have a lot of books DESIGNERS THAT INFLUENCED YOU THEN/NOW: Tibor Kalman, Wolfgang Weingart, Piet Zwart, Stefan Sagmeister, Karel Martens, Wim Crouwel, Emil Ruder, Pierre Mendell, Max Bill, Paul Rand, Saul Bass, Paula Scher, Cassandre, Karl Gerstner, Michael C. Place & The Designers Republic / Ludovic Balland, Daniel Eatock (see also p. 58–61), James Goggin (see also p. 98–101), Armand Mevis, Maureen Mooren, Leonardo Sonnoli, Willi Kunz, Geoff McFetridge, Non-Format, Laszlo Moholy-Nagy, Dexter Sinister, Sonnenzimmer, Cybu Richli + Fabienne Burri, the list goes on... PIECES OF DESIGN THAT INFLUENCED YOU THEN: I remember the moment I decided to go back and study graphic design for my Masters. I was in Switzerland taking a workshop with Weingart for the summer of 2005 and he showed us a book by one of his students – Philip Burton. That one book changed my whole perspective on what design could be. At that moment in my life I learned graphic design is really a platform to express the world visually. We, as designers, have the opportunity to create new images, and new forms of presenting and interpreting the world

RICHARD WALKER
(KK OUTLET/KESSELSKRAMER)

EDUCATION: Cambridge (UK), Regional College, Foundation / London (UK), Camberwell College of Arts, Bachelor of Arts (B.A. Hons), Graphic Design ARE YOU EMPLOYED OR SELF-EMPLOYED?: Employed PREVIOUS EMPLOYMENT: Red Square editing (London, UK), I.D magazine (London, UK), Simple Productions (London, UK), Mother (London, UK), KesselsKramer (Amsterdam, NL), Fallon (London, UK), Weiden and Kennedy (London, UK), Weiden and Kennedy (Amsterdam, NL) ARCHITECTS/BUILDINGS THAT INFLUENCED YOU THEN/NOW: Not sure how a building can influence you. The job centre in Peckham was influential in getting me a place on a QuarkXpress evening course / I like The Gherkin (London, UK) by Norman Foster MUSICIANS/ALBUMS THAT INFLUENCED YOU THEN/NOW: Having an opinion about music at college was very important. Finding bands that were new and good really mattered. The actual music was a bit secondary. I used to like a band called The Makeup at college. I also sided with Blur during the Oasis vs. Blur question / These days I listen to whatever gets played at work. Edward Sharpe and the Magnetic Zeros are worth a listen ANY OTHER INFLUENCES THEN/NOW: Scott King was my tutor at Camberwell College. I still see him and still rate him as one of the more relevant artists of our generation / The people who influence me now are the people I work with DID YOU OWN ANY SORT OF COLLECTION THEN/NOW?: I have a massive record collection YOUR MOST VALUED POSSESSION NOW: I have an original May '68 poster. It's the one with the riot policeman holding a baton. I love it but it has a big SS symbol on the shield. My wife won't have it in the house. I've tried explaining that it's actually very anti-fascist, but I see her point HOW OLD WERE YOU WHEN YOU FIRST THOUGHT OF BECOMING A DESIGNER?: I was 24 – I bumped into an old college friend of mine who was wearing a suit and carrying a portfolio. It looked like he was doing very well. He was in fact coming back from an interview at an ad agency. He didn't get the job but we got talking and he explained that it was easier to get the sort of job he was after if he was in a creative team. He suggested we started working together and we started arguing over who would be the copywriter and who would be the art director. I won the argument and that's when I got the official label. before that I wanted to be a film director. Before that I was a trainee butcher with Dewhurst's in Royston DESIGNERS THAT INFLUENCED YOU THEN/NOW: I think the biggest influences were the people I used to hang out with or share a flat with. Record covers have always been a great influence too. As I got a bit more interested in design I started buying record sleeves for the designers and not really the music. I've never been a fan of New Order but I am a fan of Peter Saville and began looking at the other work he made. That got me into other music, which got me into other designers, and so on. When I was at college I was a fan of Fluxus. I liked the fact that there was a concept in the design and it was always quite funny. They demystified art and I liked the fact that it was a collective. I also thought that Tomato were really cool. They felt culturally relevant, as they had just done the title sequence for the film Trainspotting. My knowledge of graphic design up until then was quite traditional and clean. Tomato looked like they got their hands dirty / These days my influences haven't really changed – I think you form an opinion about art and music and stuff very early on. Those are the things that help shape your taste, which in turn forms your visual personality and design outlook on life. You then take what you like from the world that fits into those taste parameters. The parameters just get bigger ARTISTS/WORKS OF ART THAT INFLUENCED YOU: The South London Gallery was next to college so I got to see a lot of Young British Artists. I think I was fascinated by how much some of this work was being sold for. Before I went to college my sense of modern art came from books like The Shock of the New – all very much out of reach. At Camberwell College, at that time, you could go to the pub and see artists that were making waves in the art world propping up the bar. It became within your reach, which for an art student was very inspiring

SANDRA HOFFMANN ROBBIANI
(VISUAL STUDIES)

EDUCATION: Vancouver (CAN), Capilano College, Diploma, Graphic Arts / Basel (CH), Schule für Gestaltung, post-graduate, Graphic Design / Zurich (CH), Hochschule der Künste, Executive Masters, Cultural Studies in Art, Design and Media / Zürich (CH), Hochschule der Künste/Plymouth University (UK), PhD (Candidate), Z-Node Planetary Collegium, Institute of Cultural Studies in the Arts (in progress) ARE YOU EMPLOYED OR SELF-EMPLOYED?: Self-employed and employed (Professor of Typography at Hochschule Darmstadt (D) ARCHITECTS/ BUILDINGS THAT INFLUENCED YOU THEN/NOW: Tadao Ando, Atelier 5, B.C. Binning, A. Erickson, Buckminster Fuller, Frank Gehry, Zaha Hadid, Herzog & de Meuron, Karl Moser, Luigi Snozzi, Livio Vacchini / Various MUSICIANS/ALBUMS THAT INFLUENCED YOU THEN/NOW: Barbara, my Baroque-oboe-playing roommate / Ousel

blackbirds (Amsel) ANY OTHER INFLUENCES THEN/NOW: Flight YOUR MOST VALUED POSSESSION THEN: A toolbox with instruments (Swann-Morton scalpel, marble, roller, Caran d'Ache pens and pencils, Racher typometre, calculating scale, Falzbein, Cementit, Kern compasses, mink paintbrushes, loupe, Juwel stapler, Prismacolor pencil crayons, Gedess pencil sharpener, bulldog clips, magnets, Omega Reissnagel drawing-pins, hole punch, stamp pad and letter stamps, technograph 777 pencils, gyro compass, burnisher, green masking tape, brown paper tape, Post-its, Minox, coloured stones, Klebeband from EPA, Pelikan plaka, sketchbooks from Rebetez, Knetgummi, Ilford canisters...) HOW OLD WERE YOU WHEN YOU FIRST THOUGHT OF BECOMING A DESIGNER?: 7 – it was then when I locked myself in the bathroom until my mother promised to drive me across the scary intersection to an afternoon drawing class DESIGNERS THAT INFLUENCED YOU THEN: Hans Arp, H.C. Berann, Donald Wills Douglas, W. A. Dwiggins, Karl Gerstner, April Greiman, Kurt Hauert, John Heartfield, Ernst Heinkel, Josef Hoffmann, Armin Hofmann, Howard Hughes, Eduard Imhof, Edward Johnston, Otto Lilienthal, Hans-Rudolf Lutz, Herbert Matter, Willy Messerschmitt, Reginald Joseph Mitchell, Stanley Morison, Bruno Munari, Paul Rand, Paul Renner, Niklaus Stoecklin, Ladislav Sutnar, Jan Tschichold, Wolfgang Weingart, Piet Zwart, et al. AUTHORS/ BOOKS THAT INFLUENCED YOU THEN/NOW: Hugo Ball, Simone de Beauvoir, John Berger, Friedrich Duerrenmatt, Eugen Gomringer, James Joyce, Birgit Kempker, R.D. Laing, Louis L'Amour, Edgar Allan Poe, Antoine de Saint-Exupéry, Susan Sontag, Gertrude Stein / John Langshaw Austin, Simon Baron-Cohen, Lewis Carroll, Emily Carr, Angela Carter, Michel Foucault, Martin Heidegger, Maurice Merleau-Ponty, Dieter Mersch, Laurie Petrou, V.S. Ramachandran, Eva Schuermann, Mary Wollstonecraft, Ludwig Wittgenstein FILMS/DIRECTORS THAT INFLUENCE YOU NOW: Das gefrorene Herz (Xavier Koller), Hoehenfeuer (Fredi M. Murer), Women without Men (Shirin Neshat), Beresina oder Die letzten Tage der Schweiz (Daniel Schmid), My Life Without Me (Isabel Coixet), My Winnipeg (Guy Maddin), films by Michael Haneke

SASCHA LOBE
(L2M3)

EDUCATION: Hochschule Pforzheim (Germany), Diplom-Designer (Dipl.-Des.), Graphic Design ARE YOU EMPLOYED OR SELF-EMPLOYED?: Self-employed and employed (Professor at Hochschule für Gestaltung Offenbach (D)) PREVIOUS EMPLOYMENT: None GENERAL COMMENT ON ALL THE ANSWERS GIVEN ON THE SUBJECT OF INFLUENCES THEN/NOW WITHIN THIS BOOK: Everything I like influences me. Everything I don't like doesn't influence me. But it's difficult to distinguish between things that motivate you and influence your thoughts, and things that are formal, stylistic influences. So in that respect I can't really distinguish between things that have fundamentally changed my work and things that merely reflect my interests. All of the names that I give here were/are points of reference for me and 'cut to the core' of my interests ARCHITECTS/ BUILDINGS THAT INFLUENCED YOU THEN/NOW:

Mies van der Rohe, Giò Ponti, Carlo Scarpa / David Chipperfield, SANAA, Valerio Olgiati, Herzog & de Meuron MUSICIANS/ALBUMS THAT INFLUENCED YOU THEN/NOW: Mozart, Miles Davis, Pixies, Tom Waits, Portis-head, Beastie Boys, Beck / Bach, Andreas Scholl, Françoise Hardy, Helge Schneider, The White Stripes, Adele, The Avett Brothers, Ezra Furman – music is too fast, ask me tomorrow and I'll write down different ones... ANY OTHER INFLUENCES THEN/NOW: My girlfriend / My wife DID YOU OWN ANY SORT OF COLLECTION THEN/NOW?: Music, books / Books, music

STEFAN SAGMEISTER
(SAGMEISTER INC.)

EDUCATION: Vienna (AT), Universität für angewandte Kunst Wien, Bachelor of Art (B.A.) / New York (USA), Pratt Institute, Master of Arts (M.A.) ARE YOU EMPLOYED OR SELF-EMPLOYED?: Self-employed ARCHITECTS/BUILDINGS THAT INFLUENCED YOU THEN/NOW: Guenther Domenig / Herzog & de Meuron MUSICIANS/ALBUMS THAT INFLUENCED YOU THEN/NOW: King Crimson / Sigur Rós

SVEN VOELKER
(SVEN VOELKER STUDIO)

EDUCATION: Bremen (D), Hochschule für Künste, Diplom-Designer (Dipl.-Designer) / London (UK), Middlesex University, Master of Arts (M.A.) ARE YOU EMPLOYED OR SELF-EMPLOYED?: Self-employed and employed (Professor at Kunsthochschule Halle (D)) PREVIOUS EMPLOYMENT: Imagination (London, UK), Plex (Berlin (D)), Professor at Hochschule für Gestaltung Karlsruhe (D) ARCHITECTS/BUILDINGS THAT INFLUENCED YOU THEN/NOW: Tadao Ando, Rem Koolhaas / SANAA MUSICIANS/ALBUMS THAT INFLUENCED YOU THEN/NOW: Metalheadz, Under-world, Björk / Manu Katche, Maximo Park, Underworld DID YOU OWN ANY SORT OF COLLECTION THEN/NOW?: A matchbox car collection / I have a beautiful collection of posters by the New York artist Lawrence Weiner. Apart from that I own a strange but large collection of pictures and objects from various and very different epochs for which I haven't found a curatorial thread yet WHAT DO YOU DISLIKE ABOUT WORKING AS A DESIGNER?: It's very difficult to enter the hermetically sealed area of art. I don't mean to design the catalogues or posters for museums or galleries, that's boring, but for a designer who is the author of his own work to publish, exhibit or sell art. Art for me is as interesting as big corporate companies for whom I worked. To combine these two areas of practice without using a pseudonym isn't easy at all

TIM BALAAM
(HYPERKIT)

EDUCATION: Ipswich (UK), Suffolk College, B-Tech, General Art and Design / London (UK), Camberwell College of Arts, Bachelor of Arts (B.A. Hons), Graphic Design / London (UK), Royal College of Art, Master of Arts (M.A.), Graphic Design ARE YOU EMPLOYED OR SELF-EMPLOYED?: Director of own company CURRENT AND/OR PREVIOUS EMPLOYMENT: None ARCHITECTS/BUILDINGS THAT INFLUENCED YOU THEN/NOW: Rem Koolhaas / MVRDV MUSICIANS/ALBUMS

THAT INFLUENCED YOU THEN/NOW: Beastie Boys / Squarepusher ANY OTHER INFLUENCES THEN/NOW: Anything and everything / Kate, my wife and Hyperkit co-founder DID YOU OWN ANY SORT OF COLLECTION THEN/NOW?: Examples of information graphics / Digital photographs of construction site furniture HOW DO YOU DEVELOP/ RESEARCH AN IDEA NOW?: Research and development is an ongoing process and everything we have seen, read and experienced dictates how we want to design as a studio. This is combined with straightforward research into subjects that are relevant to particular projects

URS LEHNI
(LEHNI-TRÜB, ROLLO PRESS, CORNER COLLEGE)

EDUCATION: Lucerne (CH), Hochschule Luzern, Bachelor of Art (B.A.) / Maastricht (NL), Jan van Eyck Academie, Post-graduate studies ARE YOU EMPLOYED OR SELF-EMPLOYED?: Self-employed and employed (Professor, Staatliche Hochschule für Gestaltung Karlsruhe (D)) HOW DO YOU DEVELOP/ RESEARCH AN IDEA NOW?: The conception of a situation within which design can happen is very close to the modes with which I also like to work in more recent projects: scores, restrictions, processes, etc.

YASMIN KHAN
(COUNTERSPACE)

EDUCATION: Los Angeles, CA (USA), University of California, UCLA, Bachelor of Arts (B.A.), Fine Art / Pasadena, CA (USA), Art Center College of Design, Bachelor of Fine Arts (B.F.A.), Graphic Design / Valencia, CA (USA), California Institute of the Arts (CalArts), Master of Fine Arts (M.F.A.), Graphic Design, ARE YOU EMPLOYED OR SELF-EMPLOYED?: Both employed (senior lecturer at Otis College of Art and Design) and self-employed MUSICIANS/ALBUMS THAT INFLUENCED YOU THEN/NOW: Dungen, MIA / Sixto Rodriguez, MIA ANY OTHER INFLUENCES THEN/NOW: Mentor, then: Denise Gonzales Crisp DID YOU OWN ANY SORT OF COLLECTION THEN/ NOW?: Books

YVES FIDALGO
(FULGURO)

EDUCATION: Lausanne (CH), ECAL – Ecole cantonale d'art de Lausanne, Bachelor of Arts (B.A.), Industrial Design ARE YOU EMPLOYED OR SELF-EMPLOYED?: Self-employed PREVIOUS EMPLOYMENT: None ARCHITECTS/ BUILDINGS THAT INFLUENCED YOU THEN/NOW: Herzog & de Meuron (Tate Modern, Prada Shop Tokyo, Basel Station Building), Diller and Scofidio (Cloud in Yverdon for Expo02 and other works), Jean Nouvel (Congress Building in Luzern, Monolith in Morat, Expo 2002) MUSICIANS/ALBUMS THAT INFLUENCED YOU THEN/NOW: Johnny Cash, Emily Jane White, Sigur Rós, The Clash, Damien Jurado, Jose Gonzales, Moriarty, Kraftwerk, Arcade Fire, God Machine, Elliott Smith DID YOU OWN ANY SORT OF COLLECTION THEN/ NOW?: Comics DESIGNERS THAT INFLUENCED YOU THEN: Ronan Bouroullec, Olivier Sidet, Florence Doléac (all our teachers at college). Also Jean Prouvé. And Castiglioni. And Charles and Ray Eames. And all the Droog stuff. Marti Guixé. Richard Hutten, Fernando and Humberto Campana

Plan B
Age of first design career thought
Hours spent designing
Idea development and research
Influential designers
Influential design pieces
Influential authors and books
Influential artists
Influential directors and films
Likes about working as a designer (only now)

Then

Plan B (hypothetical)
Would one do a design career all over again
Hours spent designing
Idea development and research
Influential designers
Influential design pieces
Influential authors and books
Influential artists
Influential directors and films
Dislikes about working as a designer

Now

ANDREAS GNASS	ANDREW STEVENS	ANNELYS DE VET	ANTÓNIO S. GOMES	BEN BRANAGAN	BERND HILPERT
No plan B, sorry	**No plan B**	**Study maths**	I remember planning to do an intensive casino croupier course while I was trying to think of plan B	I was always really into drawing and making things and knew I wanted to do something related to this	**Architecture**

BRIAN WEBB	CHRISTIAN HEUSSER	DANIEL EATOCK	DANIJELA DJOKIC	EMMI SALONEN	ÉRIC & MARIE GASPAR
Didn't know it then but a design historian	**No plan B**	**Racing-car driver**	**Researcher at the MIT**	**Photo-graphy**	**No plan B**

FONS HICKMANN	HANS DIETER REICHERT	HOLGER JACOBS	HOON KIM	HYOUN YOUL JOE	ISABELLE SWIDERSKI
Porn actor	-	There never was a plan B but looking back I might have enjoyed being a carpenter	If I had been something like colour-blind, I would have become a dentist	**Pilot, doctor, mathematician**	**Amazingly to me now, a criminal lawyer**

JAMES GOGGIN	JAN WILKER	JULIE GAYARD	KAI VON RABENAU	KEN GARLAND	KIRSTY CARTER
Artist, architect or hip-hop producer	**Architect, scuba-diving teacher**	**There was no plan B**	**Acting**	My teachers thought I would have a career in English literature or history – I loved writing, and I still write a lot in my work	A writer – I also love making books, so if I were not designing them anymore then I could have authored them

KRISTINE MATTHEWS	LARS HARMSEN	LAURENT LACOUR	LIZA ENEBEIS	LUCINDA NOBLE	MAKI SUZUKI
Astronomy (distant second)	**My dream was to be a bush pilot**	**Architecture**	**There was no plan B**	**To be honest I didn't really have a plan B**	**Being a designer was my second choice – I studied marketing**

MARC VAN DER HEIJDE	MARGARET CALVERT	MARION FINK	MARTIN LORENZ	MATTHIAS GÖRLICH	MICHAEL GEORGIOU
There was no plan B – I am still working my butt off for plan A	-	**Psychology or languages**	There was no second choice, since I was 16 – before I could have imagined being a cook	Plan B was to go into marketing – thank god this didn't happen	**Interior designer**

NIKKI GONNISSEN	OLIVER KLIMPEL	PAUL BARNES	PREM KRISHNAMURTHY	RENATA GRAW	RICHARD WALKER
There was no plan B – I always felt that there had to be a balance between design, art and society	I had applied to study journalism too. I'm glad I got into the course in art school, so much better this way!	**Historian**	**Artist, then curator**	**Graphic design is my plan B**	My cousin got me a job as a runner in a small editing company – if I had stuck with it I would have been an editor

SANDRA HOFFMANN	SASCHA LOBE	STEFAN SAGMEISTER	SVEN VOELKER	TIM BALAAM	URS LEHNI
First choice: fighter pilot	I wanted to study electrical engineering and become an engineer – that would have been the alternative to design and architecture	**Had none**	-	**Professional athlete**	I didn't really have one and my parents also didn't force me to come up with one

YASMIN KHAN	YVES FIDALGO	RANKING LIST
Writing	**Engineer**	1 NONE 2 ARCHITECT 3 PILOT, WRITER

What was your second choice of career, your plan B?

———

Then

ANDREAS GNASS
Start to be bored

ANDREW STEVENS
I realize I'm not going to become a professional footballer... if I didn't have to earn any money, I'd still do design, just without the dull bits

ANNELYS DE VET
I couldn't – even if I were to do different things I would still approach them as a designer; my métier is that of graphic design

ANTÓNIO S. GOMES
Probably start teaching full-time with the risk of becoming removed from reality and tired of hearing my own voice – if I was braver I'd take up farming

BEN BRANAGAN
Swimming in the sea

BERND HILPERT
Something simple

BRIAN WEBB
Write more books

CHRISTIAN HEUSSER
Be unemployed – on second thoughts I would wish I could earn a living by becoming a musician

DANIEL EATOCK
Play, walk, run, make, cook

DANIJELA DJOKIC
Become a writer

EMMI SALONEN
Set up a shop

ÉRIC & MARIE GASPAR
Anything we can do

FONS HICKMANN
Playing with the children

HANS DIETER REICHERT
Teaching design, talking about design

HOLGER JACOBS
Go on a very long cycling trip

HOON KIM
Run a gallery and curate exhibitions

HYOUN YOUL JOE
Well, maybe I can do something related to design: book store, café, pub, editor, publisher, etc...

ISABELLE SWIDERSKI
Make films

JAMES GOGGIN
I would just read all day. I don't think I'll stop designing...
(Full answer, p. 227)

JAN WILKER
More music and teaching

JULIE GAYARD
Photography, play music

KAI VON RABENAU
I would become a father

KEN GARLAND
What I am doing now: be a photographer – but a photographer in a design context

KIRSTY CARTER
Reading and writing

KRISTINE MATTHEWS
Get depressed

LARS HARMSEN
Travel, sail, see friends all over the world and work outside

LAURENT LACOUR
Never thought about it

LIZA ENEBEIS
There is no plan B

LUCINDA NEWTON-DUNN
Work in some kind of research/documentary -making, or do some kind of work towards environmental issues

MAKI SUZUKI
Cook, start a record label, museum, magazine, write a TV series, become a director, etc.

MARC VAN DER HEIJDE
Pursue a career in my other passion: promoting classical music through every means conceivable

MARGARET CALVERT
Paint

MARION FINK
Open a café or write a book

MARTIN LORENZ
I would paint

MATTHIAS GÖRLICH
I would most probably do something like selling books – although my...
(Full answer, p. 229)

MICHAEL GEORGIOU
Curating

NIKKI GONNISSEN
I don't know... changing the world in some way

OLIVER KLIMPEL
I would try to write more, go to another country and try to grow a beard

PAUL BARNES
Travel and bake bread

PREM KRISHNAMURTHY
Curate or run a museum or open a bar

RENATA GRAW
I would probably have to become an artist or just a world traveller (can't hurt to dream!)

RICHARD WALKER
I lie awake at night pondering this question

S. HOFFMANN ROBBIANI
Go hiking in the Alps

SASCHA LOBE
Can't stop. If I did stop, I'd probably just be lazy

STEFAN SAGMEISTER
Make documentary movies

SVEN VOELKER
-

TIM BALAAM
Sculptor

URS LEHNI
I have the romantic idea of working with wood, being a cabinet-maker or something similar – but I never really gave it a try

YASMIN KHAN
Write, teach and cook

YVES FIDALGO
Open a restaurant or bar

RANKING LIST
1 OPEN BAR / CAFÉ / SHOP, TEACH, TRAVEL, WRITE
2 MAKE ART, COOK
3 CURATE, READ

What would you do today if you stopped designing?

Now

ANDREAS GNASS	ANDREW STEVENS	ANNELYS DE VET	ANTÓNIO S. GOMES	BEN BRANAGAN	BERND HILPERT
18	16	15	19	As a teenager	19, but without a clear idea of what it was

BRIAN WEBB	CHRISTIAN HEUSSER	DANIEL EATOCK	DANIJELA DJOKIC	EMMI SALONEN	ÉRIC & MARIE GASPAR
14/15	Around 15	Young	18	19	14/17

FONS HICKMANN	HANS DIETER REICHERT	HOLGER JACOBS	HOON KIM	HYOUN YOUL JOE	ISABELLE SWIDERSKI
-	17	Probably around 5 or 6 when I started to draw, although I didn't know what a designer was then	15	20	16

JAMES GOGGIN	JAN WILKER	JULIE GAYARD	KAI VON RABENAU	KEN GARLAND	KIRSTY CARTER
Around 12	I think I was around 22, right after I started studying architecture	12	13	17	13 – I was designing all my homework in ClarisWorks and Photoshop on my Macintosh Performa; suddenly I was a graphic designer

KRISTINE MATTHEWS	LARS HARMSEN	LAURENT LACOUR	LIZA ENEBEIS	LUCINDA NOBLE	MAKI SUZUKI
9	Around 22/23	16	I must have been very young because I can't remember	18–20. Having had a very creative upbringing, I'd known I wanted to do something artistic ever since I was tiny, though	17

MARC VAN DER HEIJDE	MARGARET CALVERT	MARION FINK	MARTIN LORENZ	MATTHIAS GÖRLICH	MICHAEL GEORGIOU
Consciously, that would have been around 16	20	16	12 – I loved to draw, but did not have the balls to choose the life of an artist – it took 10 years to love the profession of being a designer	Around 22 – after some internships	20

NIKKI GONNISSEN	OLIVER KLIMPEL	PAUL BARNES	PREM KRISHNAMURTHY	RENATA GRAW	RICHARD WALKER
Around 20	Around 18 – I went to evening classes at the Art Academy Dresden; apart from life drawing we had an introduction to typography – an exciting moment	14	17, perhaps	24. I had studied industrial design before I ever thought of becoming a graphic designer	I was 24 – I bumped... (Full answer, p. 230)

SANDRA HOFFMANN	SASCHA LOBE	STEFAN SAGMEISTER	SVEN VOELKER	TIM BALAAM	URS LEHNI
7 – it was then when I locked... (Full answer, p. 231)	16	14	Around 18	18	15

YASMIN KHAN	YVES FIDALGO	AVERAGE/YOUNGEST/OLDEST			
25	18	A 16¾ Y 7 O 25			

How old were you when you first thought of becoming a designer?

Then

ANDREAS GNASS

Yes

ANDREW STEVENS

Yeah, I think so

ANNELYS DE VET

Yes

ANTÓNIO S. GOMES

Yes – there is so much I still don't know

BEN BRANAGAN

Probably

BERND HILPERT

Yes, but there are times when I have doubts

BRIAN WEBB

Yes

CHRISTIAN HEUSSER

I guess so

DANIEL EATOCK

No

DANIJELA DJOKIC

Maybe

EMMI SALONEN

Yes

ÉRIC & MARIE GASPAR

Yes

FONS HICKMANN

No

HANS DIETER REICHERT

Yes

HOLGER JACOBS

Yes

HOON KIM

Yes I would

HYOUN YOUL JOE

Yes, I am enjoying what…
(Full answer, p. 227)

ISABELLE SWIDERSKI

Yes

JAMES GOGGIN

Maybe not

JAN WILKER

Yes

JULIE GAYARD

Maybe I would have concentrated on photography instead – or a musical instrument

KAI VON RABENAU

Ah, that's a difficult question… I don't know

KEN GARLAND

Absolutely without question

KIRSTY CARTER

Yes! I love being a designer, …
(Full answer, p. 228)

KRISTINE MATTHEWS

Absolutely

LARS HARMSEN

No, I don't think so
(Full answer, p. 228)

LAURENT LACOUR

No

LIZA ENEBEIS

Yes, without a doubt

LUCINDA NEWTON-DUNN

Yes, although I remain somewhere between being a designer and an artist

MAKI SUZUKI

Yes

MARC VAN DER HEIJDE

Yes – but I still wish I had known then what I know now!

MARGARET CALVERT

Yes

MARION FINK

Yes

MARTIN LORENZ

Yes, definitely

MATTHIAS GÖRLICH

Yes

MICHAEL GEORGIOU

Certainly

NIKKI GONNISSEN

Yes

OLIVER KLIMPEL

Yes, it's a pretty good choice

PAUL BARNES

Not sure

PREM KRISHNAMURTHY

Probably

RENATA GRAW

I would probably have become a designer sooner

RICHARD WALKER

Actually, I'm an art director…

S. HOFFMANN ROBBIANI

Why not?

SASCHA LOBE

Absolutely

STEFAN SAGMEISTER

Yes

SVEN VOELKER

I would probably do it again

TIM BALAAM

Yes

URS LEHNI

I guess so, although maybe combined with another profession

YASMIN KHAN

Yes

YVES FIDALGO

Yep

YES/NO/PERHAPS

Y 39
N 3
P 8

Would you still have become a designer if you knew what you know now?

Now

ANDREAS GNASS	ANDREW STEVENS	ANNELYS DE VET	ANTÓNIO S. GOMES	BEN BRANAGAN	BERND HILPERT
4	14	24	When the deadlines were tight I worked all night	Not enough	8

BRIAN WEBB	CHRISTIAN HEUSSER	DANIEL EATOCK	DANIJELA DJOKIC	EMMI SALONEN	ÉRIC & MARIE GASPAR
12, really maybe more	10	0.3	6–16	4–5	9

FONS HICKMANN	HANS DIETER REICHERT	HOLGER JACOBS	HOON KIM	HYOUN YOUL JOE	ISABELLE SWIDERSKI
12	10	About 10	12	Over 12	6–10

JAMES GOGGIN	JAN WILKER	JULIE GAYARD	KAI VON RABENAU	KEN GARLAND	KIRSTY CARTER
Waking hours	3 (but much more talking about it)	4 (the rest I was in the canteen, café or bar)	10	4–12	I think about design and our projects all the time, it's an emormous part of my life, which I am sure is the case for most designers… (Full answer, p. 228)

KRISTINE MATTHEWS	LARS HARMSEN	LAURENT LACOUR	LIZA ENEBEIS	LUCINDA NOBLE	MAKI SUZUKI
Too many (around 11)	5	6–12	I didn't/don't have a set schedule or time limit,… (Cont. opposite – now)	7–10	10 – except weekends

MARC VAN DER HEIJDE	MARGARET CALVERT	MARION FINK	MARTIN LORENZ	MATTHIAS GÖRLICH	MICHAEL GEORGIOU
4 (on average)	About 5	8–10	14 (of unfocused sketching)	Certainly more than today	8

NIKKI GONNISSEN	OLIVER KLIMPEL	PAUL BARNES	PREM KRISHNAMURTHY	RENATA GRAW	RICHARD WALKER
A lot	7	7	4–6	Too many	As long as it takes

SANDRA HOFFMANN	SASCHA LOBE	STEFAN SAGMEISTER	SVEN VOELKER	TIM BALAAM	URS LEHNI
Ooofff!	24	16	Probably always more than 8 hours, often until deep into the night	Not sure, design only made up a small part of what I did at college	Approx. 8

YASMIN KHAN	YVES FIDALGO	AVERAGE/MOST/FEWEST
12+	Let's say 9 – but do I count in the hours spent drinking beer trying to be inspired?	A 9½+ M 24 F 3

How many hours did you spend designing each day?

Then

ANDREAS GNASS	ANDREW STEVENS	ANNELYS DE VET	ANTÓNIO S. GOMES	BEN BRANAGAN	BERND HILPERT
5	9	24	A lot fewer than I would like to	Not enough	10

BRIAN WEBB	CHRISTIAN HEUSSER	DANIEL EATOCK	DANIJELA DJOKIC	EMMI SALONEN	ÉRIC & MARIE GASPAR
6, really rather fewer	12	0.2	2	8–10	9

FONS HICKMANN	HANS DIETER REICHERT	HOLGER JACOBS	HOON KIM	HYOUN YOUL JOE	ISABELLE SWIDERSKI
7	12–14	About 12 (if admin and paperwork count as designing…)	8	It depends on projects – approx. 6 to 8	0 to 12

JAMES GOGGIN	JAN WILKER	JULIE GAYARD	KAI VON RABENAU	KEN GARLAND	KIRSTY CARTER
Waking hours	5 (plus another 5 of non-design and office stuff, like reading, talking, eating, writing, meeting, etc.)	4 (the rest I am writing mails, making calls, calculating prices or sitting in a café)	10	7	See opposite (then)

KRISTINE MATTHEWS	LARS HARMSEN	LAURENT LACOUR	LIZA ENEBEIS	LUCINDA NEWTON-DUNN	MAKI SUZUKI
Does teaching design count and running a design business? If so: 7 before kids' bedtime, 2 after (if only actually designing, about half an hour)	2–3 of design of 8–10 of work	Designing: 0.3; thinking, concepts: 4; managing: rest	…I only know that I like to start at 09:30 and keep going till 19:00, 21:00, 24:00, 02:00…	0–8, it varies – juggling being a mother and working from home	It depends on the definition – going to a talk, exhibition or trip informs the work or becomes the work, so 24/7

MARC VAN DER HEIJDE	MARGARET CALVERT	MARION FINK	MARTIN LORENZ	MATTHIAS GÖRLICH	MICHAEL GEORGIOU
8 (designing or having to do with the process of it)	Between 5 and 10	None – talking about it: 8	2 (of focused design execution)	Marginal – work has become more admin and meetings; sometimes I try to take a day off to only do design work	4

NIKKI GONNISSEN	OLIVER KLIMPEL	PAUL BARNES	PREM KRISHNAMURTHY	RENATA GRAW	RICHARD WALKER
A lot but different – now it's more thinking of solutions, strategies, approach, etc.	3	4–12	8–12	Not enough	As long as it takes

S. HOFFMANN ROBBIANI	SASCHA LOBE	STEFAN SAGMEISTER	SVEN VOELKER	TIM BALAAM	URS LEHNI
Ooofff!	24	8	6.5 (but more on the days I teach)	4	Less than 2

YASMIN KHAN	YVES FIDALGO	AVERAGE/MOST/FEWEST			
Varies, anywhere from 0–12+	Around 9 – less beer, more design	A 7- M 24 F 0			

How many hours do you spend designing each day?

Now

ANDREAS GNASS

With a piece of paper and a pen or taking a shower

ANDREW STEVENS

Discussions with peers

ANNELYS DE VET

By living

ANTÓNIO S. GOMES

Ideas usually came during the process of making or working with a certain medium

BEN BRANAGAN

Listening, talking, drawing, making, reading, writing, going to places – it depended on the nature of the project

BERND HILPERT

Thinking, reading, discussing, writing, sketching, again and again…

BRIAN WEBB

Collect information, analyze, synthesize

CHRISTIAN HEUSSER

I simply started with an idea and developed it from there

DANIEL EATOCK

Intuition

DANIJELA DJOKIC

Back to zero. Start from zero with every new project. Find the basic problem and try…
(Cont. opposite – now)

EMMI SALONEN

At college I would look at other people's work much more, and try to learn about their way of thinking, how to get to the solution

ÉRIC & MARIE GASPAR

We spent a lot of time in libraries collecting images – we stuck them in sketchbooks and eventually we found ideas from them

FONS HICKMANN

I took a shower

HANS DIETER REICHERT

Library and discussions with fellow students

HOLGER JACOBS

I spent a lot of time in the library while in college – projects were complex and research was everything…
(Full answer, p. 227)

HOON KIM

I used to research into related fields to have a good understanding between those…
(Full answer, p. 227)

HYOUN YOUL JOE

From the environment around me and based on my experience

ISABELLE SWIDERSKI

Mostly through words, bouncing ideas off fellow students, feedback from tutors, library

JAMES GOGGIN

Wholeheartedly, and excitedly

JAN WILKER

I consciously tried as many avenues as possible – I looked at everything as if it were a brain exercise

JULIE GAYARD

Writing, drawing in a sketchbook, researching within books

KAI VON RABENAU

I spent hours in the library, researching a topic – then I would start drawing sketches and outlines, focusing in on a solution

KEN GARLAND

I tended to hoard images and sooner or later they formed a coherent group

KIRSTY CARTER

Research is key to a successful project or idea; I/we spend a great deal of…
(Cont. opposite – now)

KRISTINE MATTHEWS

Brainstorm, then chase up interesting leads

LARS HARMSEN

Books and magazines, public and university libraries

LAURENT LACOUR

Visual research, thinking, discussing, searching (teamwork)

LIZA ENEBEIS

I always start writing; I describe all the images that I will create

LUCINDA NOBLE

Pretty much the same process creatively then and now – it varies of course from …
(Cont. opposite – now)

MAKI SUZUKI

Usually, there are ideas around and they are constantly developed as a reaction to a situation

MARC VAN DER HEIJDE

There is no one way. You might want to approach an idea from a visual angle…
(Cont. opposite – now)

MARGARET CALVERT

e.g. Walked around supermarkets looking at packaging, having been given a packaging brief for spices

MARION FINK

Just observing, playing around, talking to people

MARTIN LORENZ

Intuitively

MATTHIAS GÖRLICH

Then and now is pretty much the same process. I like to rethink …
(Cont. opposite – now)

MICHAEL GEORGIOU

Books

NIKKI GONNISSEN

Engage, listen, research, analyze, focus

OLIVER KLIMPEL

–

PAUL BARNES

I think life is one long research project. All the time you are being inspired by the world…
(Cont. opposite – now)

PREM KRISHNAMURTHY

Read books, isolate myself as much as possible, write

RENATA GRAW

I learned that you can never predict that something will not work unless you actually begin doing
(Cont. opposite – now)

RICHARD WALKER

I used to go and have a look at what the others were doing

SANDRA HOFFMANN

Horizontally laid-out piles of sketches and notes, snapshots…
(Cont. opposite – now)

SASCHA LOBE

'TDS': Thinking, doing…
(Cont. opposite – now)

STEFAN SAGMEISTER

Talk to client extensively

SVEN VOELKER

I did a lot of research to get to know the subject and the problem – at the time, without real Internet and without Google, this was real work

TIM BALAAM

Independent and project-specific research such as attending a talk, visiting a museum/ exhibition or reading in the library

URS LEHNI

I guess back in school we already had established similar working methods to the ones we're using now – just in a very naive way

YASMIN KHAN

Lots of visual research, identifying specific formal and/or conceptual inspiration, lots of making, assessing, reworking

YVES FIDALGO

Taking a shower

How did you develop/research an idea?

Then

ANDREAS GNASS

With a piece of paper and a pen or taking a shower

ANDREW STEVENS

Discussion with colleagues and also the web – not for ideas, but things that make the ideas manifest

ANNELYS DE VET

By living

ANTÓNIO S. GOMES

Now the idea is mostly a cognitive reaction to research, be it open research on the net or bibliographic

BEN BRANAGAN

Listening, talking, drawing, making, reading, writing, going to places – it depends on the nature of the project

BERND HILPERT

Thinking, reading, discussing, writing, sketching, again and again…

BRIAN WEBB

Collect information, analyze, synthesize

CHRISTIAN HEUSSER

We team-discuss first ideas, develop them, talk again and reconsider the various sketches – then we decide upon a strategy to follow

DANIEL EATOCK

Intuition

DANIJELA DJOKIC

…to get to the bottom of it. Focus on the essential and simple things. Challenge the established

EMMI SALONEN

I tend to find out as much as I can about the client and let the inspiration come from their stories

ÉRIC & MARIE GASPAR

It is a bit more difficult to do it like then – deadlines are very tight and we lack time

FONS HICKMANN

I take a bath

HANS DIETER REICHERT

Internet, library, experience, conversations in family and among staff

HOLGER JACOBS

I still do research but more sporadically and there is no systematic…
(Full answer, p. 227)

HOON KIM

Basically, clients and co-workers develop an idea together. I still study related…
(Full answer, p. 227)

HYOUN YOUL JOE

From the environment around me and based on my experience

ISABELLE SWIDERSKI

Lots of ugly sketches + words, travelling, walking around, bouncing ideas off collaborators and colleagues, Internet + library + life

JAMES GOGGIN

Wholeheartedly, and excitedly

JAN WILKER

It's all very 'organic' in our studio, there's no one set process

JULIE GAYARD

Talking to the client about the product and its context. Writing, drawing in a sketchbook,…
(Full answer, p. 227)

KAI VON RABENAU

No time for all this (see opposite) – now when I get a job deadlines are very tight, so I need to start on the final piece without being able to research/develop much

KEN GARLAND

Same as then plus for client work I rely on them showing me as much as possible of their material

KIRSTY CARTER

…time doing it – whether it's a trip to the British Library or a visit to Barbara…
(Full answer, p. 228)

KRISTINE MATTHEWS

Brainstorm with employees, then have them chase up interesting leads – repeat

LARS HARMSEN

Web, books, magazines, interviews

LAURENT LACOUR

Visual research, thinking, discussing, searching (teamwork)

LIZA ENEBEIS

I always start writing; I describe all the images that I will create

LUCINDA NEWTON-DUNN

…project to project but basically I strip a brief down to the basics, look up literal meanings …
(Full answer, pp. 228–229)

MAKI SUZUKI

Same as then plus we also go to a residency once per year

MARC VAN DER HEIJDE

…or very much from a textual one (to deliberately avoid starting…
(Full answer, p. 229)

MARGARET CALVERT

I start with the idea, then follow through with research, if applicable. Usually within my own…
(Full answer, p. 229)

MARION FINK

Same as then with more time pressure and less playful

MARTIN LORENZ

Intuitively

MATTHIAS GÖRLICH

…the process, for example by starting with something …
(Full answer, p. 229)

MICHAEL GEORGIOU

Brainstorm, looking around, books

NIKKI GONNISSEN

Engage, listen, analyze, focus, use different strategies, make use of experience, use of different strengths by collaborating

OLIVER KLIMPEL

I've recently tried to do more speculative work and read more – less result-driven things…
(Full answer, p. 230)

PAUL BARNES

…around – you jot it down on a piece of paper or file it in your mind and then let it grow

PREM KRISHNAMURTHY

Read books, isolate myself as much as possible, write

RENATA GRAW

…it, and it's in the moment of creation that you then discover new understanding, new meaning

RICHARD WALKER

I still do (see then)

S. HOFFMANN ROBBIANI

…Post-its, but nothing recurring or systematically organized

SASCHA LOBE

…seeing, thinking, doing, seeing…

STEFAN SAGMEISTER

Talk to client extensively

SVEN VOELKER

These days I do a lot of research independently from projects. I know which subjects interest me and I develop projects based on that

TIM BALAAM

Research and development is an ongoing process and everything we have seen, read…
(Full answer, p. 231)

URS LEHNI

The conception of a situation within which design can happen is very close to the modes with which I also like to work in…
(Full answer, p. 231)

YASMIN KHAN

Tapping into ongoing visual research and long-standing interests; lots of making, assessing and reworking; also collaboration, discussion with peers

YVES FIDALGO

See then, hasn't changed much…

How do you develop/research an idea?

Now

ANDREAS GNASS

The straight lines of Dieter Rams, the clear thoughts of Wolfgang Weingart, the conceptual thoughts of Bauhaus, the...
(Cont. opposite – now)

ANDREW STEVENS

Peter Saville, Neville Brody, Saul Bass, Margaret Calvert (pp. 150–153), Derek Birdsall, Herb Lubalin

ANNELYS DE VET

–

ANTÓNIO S. GOMES

Ed Fella, Vaughan Oliver, Neville Brody, David Carson, Sebastião Rodrigues

BEN BRANAGAN

Amongst others: Bruce Mau, Ken Garland (pp. 114–117)

BERND HILPERT

My teachers (mainly Heinz Habermann, Horst Brüning and Marc Bertier)

BRIAN WEBB

John Gorham, Push Pin Studios, US advertising, Dada, H. N. Werkman

CHRISTIAN HEUSSER

Wolfgang Weingart, Mary Vieira, Georg Staehelin

DANIEL EATOCK

Adrian Newey

DANIJELA DJOKIC

Otl Aicher, Herbert W. Kapitzki, Richard Saul Wurman, Edward Tufte, Marcello Zuffo, etc.

EMMI SALONEN

I really couldn't list designers who have influenced me. Except Mike Mills, whom I have much respect...
(Cont. opposite – now)

ÉRIC & MARIE GASPAR

Alan Fletcher

FONS HICKMANN

Uwe Loesch

HANS DIETER REICHERT

Willy Fleckhaus, Emil Ruder, Wim Crouwel, Wolfgang Weingart, Alexey Brodovitch, Hans Nienheysen, Josef Müller-Brockmann

HOLGER JACOBS

I was more influenced by visual poets such as Franz Mon and Eugen Gomringer

HOON KIM

Karel Martens, David Reinfurt, James Goggin (pp. 98–101), Paul Elliman

HYOUN YOUL JOE

Anh Graphics, Doosup Kim, Helmut Schmid, Hong Design, Image and Imagination, Kohei Sugiura, Matsuda Yukimasa,...
(Full answer, p. 227)

ISABELLE SWIDERSKI

April Greiman, Neville Brody

JAMES GOGGIN

Charles and Ray Eames, Graphic Thought Facility (pp. 30–33), Ettore Sottsass...
(Full answer p. 227)

JAN WILKER

Otl Aicher, Max Bill, Wim Crouwel, Tibor Kalman, Stefan Sagmeister (pp. 202–205)

JULIE GAYARD

Josef Müller-Brockmann, Max Bill, Mike Mills, Julian House

KAI VON RABENAU

Vaughan Oliver

KEN GARLAND

Hans Schleger

KIRSTY CARTER

Josef Müller-Brockmann

KRISTINE MATTHEWS

Tibor Kalman, Sophie Thomas, Holger Jacobs (pp. 82–85), Graphic Thought Facility (pp. 30–33), Alan Kitching, Saul Bass, Josef Müller-Brockmann

LARS HARMSEN

Neville Brody, David Carson, Vaughan Oliver

LAURENT LACOUR

Lars Müller, Ruedi Baur, Wolfgang Weingart

LIZA ENEBEIS

Tibor Kalman – I admire him for his sense of humour and unconventional observations – his approach to design still lives on

LUCINDA NOBLE

No particular influences. I've always been inspired by a general mixture of styles and approaches. Names that come to...
(Full answer, p. 229)

MAKI SUZUKI

M/M Paris, Bless, Daft Punk, Maison Martin Margiela

MARC VAN DER HEIJDE

Amongst many: Piet Zwart, Neville Brody

MARGARET CALVERT

Hans Schleger and Jock Kinneir – two designers who gave me an insight into graphic design, while I was on the Illustration course at Chelsea

MARION FINK

Otl Aicher, Wolfgang Weingart

MARTIN LORENZ

Friedrich Forssman

MATTHIAS GÖRLICH

We had our 'heroes' (all the Swiss and Dutch), but I can't name anyone in particular

MICHAEL GEORGIOU

Neville Brody, Paul Rand, Alan Fletcher, Milton Glaser

NIKKI GONNISSEN

Piet Zwart, Willem Sandberg, Neville Brody, Malcolm Garrett, Tibor Kalman, Tomato, 8vo, Gert Dumbar, Wim Crouwel, Pierre Bernard

OLIVER KLIMPEL

Otl Aicher, Wolfgang Weingart, Peter Saville, Hard Werken, Mevis and van Deursen

PAUL BARNES

Jan Tschichold, Charles Collett, Robert and George Stephenson...
(Full answer, p. 230)

PREM KRISHNAMURTHY

Robin Kinross (Design/Writing/Research), Tibor Kalman, Jan Tschichold

RENATA GRAW

Tibor Kalman, Wolfgang Weingart, Piet Zwart, Stefan Sagmeister (pp. 202–205), Wim Crouwel, Karel Martens...
(Full answer, p. 230)

RICHARD WALKER

I think the biggest influences were the people I used to hang out with/share a flat with...
(Full answer, pp. 230–231)

SANDRA HOFFMANN

Hans Arp, H.C. Berann, Donald Wills Douglas, W.A. Dwiggins, Karl Gerstner...
(Full answer, p. 231)

SASCHA LOBE

Bauhaus, Ott+Stein, Vaughan Oliver, Neville Brody, Max Bill, Bruno Munari, Charles and Ray Eames, Rei Kawakubo

STEFAN SAGMEISTER

Storm Thorgerson

SVEN VOELKER

Tibor Kalman

TIM BALAAM

Nobody in particular

URS LEHNI

Cornel Windlin

YASMIN KHAN

Metahaven, Superstudio, Genevieve Gauckler, Antoine + Manuel, Droog

YVES FIDALGO

Ronan Bouroullec, Olivier Sidet, Florence Doléac (all our tutors at college). Also Jean Prouvé. And Achille Castiglioni. And...
(Full answer, p. 231)

RANKING LIST

1 NEVILLE BRODY, WOLFGANG WEINGART
2 TIBOR KALMAN
3 JOSEF MÜLLER-BROCKMANN, MAX BILL

Which designers influenced you?

Then

ANDREAS GNASS

…'insistence' of Sandra Hoffmann (pp. 194–197) and the playfulness of Achille Castiglioni. Today this is all in my head like in a big stew

ANDREW STEVENS

–

ANNELYS DE VET

–

ANTÓNIO S. GOMES

Karl Gerstner, Victor Palla, Paulo Cantos, Lust, Vincent Perrottet

BEN BRANAGAN

Bruno Munari

BERND HILPERT

My project partners (Peter Eckart, Michel de Boer, Ahn Sang Soo, Roland Lambrette, Vincent van Baar, Zou Zhengfang, Elodie Boyer and many others)

BRIAN WEBB

Everybody, Dada, H. N. Werkman

CHRISTIAN HEUSSER

Jan Tschichold, Richard Paul Lohse, Ruedi Baur

DANIEL EATOCK

Enzo Mari

DANIJELA DJOKIC

John Maeda

EMMI SALONEN

…for. Then and now. I'm more influenced by people making things in general than just certain designers

ÉRIC & MARIE GASPAR

Alan Fletcher

FONS HICKMANN

David Lynch

HANS DIETER REICHERT

Jan Tschichold, Dieter Rams, Anthony Froshaug, Otl Aicher, Helmut Schmid, Derek Birdsall, Irma Boom, North, Harry Beck… (Full answer, p. 227)

HOLGER JACOBS

I try to avoid specific influences but respect Alan Fletcher, Karel Martens, Tibor Kalman, Lance Wyman, Graphic Thought Facility (pp. 30–33) a lot

HOON KIM

Rei Kawakubo, Kenya Hara

HYOUN YOUL JOE

Antoni Muntadas, Daniel Harding and Tomas Celizna, Daniel Eatock (pp. 58–61), Lehni-Trüb (pp. 214–217)… (Full answer, p. 227)

ISABELLE SWIDERSKI

Swiss Modernists

JAMES GOGGIN

See then, plus Bruno Munari, Sori Yanagi, Enzo Mari, W. A. Dwiggins and countless others

JAN WILKER

David Oreilly, Elliott Earls, Norm, Experimental Jetset

JULIE GAYARD

Max Bill, Josef Müller-Brockmann, Mike Mills, Julian House and Dutch designers: Metahaven, Experimental Jetset

KAI VON RABENAU

Mike Meiré

KEN GARLAND

Piero della Francesca

KIRSTY CARTER

Derek Birdsall

KRISTINE MATTHEWS

See then + Rosa Loves, We Are What We Do, Droog, Sennep, Hyperkit (pp. 210–213), Non-Format, Cassie Klingler, Brighten the Corners (p. 256)

LARS HARMSEN

–

LAURENT LACOUR

A lot

LIZA ENEBEIS

Recent extremely talented graduates from The Hague and Rotterdam Academy – I am hoping they will be the next ones to influence all of us

LUCINDA NEWTON-DUNN

See then + names that come to mind now: Eley Kishimoto, Lena Corwin, Marimekko, Bauhaus, Anni Albers, Charles and Ray Eames

MAKI SUZUKI

The people who influence us today are people we work with: Alex Rich, Yuri Suzuki, Martino Gamper, Fabien Cappello

---

MARC VAN DER HEIJDE

Amongst many: Lex Reitsma, Piet Gerards

MARGARET CALVERT

Adrian Frutiger for his passion and commitment, and Thomas Heatherwick for his originality and sense of fun

MARION FINK

Maison Martin Margiela

MARTIN LORENZ

Kurt Schwitters

MATTHIAS GÖRLICH

There are designers whom I respect for their approach e.g. Urs Lehni (pp. 214–217) for rethinking… (Full answer, p. 229)

MICHAEL GEORGIOU

Alan Fletcher, Paul Rand, Fons Hickmann (pp. 74–77), KesselsKramer (pp. 190–193), Graphic Thought Facility (pp. 30–33)

NIKKI GONNISSEN

Wim Crouwel, Jurgen Bey, De Designpolitie, Pierre di Sciullo, Catherine Zask, Paul Cox, Metahaven, etc.

OLIVER KLIMPEL

Memphis style, Barney Bubbles, Rei Kawakubo, Bart de Baets, Stewart Bailey

PAUL BARNES

Probably the same as then, but even more

PREM KRISHNAMURTHY

Anthony Froshaug, Norman Potter, Klaus Wittkugel, Will Burtin

RENATA GRAW

Ludovic Balland, Daniel Eatock (pp. 58–61), James Goggin (pp. 98–101), Armand Mevis, Maureen Mooren… (Full answer, p. 230)

RICHARD WALKER

These days my influences haven't really changed – I think you form an opinion… (Full answer, pp. 230–231)

S. HOFFMANN ROBBIANI

Wolf Hirth and Martin Schempp, Bertrand Piccard

SASCHA LOBE

'Inspired' rather than 'influenced': 2×4, Spin, Fanette Mellier, Pam&Jenny, Phillipe Apeloig, Droog, Ronan and Erwan Bouroullec

STEFAN SAGMEISTER

Tibor Kalman

SVEN VOELKER

Allen Ruppersberg, Otl Aicher, John Warwicker, Bruno Munari, Anton Stankowski, Helmut Smits, Daniel Eatock and so many more…

TIM BALAAM

Charles and Ray Eames

URS LEHNI

Bruno Munari

YASMIN KHAN

Paperrad, Beige, Metahaven, Hella Jongerius, Keiichi Tanaami

YVES FIDALGO

As you go along, your influences are not so definite – there are so many that I really find it wrong to name one over another

RANKING LIST

1 BRUNO MUNARI, DANIEL VAN DER VELDEN (METAHAVEN)
2 ALAN FLETCHER, CHARLES AND RAY EAMES, DANIEL EATOCK, EXPERIMENTAL JETSET, GRAPHIC THOUGHT FACILITY, JAN TSCHICHOLD, PAUL RAND
3 ANTHONY FROSHAUG, ENZO MARI, KAREL MARTENS, MAX BILL, RICHARD PAUL LOHSE, TIBOR KALMAN, URS LEHNI (LEHNI-TRÜB)

Which designers influence you?

Now

ANDREAS GNASS	ANDREW STEVENS	ANNELYS DE VET	ANTONIO S. GOMES	BEN BRANAGAN	BERND HILPERT
Everyday products	Gastrotypographicalassemblage by Lou Dorfsman and Herb Lubalin (1966)	-	**Mo'Wax CD packaging, Vladimir Mayakovsky (For the Voice, 1923)**	**The record cover to TNT by Tortoise**	Every day I saw design that had an effect on my projects. Then, more objects were classified as 'design'

BRIAN WEBB	CHRISTIAN HEUSSER	DANIEL EATOCK	DANIJELA DJOKIC	EMMI SALONEN	ÉRIC & MARIE GASPAR
'Found' lettering, graphics and type specimens	xtre-em poster by Georg Staehelin (1997)	**Post-it note**	**Victor Vasarely drawings**	**The book Graphic Agitation (Liz McQuiston)**	**The Valentine typewriter for Olivetti by Ettore Sottsass (1969)**

FONS HICKMANN	HANS DIETER REICHERT	HOLGER JACOBS	HOON KIM	HYOUN YOUL JOE	ISABELLE SWIDERSKI
Dildos	Twen (magazine) and book covers (Surkamp Verlag) by Willy Fleckhaus and books Typography (Emil Ruder), ypography Today' (Helmut Schmid)	The poem 'silence' or 'silencio' (Eugen Gomringer) and kitschy Japanese magazines	A British poster, Keep Calm and Carry On, various Dutch design	-	-

JAMES GOGGIN	JAN WILKER	JULIE GAYARD	KAI VON RABENAU	KEN GARLAND	KIRSTY CARTER
Olivetti Valentine typewriter, Ettore Sottsass	Whatever the designers that are mentioned on the spread before did	**Film by Hans Richter: Rhythm 23**	**4AD record covers**	-	Common Worship for the Church of England designed by Derek Birdsall

KRISTINE MATTHEWS	LARS HARMSEN	LAURENT LACOUR	LIZA ENEBEIS	LUCINDA NOBLE	MAKI SUZUKI
Anything by Tibor Kalman (esp. office map for studio tours), anything by Charles and Ray Eames (esp. House of Cards and Power of Ten)	**The early campaigns for Benetton by Oliviero Toscani**	**Transfer (book by Lars Müller Publishers)**	I was in love with Florent by Tibor Kalman for a long time	I can't remember any pieces that inspired me in particular	**the PIL record, Album**

MARC VAN DER HEIJDE	MARGARET CALVERT	MARION FINK	MARTIN LORENZ	MATTHIAS GÖRLICH	MICHAEL GEORGIOU
Within the context of my student work (p. 148): the typographical posters of Ton Homburg (Opera) for the… (Full answer, p. 229)	-	Work for the Olympic Games 1972 by Otl Aicher and Swiss poster design from the 1960s/1970s by Armin Hofmann	**TC 100 by Hans (Nick) Roericht**	-	-

NIKKI GONNISSEN	OLIVER KLIMPEL	PAUL BARNES	PREM KRISHNAMURTHY	RENATA GRAW	RICHARD WALKER
-	The posters designed by Wolfgang Weingart	-	**Too many to name**	I remember the moment I decided to go back and… (Full answer, p. 230)	I've always liked functional design e. g. audience survey maps

SANDRA HOFFMANN	SASCHA LOBE	STEFAN SAGMEISTER	SVEN VOELKER	TIM BALAAM	URS LEHNI
Avro (Aero, Anson, Lancaster), Schiff nach Europa, Solar Impulse	**Nefertiti bust (Thutmose)**	King Crimson album cover for In the Court of the Crimson King	**Apple PowerBook**	**Lego**	-

YASMIN KHAN	YVES FIDALGO				

ANDREAS GNASS

Everyday products

ANDREW STEVENS

None

ANNELYS DE VET

-

ANTÓNIO S. GOMES

XTC's GO TO album cover, Whole Earth Catalogue

BEN BRANAGAN

-

BERND HILPERT

Every day I see design that has an effect on my projects. Now, more the things of daily… (Full answer, p. 226)

BRIAN WEBB

'Found' lettering, graphics and type specimens plus everything I can't do

CHRISTIAN HEUSSER

La cinémathèque française: Projected guidance system in the museum of cinematography in Bercy, Paris (F)

DANIEL EATOCK

Post-it note and Pritt Stick

DANIJELA DJOKIC

Generative Design

EMMI SALONEN

I tend to look at notebooks and stationery in general

ÉRIC & MARIE GASPAR

Five Tyres Remoulded by Richard Hamilton (1972)

FONS HICKMANN

UFOs

HANS DIETER REICHERT

Tractatus Logico-Philosophicus (Ludwig Wittgenstein), Bible, Die Neue Typography (Jan Tschichold), Typography (Otl Aicher)

HOLGER JACOBS

'68 Olympics identity (Lance Wymans)

HOON KIM

Fashion design, architecture, novels are more inspiring than graphic design

HYOUN YOUL JOE

-

ISABELLE SWIDERSKI

-

JAMES GOGGIN

Formosa perpetual calendar, Enzo Mari for Danese

JAN WILKER

Whatever the designers that are mentioned on the spread before did

JULIE GAYARD

Best wishes postcards from Josef and Anni Albers

KAI VON RABENAU

032c and Brand Eins magazines

KEN GARLAND

-

KIRSTY CARTER

Monty Python Catalogues designed by Derek Birdsall

KRISTINE MATTHEWS

The Reverse Ark by Future Farmers and Lego

LARS HARMSEN

-

LAURENT LACOUR

Established & Sons (product and graphic design)

LIZA ENEBEIS

Although I still love Tibor Kalman's work, I am not only drawn to one piece of work by one person, it can be anything I see around me

LUCINDA NEWTON-DUNN

The beautiful, simple graphics printed on Japanese vegetable boxes

MAKI SUZUKI

The Kon-Tiki raft

MARC VAN DER HEIJDE

Within the context of my professional work (p. 149): I love the animation Phillippe Apeloig made for the Mois du graphisme d'Echirolles

MARGARET CALVERT

-

MARION FINK

-

MARTIN LORENZ

Fröbelgaben (Friedrich Fröbel)

MATTHIAS GÖRLICH

-

MICHAEL GEORGIOU

-

NIKKI GONNISSEN

'68 Olympics identity (Lance Wymans) – a mix between psychedelic design of that time and old Mexican designs (local/global mix)

OLIVER KLIMPEL

Ringier Annual Report designed by Fischli & Weiss and The Prisoner (film series) by Patrick McGoohan

PAUL BARNES

-

PREM KRISHNAMURTHY

Too many to name

RENATA GRAW

-

RICHARD WALKER

I like Boris bikes

S. HOFFMANN ROBBIANI

Hardoy Butterfly Chair, Gordon Smith House

SASCHA LOBE

Premier case (AG Franzoni)

STEFAN SAGMEISTER

Seed Magazine

SVEN VOELKER

iPhone

TIM BALAAM

Algues by Ronan and Erwan Bouroullec

URS LEHNI

-

YASMIN KHAN

OZ magazine, Salvador Dalí's Les Diners de Gala cookbook

YVES FIDALGO

Maybe Jean Prouvé's pieces

Which pieces of design influence you?

Now

ANDREAS GNASS

e.g.
Marshall
McLuhan

ANDREW STEVENS

Jon Savage
(England's
Dreaming)

ANNELYS DE VET

Isabelle Allende,
Connie Palmen,
J.D. Salinger,
Sigmund Freud,
Paulo Coelho,
Don DeLillo

ANTÓNIO S. GOMES

Marshall McLuhan
(Understanding
Media), Gillo Dorfles
(As Oscilações do
Gosto), William Gibson
(Neuromancer),
Douglas Coupland

BEN BRANAGAN

Italo Calvino
(If on a Winter's
Night a
Traveller), Arthur
C. Clarke (2001)

BERND HILPERT

I never
read very
much…

BRIAN WEBB

Harper Lee (To Kill
a Mockingbird),
Herbert Spencer
(Pioneers of Modern
Typography)

CHRISTIAN HEUSSER

Ulf
Poschardt
(DJ Culture)

DANIEL EATOCK

Lucy R. Lippard
(Six Years: the
dematerialization
of the art object)

DANIJELA DJOKIC

Marshall
McLuhan

EMMI SALONEN

Sociology
books

ÉRIC & MARIE GASPAR

Christopher
Alexander
(A Pattern
Language)

FONS HICKMANN

Mikhail
Bulgakov

HANS DIETER REICHERT

Herman Hesse, Max
Frisch, Max Bense,
Umberto Eco,
Walter Benjamin,
James Joyce,
Norman Potter

HOLGER JACOBS

Junichiro
Tanizaki (In
Praise of
Shadows)

HOON KIM

Georges Perec,
Haruki
Murakami,
Norman Potter

HYOUN YOUL JOE

Seigo Matsuoka (The
Editorial Engineering of
Knowledge), Matsuda
Yukimasa (Code, Zero,
Designscape), John
Berger, Philip B. Meggs

ISABELLE SWIDERSKI

Jeanette
Winterson,
Baudelaire,
Balzac, Voltaire

JAMES GOGGIN

Georges Perec, Lucy
Lippard, Marc Augé,
Zygmunt Bauman,
Paul Auster, Haruki
Murakami, David
Mitchell, J.D. Salinger

JAN WILKER

Franz Kafka
(Kurzgeschichten),
Arthur Schnitzler
(Der Weg ins Freie,
Traumnovelle)

JULIE GAYARD

–

KAI VON RABENAU

Graham Greene,
Salman Rushdie,
Max Frisch

KEN GARLAND

Evelyn Waugh
(Decline and
Fall)

KIRSTY CARTER

Georges
Perec

KRISTINE MATTHEWS

J.D. Salinger (Raise
High the Roof Beam,
Carpenters and Nine
Stories), Paul Auster,
Chuck Palahniuk (Fight
Club), Donna Tartt
(The Secret History)

LARS HARMSEN

Neville Brody (The
Graphic Language),
Emigre, Face,
Tempo, Wiener
(all magazines)

LAURENT LACOUR

Lars Müller,
Ruedi Baur,
Wolfgang
Weingart

LIZA ENEBEIS

Marshall McLuhan
(Understanding Media),
John Berger (Ways of
Seeing), Harold Evans
(Pictures on a Page)

LUCINDA NOBLE

John Pawson
(Minimum), Edward
Tufte, Haruki
Murakami, Paul
Auster

MAKI SUZUKI

Irvine
Welsh
(Filth)

MARC VAN DER HEIJDE

Oscar Wilde
(The Picture
of Dorian
Gray)

MARGARET CALVERT

–

MARION FINK

Jean Baudrillard,
Marshall McLuhan,
Charles and Ray
Eames (The Powers
of Ten)

MARTIN LORENZ

Douglas Adams
(Hitchhiker's
Guide to the
Galaxy)

MATTHIAS GÖRLICH

Probably all the coffee-
table books from Die
Gestalten Verlag
(Berlin) but also some
of the older Swiss
design books for the
visuals

MICHAEL GEORGIOU

George Orwell
(1984), George
Seferis, Oscar
Wilde

NIKKI GONNISSEN

Claes Oldenburg
(Notes in Hand), Jan
Brand (Words and
the images), Ovid
(Metamorphoses)

OLIVER KLIMPEL

Jean Baudrillard,
José Antonio
Muñoz & Carlos
Sampayo, Paul
Scherbarth

PAUL BARNES

Jan Tschichold
(Typographische
Gestaltung), Karl
Gerstner (Designing
Programmes)

PREM KRISHNAMURTHY

Robin Kinross, Italo
Calvino, Georges
Perec, John Berger,
Martin Heidegger

RENATA GRAW

Robert Venturi
(Learning from
Las Vegas)

RICHARD WALKER

I haven't /
don't read
much…

(Cont. opposite – now)

SANDRA HOFFMANN

Hugo Ball,
Simone de
Beauvoir, John
Berger…

(Full answer, p. 231)

SASCHA LOBE

Robert M. Pirsig,
Roland Barthes,
Paul Virilio,
Wolfgang Welsch,
Marcel Proust

STEFAN SAGMEISTER

Tom Wolfe

SVEN VOELKER

Salman Rushdie
(Haroun and the
Sea of Stories)

TIM BALAAM

Le Corbusier
(Towards
a New
Architecture)

URS LEHNI

Friedrich
Glauser

YASMIN KHAN

Miranda
July, MFK
Fisher

YVES FIDALGO

Don't
remember

RANKING LIST

1 MARSHALL MCLUHAN
2 GEORGES PEREC, JOHN BERGER
3 HARUKI MURAKAMI, PAUL AUSTER, J.D. SALINGER

Which authors/books
influenced you?

Then

ANDREAS GNASS

e.g. Wolf Lotter

ANDREW STEVENS

None

ANNELYS DE VET

Rüdiger Safranski, Alain Badiou, Peter Sloterdijk, Octavio Paz, Mahmoud Darwish, Bas Heijne, Anna Tilroe, Roland Barthes, Paul Virilio

ANTÓNIO S. GOMES

Friedrich Kittler (Gramophone, Film, Typewriter), Neal Stephenson (Snow Crash), Hakim Bey (Temporary Autonomous Zones)

BEN BRANAGAN

Italo Calvino (Mr Palomar), Salman Rushdie (Midnight's Children)

BERND HILPERT

I never read very much…

BRIAN WEBB

Harper Lee (To Kill a Mockingbird), Herbert Spencer (Pioneers of Modern Typography)

CHRISTIAN HEUSSER

John Irving (Hotel New Hampshire)

DANIEL EATOCK

All books

DANIJELA DJOKIC

John Maeda

EMMI SALONEN

Sociology books

ÉRIC & MARIE GASPAR

Fernando Pessoa (The Book of Disquiet)

FONS HICKMANN

Matthias Feldbacken

HANS DIETER REICHERT

Marshall McLuhan, Vilém Flusser, William of Ockham, Ludwig Wittgenstein

HOLGER JACOBS

Graham Harding and Paul Walton (The Bluffer's Guide to Marketing) – for very practical reasons

HOON KIM

Georges Perec, Haruki Murakami, Norman Potter

HYOUN YOUL JOE

George Kubler (The Shape of Time), Jan van Toorn (Design beyond Design), C. Danto (After the End of Art), Suksan Tak (Korean Nationalism, Korean Identity)

ISABELLE SWIDERSKI

Muriel Barbery, Michael Cunningham, Daniel Pennac

JAMES GOGGIN

Brian Holmes, Owen Hatherley, Hari Kunzru, Tom McCarthy, Boris Groys, Hito Steyerl, Vladimir Nabokov

JAN WILKER

David Foster Wallace

JULIE GAYARD

-

KAI VON RABENAU

David Foster Wallace, John le Carré, Leo Tolstoy, McSweeney's (Journal)

KEN GARLAND

Cormac McCarthy (The Road)

KIRSTY CARTER

Eric Gill (Essay on Typography)

KRISTINE MATTHEWS

Richard Scarry (What Do People Do All Day?), Truman Capote (In Cold Blood)

LARS HARMSEN

All the hundreds of magazines and books we receive monthly because of our blog and magazine, Slanted

LAURENT LACOUR

A lot

LIZA ENEBEIS

Recently I read Andy Warhol (From A to B and Back Again). I am not sure if it influenced me but I enjoyed it

LUCINDA NEWTON-DUNN

Illustrated children's books (1940s–80s) and photography books such as those of Rinko Kawauchi

MAKI SUZUKI

Romain Gary (The Roots of Heaven)

MARC VAN DER HEIJDE

Herman Hesse (Siddharta)

MARGARET CALVERT

Herbert Spencer (Pioneers of Modern Typography)

MARION FINK

Karl Gerstner, Horst Bredekamp, Gottfried Böhm

MARTIN LORENZ

Karl Gerstner (Programme Gestalten)

MATTHIAS GÖRLICH

Certainly Tomás Maldonado (Umwelt und Revolte) and some other more theoretical books … (Full answer, p. 230)

MICHAEL GEORGIOU

Steven Heller

NIKKI GONNISSEN

At the moment I read Elias Canetti (Crowds and Power) and I love to read novels

OLIVER KLIMPEL

David Simon, F. Scott Fitzgerald, Stephen Bayley

PAUL BARNES

Jan Tschichold (Typographische Gestaltung), Robin Kinross (Modern Typography)

PREM KRISHNAMURTHY

Vikram Chandra, Orhan Pamuk, W.G. Sebald, Bruno Latour, Boris Groys, Michael Pollan

RENATA GRAW

Paul Rand (Conversations with Students), Michael Beirut (Seventy-nine Short Essays on Design)

RICHARD WALKER

…but I have a great bookshelf, which is full of books I bought by the metre

S. HOFFMANN ROBBIANI

John Langshaw Austin, Simon Baron-Cohen, Lewis Carroll… (Full answer, p. 231)

SASCHA LOBE

Dick Francis, Christian Kracht, Ian McEwan, Haruki Murakami, Jason Starr

STEFAN SAGMEISTER

Jonathan Franzen

SVEN VOELKER

Derek Jarman (Chroma)

TIM BALAAM

Kenya Hara (Designing Design)

URS LEHNI

Italo Calvino

YASMIN KHAN

Jennifer Egan

YVES FIDALGO

Jorn Riel

Which authors/books influence you?

Now

ANDREAS GNASS

Lienhard von Monkiewitsch, Kasimir Malewitsch,...
(Cont. opposite – now)

ANDREW STEVENS

Photographers Paul Reas, Paul Graham, Martin Parr

ANNELYS DE VET

Gilbert and George, Fluxus, Daan van Golden, H.N. Werkman, Barbara Kruger, Fischli and Weiss, Willem Sandberg, Tracey Emin, Pippilotti Rist

ANTÓNIO S. GOMES

Gary Hill (Tall Ships), John Baldessari (The Back of all the Trucks), Chuck Close (Portraits), Gerhard Richter (Abstract Paintings), Tony Oursler (Eyes)

BEN BRANAGAN

Bernd and Hilla Becher, Raymond Pettibon, Michael Landy (Breakdown)

BERND HILPERT

Many – as a part of daily awareness – but no specific influences

BRIAN WEBB

Pop artists, Peter Blake, Ron Kitaj

CHRISTIAN HEUSSER

Nam June Paik

DANIEL EATOCK

Ed Ruscha

DANIJELA DJOKIC

Herbert W. Kapitzki

EMMI SALONEN

Street art

ÉRIC & MARIE GASPAR

Richard Hamilton

FONS HICKMANN

-

HANS DIETER REICHERT

Max Bill, Paul Lohse, Karl Gerstner, Josef Albers, Hannah Höch, Piet Mondrian, Kurt Schwitters, John Heartfield

HOLGER JACOBS

Bruce Nauman

HOON KIM

Sol LeWitt, Richard Serra, Bruno Munari, Max Neuhaus, Ryoji Ikeda, Casten Nicolai

HYOUN YOUL JOE

-

ISABELLE SWIDERSKI

Picasso, Degas, Rodin, Annie Leibovitz

JAMES GOGGIN

Francis Alÿs, On Kawara, Gabriel Orozco, Alighiero e Boetti, Olafur Eliasson

JAN WILKER

David Hockney

JULIE GAYARD

Marcel Broodthaers (Atlas), Sol LeWitt (Variations of an Incomplete Open Cube), John Baldessari

KAI VON RABENAU

Douglas Brothers, Paolo Roversi, Andreas Gursky

KEN GARLAND

William Turner

KIRSTY CARTER

Marcel Duchamp

KRISTINE MATTHEWS

David Shrigley, Justin Knowles, Fluxus artists, Andy Warhol

LARS HARMSEN

Damien Hirst, Nick Night, Jean-Michel Basquiat, Jean Tinguely, Robert Rauschenberg, Marcel Duchamp

LAURENT LACOUR

Roman Signer

LIZA ENEBEIS

The Chapman brothers

LUCINDA NOBLE

James Turrell, Mark Dion, Ben Nicholson, Andy Goldsworthy, Ellsworth Kelly, Piero Manzoni, Cornelia Parker, 'Thinking Aloud' (Richard Wentworth)

MAKI SUZUKI

Yves Klein, Piero Manzoni, Joseph Kosuth, Gordon Matta-Clark, Jeff Koons, Marcel Duchamp but mostly Édouard Manet

MARC VAN DER HEIJDE

Jan Dibbets

MARGARET CALVERT

Fred Brill, Leonard Rosamund and Brian Robb

MARION FINK

Anish Kapoor, Tacita Dean

MARTIN LORENZ

Pablo Picasso

MATTHIAS GÖRLICH

Concrete Art, Karl Gerstner, Richard Paul Lohse, Charlotte Posenenske, Mark Lombardi, George Maciunas

MICHAEL GEORGIOU

Andy Warhol, Paul Klee, David Hockney

NIKKI GONNISSEN

Claes Oldenburg (giant objects and soft sculptures like hamburgers, etc....
(Full answer, p. 230)

OLIVER KLIMPEL

Fischli and Weiss, Lyonel Feininger, Mike Kelley

PAUL BARNES

Too many to mention

PREM KRISHNAMURTHY

Chauncey Hare, Eugene Atget, Gregory Crewdson, Eleanor Antin

RENATA GRAW

There are so many...: Donald Judd, Sol LeWitt, Marina Abramovitz...
(Cont. opposite – now)

RICHARD WALKER

The South London Gallery was next to college so I got to see a lot of 'young British artists'...
(Full answer, p. 231)

SANDRA HOFFMANN

Monika Dillier, General Idea, Monique Jacot, Frans Masereel plus in part see answer p. 242

SASCHA LOBE

Blinky Palermo, Lawrence Weiner, Bernd and Hilla Becher, Jenny Holzer, Donald Judd, Felix Gonzalez-Torres

STEFAN SAGMEISTER

Vienna Actionists

SVEN VOELKER

Peter Greenaway

TIM BALAAM

Dan Graham

URS LEHNI

Martin Kippenberger

YASMIN KHAN

Matt Barney, Kara Walker

YVES FIDALGO

Things between then and now have got mixed up; I can't really separate them: Damien Hirst, Wolfgang Tillmans...
(Cont. opposite – now)

RANKING LIST

1 FLUXUS (GEORGE MACIUNAS), MARCEL DUCHAMP, SOL LEWITT
2 ANDREAS GURSKY, ANDY WARHOL, ANISH KAPOOR, BERND & HILLA BECHER, DAMIEN HIRST, DONALD JUDD, DAVID HOCKNEY, FISCHLI & WEISS, JOHN BALDESSARI, KURT SCHWITTERS, KARL GERSTNER, MARTIN PARR, OLAFUR ELIASSON, PIERO MANZONI, PABLO PICASSO
3 ALL THE OTHER ARTISTS LISTED

Which artists/works of art influenced you?

Then

ANDREAS GNASS

...Kurt Schwitters, Eadweard Muybridge

ANDREW STEVENS

–

ANNELYS DE VET

Lawrence Weiner, John Cage, Barbara Kruger, Hans Haacke, Jenny Holzer, Atlas Group, Khaled Hourani, Peter Friedle, Ai Weiwei, Francis Alÿs

ANTONIO S. GOMES

Pavel Pepperstein, John Stezaker (Collages), Karl Gerstner (Color Sound), Janet Cardiff (Forty-Part Motet), Allan Ruppersberg (The Singing Posters)

BEN BRANAGAN

–

BERND HILPERT

Many – as a part of daily awareness – but no specific influences

BRIAN WEBB

Paul Nash

CHRISTIAN HEUSSER

Jean-Michel Basquiat

DANIEL EATOCK

Anders Jakobsen

DANIJELA DJOKIC

Sol LeWitt

EMMI SALONEN

Elsa Salonen

ÉRIC & MARIE GASPAR

Marcel Duchamp

FONS HICKMANN

–

HANS DIETER REICHERT

Joseph Beuys, Gerhard Richter, Henry Moore, Antony Gormley, Barbara Hepworth, Ben Nicholson

HOLGER JACOBS

Victor Vasarely

HOON KIM

Alexander McQueen, Yoshitomo Nara

HYOUN YOUL JOE

–

ISABELLE SWIDERSKI

Wolfgang Tillmans, Rachel Whiteread, Louise Bourgeois, Roni Horn, Jenny Holzer

JAMES GOGGIN

See then, plus a seemingly infinite list that could include Nathan Coley, Dora García...
(Full answer, p. 227)

JAN WILKER

–

JULIE GAYARD

Same as then plus the work of Josef + Anni Albers. And Line Describing a Cone by Anthony McCall

KAI VON RABENAU

Mark Borthwick, James Turrell, Ryan McGinley

KEN GARLAND

Piero de la Francesca, Anish Kapoor

KIRSTY CARTER

Marcel Duchamp – I find endless joy and discovery in his work

KRISTINE MATTHEWS

See then, plus Clare Patey (curator/artist), Future Farmers, Tom Heatherwick, Antony Gormley, Rachel Whiteread, Banksy

LARS HARMSEN

Andreas Gursky, Santiago Sierra

LAURENT LACOUR

Olafur Eliasson

LIZA ENEBEIS

The Chapman brothers and recently I am in awe of Miro's engravings

LUCINDA NEWTON-DUNN

Donald Judd, Ellsworth Kelly, Bernd and Hilla Becher

MAKI SUZUKI

Today the people we work with influence us: Aurélien Froment...
(Full answer, p. 229)

MARC VAN DER HEIJDE

Anish Kapoor

MARGARET CALVERT

Henri Matisse, Piet Mondrian and Andy Warhol

MARION FINK

Thomas Demand, Olafur Eliasson

MARTIN LORENZ

Pablo Picasso

MATTHIAS GÖRLICH

Situationist movement and how it has developed since its death, Haroun Farocki, Raqs Media Collective

MICHAEL GEORGIOU

I see many different things and I get influenced by a piece of art or a detail in it

NIKKI GONNISSEN

John Baldessari for his use of photos and signs, playing with context...
(Full answer, p. 230)

OLIVER KLIMPEL

John Baldessari, Helmut Smits, Joseph Grigely, Lucy McKenzie

PAUL BARNES

Too many to mention (even more...)

PREM KRISHNAMURTHY

Amie Siegel, Christian Marclay, Joachim Koester, Matthew Buckingham

RENATA GRAW

...Carl Andre, Ilya Kabakov, Wassily Kandinsky, Marcel Duchamp, Robert Smithson and so on

RICHARD WALKER

I like Stanley Spencer and Francis Bacon now – both dead

S. HOFFMANN ROBBIANI

Della Robbia, Kirsten Johannsen, Ferdinand Hodler, Alex Hanimann, Shirin Neshat, Ursula Stalder, Eduard Spelterini, Kara Walker, Rémy Zaugg

SASCHA LOBE

Joseph Beuys, Roni Horn, Ed Ruscha, John Baldessari, Marina Abramovic, Dieter Roth

STEFAN SAGMEISTER

Jenny Holzer

SVEN VOELKER

Max Bill, Derek Jarman, Lawrence Weiner, Wolfgang Tillmans

TIM BALAAM

Donald Judd

URS LEHNI

Triin Tamm

YASMIN KHAN

Olafur Eliasson, Sophie Calle

YVES FIDALGO

...Andreas Gursky, Anish Kapoor, Olaf Breuning, Olafur Eliasson, Thomas Demand, William Eggleston, Martin Parr, Pierrick Sorin

RANKING LIST

1 JOHN BALDESSARI, OLAFUR ELIASSON
2 ANISH KAPOOR, JENNY HOLZER, MARCEL DUCHAMP, WOLFGANG TILLMANS
3 ANTONY GORMLEY, ANDREAS GURSKY, ANDY WARHOL, DONALD JUDD, FRANCIS ALÿS, JOSEPH BEUYS, LAWRENCE WEINER, RACHEL WHITEREAD, RONI HORN, SOL LEWITT, THOMAS DEMAND

Which artists/works of art influence you?

Now

ANDREAS GNASS	ANDREW STEVENS	ANNELYS DE VET	ANTÓNIO S. GOMES	BEN BRANAGAN	BERND HILPERT
Coen Brothers, David Lynch	Blade Runner (Ridley Scott), 2001– A Space Odyssey (Stanley Kubrick), Brazil (Terry Gilliam)	–	The Falls, A Walk Through H (Peter Greenaway), O Anjo Exterminador, The Discreet Charm of the Bourgeoisie (Luis Buñuel)	La Haine (Mathieu Kassovitz)	David Lynch

BRIAN WEBB	CHRISTIAN HEUSSER	DANIEL EATOCK	DANIJELA DJOKIC	EMMI SALONEN	ÉRIC & MARIE GASPAR
Some Like it Hot (Billy Wilder)	Björk's music video – All is Full of Love (Chris Cunningham)	Stan Brakhage, Andy Warhol	Seven (David Fincher)	Twin Peaks (David Lynch)	Stan Brakhage, Ernie Gehr, Peter Kubelka, Jonas Mekas

FONS HICKMANN	HANS DIETER REICHERT	HOLGER JACOBS	HOON KIM	HYOUN YOUL JOE	ISABELLE SWIDERSKI
Jean-Luc Godard	Jacques Tati (films by and with), Mephisto with Gustaf Gründgens	Stalker (Andrei Tarkovsky)	–	–	NYPD Blue, ER, Louis Malle, Pedro Almodóvar

JAMES GOGGIN	JAN WILKER	JULIE GAYARD	KAI VON RABENAU	KEN GARLAND	KIRSTY CARTER
Jim Jarmusch, Aki Kaurismäki, Wong Kar-Wai, Patrick Keiller, among others	The Matrix (Wachowski Brothers), South Park	Jean-Luc Godard, John Cassavetes	Wim Wenders, Brothers Quay, Peter Greenaway	Citizen Kane (Orson Welles)	Jacques Tati

KRISTINE MATTHEWS	LARS HARMSEN	LAURENT LACOUR	LIZA ENEBEIS	LUCINDA NOBLE	MAKI SUZUKI
Blade Runner (Ridley Scott), Koyaanisqatsi (Godfrey Reggio), Strictly Ballroom (Baz Luhrmann), Breakfast at Tiffany's (Blake Edwards)	Werner Herzog, Wim Wenders, Francis Ford Coppola	Roman Signer, Fischli and Weiss	In the Mood for Love (Wong Kar-Wai), The Pillow Book (Peter Greenaway)	Many of the films Al Rees (lecturer at Royal College of Art, London, UK) used to show in his film seminars – experimental clips, short films, etc.	Twin Peaks (David Lynch)

MARC VAN DER HEIJDE	MARGARET CALVERT	MARION FINK	MARTIN LORENZ	MATTHIAS GÖRLICH	MICHAEL GEORGIOU
Films by Tim Burton (still now)	–	Koyaanisqatsi (Godfrey Reggio)	Being John Malkovich (Spike Jonze)	–	Fantasia and Mary Poppins (Walt Disney), Ingmar Bergman, Luchino Visconti, Pedro Almodóvar, B&W Greek movies

NIKKI GONNISSEN	OLIVER KLIMPEL	PAUL BARNES	PREM KRISHNAMURTHY	RENATA GRAW	RICHARD WALKER
The Dear Hunter (Michael Cimino), Federico Fellini	Lars von Trier, Eric Rohmer, Werner Herzog	–	David Lynch, Wong Kar-Wai	Luis Buñuel, Jacques Tati, Orson Welles	Star Wars (George Lucas), old Laurel and Hardy films

SANDRA HOFFMANN	SASCHA LOBE	STEFAN SAGMEISTER	SVEN VOELKER	TIM BALAAM	URS LEHNI
The Adjuster (Atom Egoyan), The Hockey Sweater (Sheldon Cohen), Naked Lunch (David Cronenberg), Jacques Tati	All of Stanley Kubrick's films	The African Queen (John Huston)	Peter Greenaway	Star Wars (George Lucas)	Twin Peaks (David Lynch)

YASMIN KHAN	YVES FIDALGO	RANKING LIST
–	David Lynch, Quentin Tarantino, François Truffaut, Marco Ferreri, Jacques Tati, Nick Park, Paul Thomas Anderson	1 DAVID LYNCH (TWIN PEAKS) 2 JACQUES TATI 3 PETER GREENAWAY

Which films/directors influenced you?

Then

ANDREAS GNASS	ANDREW STEVENS	ANNELYS DE VET	ANTÓNIO S. GOMES	BEN BRANAGAN	BERND HILPERT
It's rather the beauty or energy of some scenes (e.g. Paris, Texas; Bullitt; Fargo; 2001) than specific directors/films	–	–	The Flicker (Tony Conrad), Encyclopedia Britannica (John Latham)	Curb Your Enthusiasm (Larry David)	–

BRIAN WEBB	CHRISTIAN HEUSSER	DANIEL EATOCK	DANIJELA DJOKIC	EMMI SALONEN	ÉRIC & MARIE GASPAR
Some Like it Hot (Billy Wilder)	Lost in Translation (Sofia Coppola)	Shane Meadows	Avatar (James Cameron)	Deadwood (David Milch)	Joâo César Monteiro, Andrei Tarkovski

FONS HICKMANN	HANS DIETER REICHERT	HOLGER JACOBS	HOON KIM	HYOUN YOUL JOE	ISABELLE SWIDERSKI
Lars von Trier	2001 (Stanley Kubrick), Little Fockers (Paul Weitz), Taxi Driver (Martin Scorsese), The Mission (Roland Joffé), The Deer Hunter (Michael Cimino)	My Neighbour Totoro (Japanese animation by Studio Ghibli)	–	–	John Cassavetes, Terence Malick, Krzysztof Kieslowski, The West Wing (Aaron Sorkin) and anything else written by him

JAMES GOGGIN	JAN WILKER	JULIE GAYARD	KAI VON RABENAU	KEN GARLAND	KIRSTY CARTER
Patrick Keiller, Adam Curtis, David Simon, Michael Haneke, Lynne Ramsay, among others	Valhalla Rising (Nicolas Winding Refn), Breaking Bad (Vince Gilligan)	Gus Van Sant, Agnès Varda	Christoph Hochhäusler, David Simon, Miranda July	No Country for Old Men (Coen Brothers)	John Smith – very funny and brilliant filmmaker

KRISTINE MATTHEWS	LARS HARMSEN	LAURENT LACOUR	LIZA ENEBEIS	LUCINDA NEWTON-DUNN	MAKI SUZUKI
The Royal Tenenbaums (Wes Anderson), Matt Harding, The Wire (David Simon), Everynone	Coen Brothers	Spike Jonze, David Lynch	Zabriskie Point (Michelangelo Antonioni)	Documentary and short films	The Wire (David Simon)

MARC VAN DER HEIJDE	MARGARET CALVERT	MARION FINK	MARTIN LORENZ	MATTHIAS GÖRLICH	MICHAEL GEORGIOU
Films by Mike Leigh because of their honesty and films by the Coen Brothers because of their weirdness	–	Match Point (Woody Allen)	The Life Aquatic with Steve Zissou (Wes Anderson)	–	Mike Leigh

NIKKI GONNISSEN	OLIVER KLIMPEL	PAUL BARNES	PREM KRISHNAMURTHY	RENATA GRAW	RICHARD WALKER
Dogville (Lars von Trier)	John Smith, Helmuth Costard, Patrick Keiller	–	Jean-Luc Godard, Amie Siegel	Michel Gondry, Godfrey Reggio	I thought the Kite Runner (Marc Forster) was quite good

S. HOFFMANN ROBBIANI	SASCHA LOBE	STEFAN SAGMEISTER	SVEN VOELKER	TIM BALAAM	URS LEHNI
Das gefrorene Herz (Xavier Koller), Hoehenfeuer (Fredi M. Murer), Women without Men… (Full answer, p. 231)	All of Stanley Kubrick's films	Adaptation (Spike Jonze)	Alfred Hitchcock	Playtime (Jacques Tati)	The Wire (David Simon)

YASMIN KHAN	YVES FIDALGO	RANKING LIST
–	Federico Fellini, Jean-Pierre Jeunet, Wes Anderson, John Ford, Alfred Hitchcock, Sidney Lumet, Stanley Kubrick, Coen Brothers	1 DAVID SIMON (THE WIRE) 2 COEN BROTHERS 3 STANLEY KUBRICK

Which films/directors influence you?

Now

ANDREAS GNASS

Dealing with different themes and interacting with different characters on every project

ANDREW STEVENS

Challenging problems, nice clients and subject matter. A chance to find out about other artists and designers. Hard job to complain about really

ANNELYS DE VET

Being able to act within the power fields that shift our social structures

ANTÓNIO S. GOMES

Making things work. The jack-of-all-trades quality and I like inventing tools (ideas)

BEN BRANAGAN

Making things, researching subjects, working for myself

BERND HILPERT

You have the chance to follow your interests and you can bring in your personal ideas

BRIAN WEBB

No two days / jobs are the same and solving the problem

CHRISTIAN HEUSSER

With every new project you have to find new ways to tackle the different problems that arise

DANIEL EATOCK

The idea

DANIJELA DJOKIC

The variety of interesting subjects and the permanent learning process

EMMI SALONEN

How I keep learning

ÉRIC & MARIE GASPAR

Independence

FONS HICKMANN

Almost everything

HANS DIETER REICHERT

Creating and helping to communicate, helping to explain contents visually, serving society

HOLGER JACOBS

The variety – I am not interested in a specific subject, so I enjoy working on different challenges for clients to getting my head around them

HOON KIM

Being creative and visionary

HYOUN YOUL JOE

Making typefaces, dealing with type, systemizing & editing contents, working with artists, photographers, curators & editors

ISABELLE SWIDERSKI

Every project is an opportunity to learn on so many different levels

JAMES GOGGIN

How it involves so much that isn't design

JAN WILKER

The openness – to be able to steadily invent your own area of work, to create in seemingly unlimited situations & environments

JULIE GAYARD

To communicate something visually and the craft side of it like going to the printers & discussing ways of making things

KAI VON RABENAU

Being flexible, being my own boss, working creatively & visually, meeting a lot of people + the variety of work I get to do

KEN GARLAND

Everything

KIRSTY CARTER

The very talented people I work with

KRISTINE MATTHEWS

It is what I would do in my spare time anyway, but I get to make a living at it

LARS HARMSEN

Working with the people in my studio; I am very happy to have such great partners – Uli Weiß and Florian Gaertner…
(Full answer, p. 228)

LAURENT LACOUR

Freedom (sometimes), creative approach

LIZA ENEBEIS

I can research so many different fields that are not directly linked to design

LUCINDA NOBLE

I truly love what I do and it comes from the core…
(Full answer, p. 228)

MAKI SUZUKI

The constant need to help destroy the service-related role of the designer

MARC VAN DER HEIJDE

The fact that every job puts you in a different situation, poses new questions and makes you think again

MARGARET CALVERT

The process

MARION FINK

Work is life and life is work

MARTIN LORENZ

There is no clear definition of what a designer does, so everyone can find their own approach…
(Full answer, p. 229)

MATTHIAS GÖRLICH

I like to produce something useful where there was nothing existing before

MICHAEL GEORGIOU

The diversity of the projects

NIKKI GONNISSEN

The fact that I can go deep into a specific subject for a relatively short period of time…
(Full answer, p. 230)

OLIVER KLIMPEL

Many possibilities and the flexibility – the links to many other fields and that you don't need a big set-up in order to run a design studio

PAUL BARNES

The freedom and the restrictions

PREM KRISHNAMURTHY

The combination of multiple tasks, bodies of knowledge, contexts, people

RENATA GRAW

I love the 'making' part of being a designer – it is both scary and exhilarating

RICHARD WALKER

Coming to work in an inspiring place, working with other people, solving problems & striving to make my clients famous

SANDRA HOFFMANN

The variability of projects, contents, challenges, outcomes, forms, colours

SASCHA LOBE

Putting my own ideas into practice & still being able to integrate overarching processes. Being able to 'play to' all of the senses – including the brain

STEFAN SAGMEISTER

That it is an incredibly wide field, with lots of opportunity for change

SVEN VOELKER

One can deal with a lot of different things, be independent and get very, very rich

TIM BALAAM

The process of convincing the client to go with our proposed solution

URS LEHNI

The definition of what you're supposed to do as a designer is very blurry, so you can come up with your own definition

YASMIN KHAN

Practice can change as interests change

YVES FIDALGO

Up to now we have never been bored by any project – that's something very valuable

What do you like about working as a designer?

Now

ANDREAS GNASS	ANDREW STEVENS	ANNELYS DE VET	ANTÓNIO S. GOMES	BEN BRANAGAN	BERND HILPERT
The relationship between money and time	Emailing, organizing and planning	Too many hours spent behind the computer	Proofreading – then again it can be fun sometimes	Projects that don't happen, managing other people's expectations	Sometimes personal involvement can be too great

BRIAN WEBB	CHRISTIAN HEUSSER	DANIEL EATOCK	DANIJELA DJOKIC	EMMI SALONEN	ÉRIC & MARIE GASPAR
Dealing with money	That my own ego still stands in the way when dealing with clients… (Full answer, p. 226)	The brief	Permanently starting from zero, the exhausting mental brainwork and sitting in front of a computer	The time spent sitting still	Resistance of materials, and more sadly – clients

FONS HICKMANN	HANS DIETER REICHERT	HOLGER JACOBS	HOON KIM	HYOUN YOUL JOE	ISABELLE SWIDERSKI
The name of the profession	Deadlines, misunderstanding the work of a designer	When clients (or their marketing departments) are trying to control every small step of a project and ask for constant PDF updates	Being sensitive and meticulous	Obsession	Having to deal with people who either don't like their job or don't respect others. Having to constantly explain the value of design

JAMES GOGGIN	JAN WILKER	JULIE GAYARD	KAI VON RABENAU	KEN GARLAND	KIRSTY CARTER
The lack of trust	Its preference of experiences over knowledge	Sitting in front of the computer all day, being only an operator to a client, having to persuade clients and having to find new jobs	I hate long working hours, financial insecurity, many of the jobs I have to do plus having to network and promote myself	Nothing	-

KRISTINE MATTHEWS	LARS HARMSEN	LAURENT LACOUR	LIZA ENEBEIS	LUCINDA NEWTON-DUNN	MAKI SUZUKI
Worrying that my work could be better if I could push myself harder	Email sucks, I am not made for long meetings, I hate to spoil so much life-time on a computer	Poorly paying, idiotic clients	-	That I cannot easily separate my work from my day-to-day life, which can be… (Full answer, p. 228)	Nothing

MARC VAN DER HEIJDE	MARGARET CALVERT	MARION FINK	MARTIN LORENZ	MATTHIAS GÖRLICH	MICHAEL GEORGIOU
Nothing is ever good enough	Meetings and administration	Work is life and life is work	There is no clear definition of what a designer does, so nearly everyone can work as a designer (Full answer, p. 229)	Some of the working habits that I have adopted	Training clients

NIKKI GONNISSEN	OLIVER KLIMPEL	PAUL BARNES	PREM KRISHNAMURTHY	RENATA GRAW	RICHARD WALKER
Projects were it is too difficult to come to the essence because of difficult hierarchical structures within organization	The self-centredness, the idea that constant networking might be necessary, finding new clients plus sometimes: the hard work	Too much time spent in front of computers	The narrow focus of much of the profession and many clients	I personally dislike having to 'sell' design	Nothing really – meetings can drag on a bit

S. HOFFMANN ROBBIANI	SASCHA LOBE	STEFAN SAGMEISTER	SVEN VOELKER	TIM BALAAM	URS LEHNI
Objectification, waste production, consumption endorsement	The pay	Badly organized clients	It's very difficult to enter the hermetically sealed area of art. I don't mean to design… (Full answer, p. 231)	The process of convincing the client to go with our proposed solution	That designers often complain about being designers

YASMIN KHAN	YVES FIDALGO
Being underpaid	The commercial part of it

What do you dislike about working as a designer?

Now

ANDREAS GNASS
U9 VISUELLE ALLIANZ
u9@u9.net
www.u9.net
Fichtestr. 15a
63071 Offenbach am Main
Germany
T +49 (0)69 8 01 01 50

ANDREW STEVENS
GRAPHIC THOUGHT FACILITY
info@graphicthoughtfacility.com
www.graphicthoughtfacility.com
23–24 Easton Street
London WC1X 0DS
United Kingdom
T +44 (0)20 7837 2525

ANNELYS DE VET
there@annelysdevet.nl
www.annelysdevet.nl
Wielemans Ceuppenslaan 33
1190 Brussels
Belgium

ANTÓNIO SILVEIRA GOMES
(BARBARA SAYS...PROJECTO PRÓPRIO)
projectoproprio@gmail.com
www.barbarasays.com
R. Marquês Ponte do Lima 23 4°
1100-337 Lisboa
Portugal
T +35 (0)121 3472 707

BEN BRANAGAN
ben@benbranagan.co.uk
www.benbranagan.co.uk

BERND HILPERT
UNIT-DESIGN
info@unit-design.de
www.unit-design.de
Holbeinstraße 25
60596 Frankfurt am Main
Germany
T +49 (0)69 6 6057 880

BRIAN WEBB
WEBB & WEBB DESIGN
design@webbandwebb.co.uk
www.webbandwebb.co.uk
16H Perseverance Works
38 Kingsland Road
London E2 8DD
United Kingdom
T +44 (0)207 739 7895

CHRISTIAN HEUSSER
EQUIPO
info@equipo.ch
www.equipo.ch
Amerbachstraße 53
4057 Basel
T +41 (0)61 681 4568
Switzerland

DANIEL EATOCK
daniel@eatock.com
www.eatock.com
7 Minerva Street
London E2 9EH
United Kingdom

DANIJELA DJOKIC
PROJEKTTRIANGLE
ddjokic@projekttriangle.com
www.projekttriangle.com
Humboldtstraße 4
70178 Stuttgart
Germany
T +49 (0)711 6 20 09 30

EMMI SALONEN
STUDIO EMMI
hello@emmi.co.uk
www.emmi.co.uk
Unit 110, Cremer Business
Centre
37 Cremer Street
London E2 8HD
United Kingdom
T +44 (0)77 5200 1311

ÉRIC & MARIE GASPAR
ÉRICANDMARIE
info@ericandmarie.com
www.ericandmarie.com
45 avenue Montaigne
75008 Paris
France
T +33 (0)14 723 5127

FONS HICKMANN
FONS HICKMANN M23
m23@fonshickmann.com
www.fonshickmann.com
Mariannenplatz 23
10997 Berlin
T +49 (0)30 6951 8501

HANS DIETER REICHERT
HDR VISUAL COMMUNICATION
hans@baselinemagazine.com
www.baselinemagazine.com
Bradbourne House
East Malling
Kent ME19 6DZ
United Kingdom
T +44 (0)173 287 5200

HOLGER JACOBS
MIND DESIGN
info@minddesign.co.uk
www.minddesign.co.uk
Unit 33A, Regents Studios
8 Andrews Road
London E8 4QN
United Kingdom
T +44 (0)207 254 2114

HOON KIM
WHY NOT SMILE
mail@whynotsmile.com
www.whynotsmile.com
10 Jay Street, Ste 801A
Brooklyn, NY 11201
USA
T +1 347 234 5312

HYOUN YOUL JOE
HEY JOE
youljoe@gmail.com
www.hyjoe.net
394-74 Seokyo-Dong 3F
Mapo-Gu, Seoul,
South Korea
T +82 10 8857 9374

ISABELLE SWIDERSKI
SEVEN25
studio@seven25.com
www.seven25.com
309E-896 Cambie Street
Vancouver, BC V6B 2P6
Canada
T +1 604 685 0097

JAMES GOGGIN
PRACTISE
jgoggin@mcachicago.org
studio@practise.co.uk
www.mcachicago.org
www.practise.co.uk
Director of Design, Publishing
and New Media
Museum of Contemporary
Art Chicago
220 East Chicago Avenue
Chicago IL 60611
USA
T +1 312 397 4071

JAN WILKER
KARLSSONWILKER
tellmewhy@karlssonwilker.com
www.karlssonwilker.com
536 6th avenue
New York City, NY 10011
USA
T +1 212 929 8064

JULIE GAYARD
JUTOJO
info@jutojo.de
www.jutojo.de
Brunnenstrasse 191
10119 Berlin
Germany
T +49 (0)30 2809 3946

KAI VON RABENAU
MONO.GRAPHIE
www.mono-graphie.com
www.mono-blog.com
www.mono-kultur.com
www.mono-gramm.com
Berlin/London
Germany/United Kingdom

KEN GARLAND
ken.garland@talk21.com
www.kengarland.co.uk
London
United Kingdom

KIRSTY CARTER
A PRACTICE FOR EVERYDAY LIFE
m@apracticeforeverydaylife.com
apracticeforeverydaylife.com
Unit 16, 5 Durham Yard
London E2 6QF
United Kingdom
T +44 (0)20 7739 9975

KRISTINE MATTHEWS
STUDIO MATTHEWS
info@studiomatthews.com
www.studiomatthews.com
1517 12th Avenue, Unit 202
Seattle, WA 98122
USA
T +1 206 499 9978

LARS HARMSEN
MAGMA BRAND DESIGN
info@magmabranddesign.de
www.magmabranddesign.de
www.slanted.de
Wendstraße 4
76185 Karlsruhe
Germany
T +49 (0)721 824 8580

LAURENT LACOUR
HAUSER LACOUR
info@hauserlacour.de
www.hauserlacour.de
Westendstraße 84
60325 Frankfurt am Main
Germany
T +49 (0)69 8090 9990

Adresses and contact information

Now

LIZA ENEBEIS
STUDIO DUMBAR/TYPERADIO
info@studiodumbar.com
www.studiodumbar.com
dj@typeradio.org
www.typeradio.org
Studio Dumbar
Lloydstraat 21
3024 EA Rotterdam
The Netherlands
T +31 (0)10 448 22 22
Typeradio
Groenewegje 137
2515 LR Den Haag
The Netherlands
T +31 (0)70 427 8115

LUCINDA NEWTON-DUNN
SPACE-TO-THINK
lucinda@space-to-think.com
www.space-to-think.com

MAKI SUZUKI
ÅBÄKE
abakesemail@gmail.com
www.abake.fr
Unit 73b, Regents Studios
8 Andrews Road
London E8 4QN
United Kingdom

MARC VAN DER HEIJDE
STUDIO DUMBAR
info@studiodumbar.com
www.studiodumbar.com
Lloydstraat 21
3024 EA Rotterdam
The Netherlands
T +31 (0)10 448 22 22

MARGARET CALVERT
http://en.wikipedia.org/wiki/
    Margaret_Calvert

MARION FINK
marion.fink@fhnw.ch
www.fhnw.ch
Fachhochschule
Nordwestschweiz, Hochschule
für Gestaltung und Kunst,
Institut Visuelle
Kommunikation
Vogelsangstraße 15
4058 Basel
Switzerland
T +41 (0)61 695 6751

MARTIN LORENZ
TWOPOINTS.NET
info@twopoints.net
www.twopoints.net
Via Laietana 37
4ª Planta / Despacho 32
08003 Barcelona
Spain
T +34 (0)93 318 5372

MATTHIAS GÖRLICH
STUDIO MATTHIAS GÖRLICH
studio@mgoerlich.com
www.mgoerlich.com
Soderstraße 16a
64283 Darmstadt
Germany
T +49 (0)6151 785 9780

MICHAEL GEORGIOU
G DESIGN STUDIO
g@georgiougavrilakis.com
www.georgiougavrilakis.com
Miaouli 6, Monastiraki
105 54, Athens
Greece
T +30 (0)210 322 3636

NIKKI GONNISSEN
THONIK
studio@thonik.nl
www.thonik.nl
Vijzelstraat 72, 4.52
1017 HL Amsterdam
The Netherlands
T +31 (0)20 468 3525

OLIVER KLIMPEL
BÜRO INTERNATIONAL
info@burointernational.co.uk
www.burointernational.co.uk
34 Brougham Road
London E8 4PD
United Kingdom
T +44 (0)20 7241 6323

PAUL BARNES
paul@moderntypography.com
info@commercialtype.com
www.moderntypography.com
www.commercialtype.com
45 Benbow Road
London, W6 0AU
United Kingdom
T +44 (0)20 8563 1228

PREM KRISHNAMURTHY
PROJECT PROJECTS
project@projectprojects.com
www.projectprojects.com
161 Bowery, 2nd Floor
New York, NY 10002
USA
T +1 212 509 0636

RENATA GRAW
PLURAL
hello@weareplural.com
www.weareplural.com
1310 N Clybourn Ave
Second Floor
Chicago, IL 60610
USA
T +1 312 804 4020

RICHARD WALKER
KK OUTLET/KESSELSKRAMER
info@kkoutlet.com
www.kkoutlet.com
42 Hoxton Square
London N1 6PB
United Kingdom
T +44 (0)20 7033 7680

SANDRA HOFFMANN ROBBIANI
VISUAL STUDIES
s.e.hoffmann@bluewin.ch
www.otherwords.ch
Wasserwerkgasse 7
3011 Berne
Switzerland
T +41 (0)76 316 25 45

SASCHA LOBE
L2M3
info@L2M3.com
www.L2M3.com
Hoelderlinstrasse 57
70193 Stuttgart
Germany
T +49 (0)711 99 33 91 60

STEFAN SAGMEISTER
SAGMEISTER INC.
info@sagmeister.com
www.sagmeister.com
206 West 23rd Street, 4th floor
New York, NY 10011
USA
T +1 212 647 1789

SVEN VOELKER
SVEN VOELKER STUDIO
studio@svenvoelker.com
www.svenvoelker.com
Steinstraße 37
10119 Berlin
Germany
T +49 (0)30 23 45 57 86

TIM BALAAM
HYPERKIT
info@hyperkit.co.uk
www.hyperkit.co.uk
822 Parkhall
40 Marcell Road
London SE21 8EN
United Kingdom
T +44 (0)20 7407 8982

URS LEHNI
LEHNI-TRÜB/ROLLO PRESS/
CORNER COLLEGE
office@lehni-trueb.ch
www.lehni-trueb.ch
www.rollo-press.com
www.corner-college.com
Gasometerstraße 32
8005 Zürich
Switzerland
T +41 44 272 95 42

YASMIN KHAN
COUNTERSPACE
yasmin@counterspace.net
counterspace.net
99 N. Hill St.
Los Angeles, CA 90019
USA

YVES FIDALGO
FULGURO
www.fulguro.ch
info@fulguro.ch
Rue du Maupas 28
1004 Lausanne
Switzerland
T +41 (0)21 646 7558

FRANK PHILIPPIN

Frank was born in Stuttgart, Germany, in 1967. He first thought of becoming a graphic designer during a 20-month-long civil service stint at a local magazine, where he tried to mimic the style of Neville Brody and David Carson. In 1994, after repeated rejections from the German education system, Frank travelled to London and took a Bachelor of Arts (Hons) course in Graphic Design at Camberwell College of Arts, London (UK). There, he discovered (German) modernism and the work of Jan Tschichold. He also discovered a less Germanic, quirkier approach to design.

During his studies he made an installation about silence, carried out a photographic experiment in Trafalgar Square and involved his peers' mothers in his degree show. Each day, Frank woke up at 09:30, walked to college, spent about six hours a day designing and for dinner often cooked lasagne, which he ate with a tomato and mozzarella salad. He weighed 74 kilos and did no exercise. His most valued possessions were his (cheap) fold-down table and a collection of tapes, which were sent to him regularly by his friend Rainer.

In 1997 Frank began a Master of Arts course in Graphic Design at the Royal College of Art in London, where he worked on a film about the colour green and an installation about the colour white. He also designed his graduating year's (manifesto) poster, was shortlisted for the Millennium Stamp and won the Colonel Varley Memorial Award.

After graduating, Frank completed a one-year research project on 'small print' at the Helen Hamlyn Centre in Lo

BILLY KIOSOGLOU

Billy was born in Athens, Greece, in 1973. He first thought of becoming a designer while making covers for compilation tapes on his bedroom floor. In 1992 Billy moved to the UK for a Foundation Course at Kingston University, where he discovered the books of Franz Masereel and lino-cut printing. In 1993 he enrolled on a Bachelor of Arts (Hons) course in Graphic Design at Bath College of Higher Education (UK), where he started illustrating and binding his own books. After a year in Bath, Billy moved to Camberwell College of Arts in London (UK) in 1995.

During his course he used a scalpel, an A3 typewriter and his flatmate Frank to teach himself the fundamentals of design. Each day, Billy got up at 11:00, walked to college, spent about two hours designing, and usually cooked Pastitsio with a tomato and feta salad. He weighed 69 kilos and did no exercise. His most valued possession was his double cassette player.

In 1997 Billy went to Greece to complete his military service and, after two years of staring at the walls of an underground army bunker on a Greek island, he returned to London for a Master of Arts course in Communication Art and Design at the Royal College of Art (UK) in 1999. There he produced a giant sheet of writing paper, designed his year-

BRIGHTEN THE CORNERS

During their studies Frank and Billy worked together on several projects, including an installation in their own house and three handmade, (very) limited-edition books by Franz Kafka, Albert Camus and Marguerite Duras.

In 1998 they proudly gave their copy of The New York Trilogy to Paul Auster and Fahrenheit 451 to Ray Bradbury, who complimented them on a 'beautiful book, which opens like a butterfly'. He also politely reminded them that it is he who holds the copyright for his text...

In 1999 Frank and Billy brought their faith in their acquired design skills to their current practice, Brighten the Corners. Over the years, they have worked on several projects, large and small, switching between the public sector, the corporate sector and cultural environments. Clients include Anish Kapoor, the British Council, Goethe-Institut, Italian Cultural Institute, German Post Office, Fraunhofer-Institut, Laurence King Publishing, Skira Editore, Frieze, and Bolles + Wilson architects. For more information please visit www.brightenthecorners.com.

Today, Frank is based in the Odenwald region near Darmstadt with his wife Sybille and two children Emil and Juno. He frequently visits London to meet Billy, and Stuttgart for some Maultaschen and music from Rainer's second-hand record shop. If Frank ever stopped designing, he'd take up gardening.

HOCHSCHULE DARMSTADT

Frank has been teaching since 1998, when he started as a visiting lecturer at North East Worcestershire College in Redditch, where he met Adrian Spaak (see also acknowledgements, page 4). Further work as visiting lecturer followed, in most cases for a period of up to two years, at Maidstone College, Kingston University and the University of Brighton (all in the UK) and the Merz Akademie in Stuttgart (Germany). Since 2006 Frank has been a professor of Communication Design at the Faculy of Design at the Hochschule Darmstadt (Germany).

In his courses, Frank stresses the importance of concept-driven design to his students, but is also interested in getting them to develop genuine responses to subject matter rather than formulaic ones. His students are therefore encouraged to follow their personal observations and thoughts, ask questions, use their sense of humour, and not dismiss more poetic or abstract paths to a graphic solution. As he likes to say, 'Design isn't just a discipline, it is something done for people by people and, as such, is (or should be) deeply humane.'

BRIGHTEN THE CORNERS
london@brightenthecorners.com
darmstadt@brightenthecorners.com
www.brightenthecorners.com

HOCHSCHULE DARMSTADT
FACULTY OF DESIGN
frank.philippin@h-da.de
www.fbg.h-da.de